AXEL

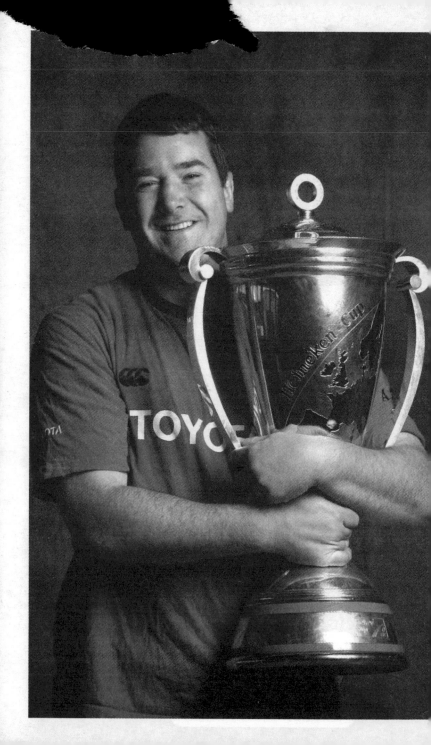

AXEL

A MEMOIR

ANTHONY FOLEY

HACHETTE
BOOKS
IRELAND

First published in 2008 by Hachette Books Ireland
First published in paperback in 2009 by Hachette Books Ireland

A division of Hachette UK Ltd

2

A CIP catalogue record for this title is available from the British Library.

ISBN 978 0 340 97767 5

Typeset in Adobe Garamond by Hachette Books Ireland
Cover and text design by Anú Design, Tara
Printed and bound by CPI Group (UK) Ltd, Croydon, CR0 4YY

Hachette Books Ireland
8 Castlecourt Centre
Castleknock
Dublin 15
Ireland

www.hbgi.ie

A division of Hachette UK LTD, 338 Euston Road, London NW1 3BH, England

Contents

Acknowledgements IX

Foreword by Keith Wood XI

Prologue XIII

1   Early doors – Killaloe 1

2   Dad 12

3   Boarder rules 27

4   Clubbing it 45

5   Capped with the Under-14s 56

6   Notes on a debut 68

7   A heavy fall 79

8   Arrested development 91

9   Hard yards 107

10 Helping hands 120

11 London calling 132

12 Hard-luck stories 148

13   Changing of the guard 160

14   Miraculous 175

15   Crashing down under, climbing back up 187

16   Surplus to requirements 202

17   Getting there 213

18   Being there 225

19   A proper ending 236

Statistical record 243

Index 251

To Olive, Tony and Dan

and to Mam, Dad, Rosie and Orla

Acknowledgements

A special thanks to all who contributed to the putting together of this book, particularly to Peter O'Reilly, for his patience and professionalism and for his ability to turn countless interviews into a well-structured and entertaining read.

Thanks to all at Hachette Books Ireland, especially to my editor, Claire Rourke, for her enthusiasm and expertise, and to Breda Purdue for her efforts in promoting the book.

Thanks also to Keith Wood, Killian Keane and Brendan Fanning for casting a critical eye over the manuscript and offering considered advice.

To John Baker, sincere thanks for his guidance and help and to Des Daly for compiling the statistical record.

My sister Rosie was incredibly helpful in arranging a vast collection of newspaper cuttings, scrapbooks and family photographs for Peter and Claire. Thanks, Rosie.

The same goes for Olive, Mam, Dad and Orla and various friends and team-mates who provided colour and clarified details: David Corkery, Mick Galwey, Brian O'Brien, Donncha O'Callaghan, Paul O'Connell, Niall O'Donovan, Shaun Payne and Niall Woods.

And, finally, thanks to all the supporters out there, be they Shannon, Munster or Ireland – or all three – who were there in good times and bad.

Anthony Foley
August 2008

Foreword

I first met Anthony Foley when his family arrived in Killaloe in 1979. We had a shared heritage, as our fathers were both proud Limerick men and Irish international rugby players. It was only natural that when the Foleys were renovating their new business and home – their pub at the end of our street – they should stay with us and become part of the extended family. United by a fanaticism for sport, Anthony and I became firm friends.

The young Foley took a long time to grow into his body but when he did, he had already laid down the foundations of his rugby career with his father, Brendan. I remember calling to their house on one of those glorious summer days that only occur in our youth. It was twenty-five degrees outside and about forty inside, yet the curtains were closed and father and son were scrutinising past games on video. A journey had begun and, with this constant repetition, Anthony began to understand those games and the game intimately.

As he got older, he put his prep work to use. In St Munchin's, he picked from the base, he kicked for touch, he took long-range speculative kicks at goal. He did whatever was required and did it not in a showy-off way but because he was just the best at it. He understood very early that he was never fleet of foot (I was never slow to point it out to him) but, rather than see his lack of pace as a hindrance, he took it as an opportunity.

His lack of pace necessitated a sixth sense, and Foley had it in spades. He had the uncanny ability to be in the right place at the right time. It was a bit freaky really, as he shouldn't have been able to get there when fitter and faster players were nowhere to be seen. But all those hours with his old man had taught him to read the game perfectly. There is no higher praise I can give him.

He is, as I have always said, the smartest rugby player I have had the honour of playing with and against. There were more talented, more skilful players, but none that maximised their talent so fully. Foley invariably did the right thing on a rugby field because he understood the game. He rarely had to think about what to do; he knew what to do.

Anthony had an excellent international career but it is his constancy with Munster that will be remembered most. His longevity is without parallel but it was his standard over the years that beggars belief. There are very few games that stand out and for any other player this would be a criticism. But for Anthony, it is recognition of his worth, of the knowledge that there was one thing you could always rely on.

He has been with Munster for fourteen years. His attitude has brought a flock of new supporters to the cause because they recognise the elements they would like to see in themselves. Heart, honesty, determination and teamwork. These are words that are rarely ascribable to individuals but they sit very comfortably on the shoulders of Anthony Foley.

Keith Wood
July 2008

Prologue

4.15 p.m., Saturday, 24 May 2008

North Dressing Room, Millennium Stadium, Cardiff

Time to be making myself scarce. Only forty-five minutes to kick-off and I feel like I've outstayed my welcome. This long, low-ceilinged room holds special memories. The last time I was in here, we were roaring and hugging and singing and jumping. Now, two years on, almost to the day, it's quiet enough to hear the hiss of iPods above the clack of studs. I'm no good to anyone here. Time to grab Shaun Payne and go. We can kill half an hour in one of the corporate boxes upstairs.

It has been a strange couple of days for both of us. Same hotel as 2006 – The Vale of Glamorgan, twenty minutes outside Cardiff – same bus journey into the city, same sea of red as we pull into Westgate Street. Just no nerves. We played golf yesterday for Christ's sake, and even considered a quick round at the Vale of Glamorgan this morning. We aren't here in any official capacity. Payney is the manager-in-waiting and will act as an extra pair of eyes, ears and hands if needs be. I said a few words to the squad last night – nothing too emotional, obvious stuff really. Now I wonder if I've been brought along for the players' benefit or for my own. Payney and I are both part of the set-up and yet separate at the same time.

It's strange to watch the rituals and routines as an observer. Hayes is getting his pre-match rub in the treatment room off to the side. Donncha is laying out his accoutrements – the towel to stand on, the new pair of white socks to go under his match socks, and so on. Our Kiwi centres, Rua and Mafs, have their match jerseys hanging up with the fronts facing out, different from everyone else. It's all just the same as normal. And I'm here wearing a suit.

I'd seen this coming, of course, just as I'd seen it coming that I'd be on the bench for the quarter-final in Gloucester. Quinny had been playing out of his skin, while Wally and Leams had done well in the Six Nations. You didn't need to be good at maths to figure out I was struggling. Then, for the semi in Coventry, I didn't even make the bench. Paulie asked me afterwards was I shocked. Nah. When you've been around the game as long as I have, you pick up on things, hear nuances in casual comments. It still hurts when you're given the news. As I said to Paulie, it's like seeing the lights of a car coming from ten miles away and still being run over.

I knew for certain when the mobile rang on the Monday evening before the final and 'Deccie' came up on the screen.

'You're not ringing to give me good news.'

'No. How did you know?'

'You never ring to give good news.'

I wasn't being grumpy. When a decision like that is made by somebody you respect, you take it on the chin. You know he's done it for what he believes is the good of the team. Like I said, I'd seen it coming, especially when he'd made me captain for the last, meaningless, Magners League game of the season, against

Glasgow in Cork, seven days before the Heineken final. That was strictly Second XV stuff. We lost, too, just as we lost my second-last game, my 200th for Munster, against Ulster in Ravenhill. Not the ideal send-off, I'll admit. I'd have liked to finish with a win. One of the things I'll really miss is that feeling when you're back in the changing room, fifteen minutes after the final whistle, and you've won, and there's this togetherness, this warmth.

To be honest, though, what I'll miss most of all is the day-to-day crack, the banter. Some of the slagging can be vicious. The rule is, when you drive into training at the University of Limerick, you leave your feelings at the gate. When Anthony Horgan got caught from behind by an All Blacks second row at Lansdowne Road, he was crucified. He lost his place in the Ireland team after that game, but he got zero sympathy when he arrived back to Munster training with his tail between his legs. Quicksand under the West Stand, Hoggy? It's not just rugby slags. Payney likes to watch his change, makes a budget every time he leaves the house. When he stumbled before scoring a try a couple of years ago, someone suggested he'd spotted a euro coin in the grass just short of the goal-line.

Newcomers are particularly vulnerable. Paul Warwick was only with us a couple of games when he missed a penalty in front of the posts against Cardiff and we lost by two points. That's a €400 win-bonus you owe the lot of us, son. Dougie Howlett hadn't even been introduced to the squad when he was getting abuse. This was a couple of months after he'd got in trouble with the police at a Heathrow airport hotel for a drunken dance on a couple of cars, a high-profile incident after which Dougie made a tearful apology to the entire Kiwi nation via his website. When he came to Limerick on a reccie, Quinny spotted him watching us train and immediately put on his traffic-cop voice: 'PLEASE STEP AWAY FROM THE VEHICLES!' Nothing is sacred. If a fella has been blown out by his girlfriend, we'll let him lick his wounds for an hour or two and then get stuck into him. It's actually a form of caring. Say nothing and there's an awkwardness that can fester. Best to get it out in the open.

I'd be pretty merciless with the abuse but then I get plenty of it myself. They slag me about the way I speak, with a lisp. When you hear them mimicking you with, 'We'll have to thet out our thtall early doorth,' you start choosing your words more carefully. I even get slagged about the way I breathe. There have been so many nose-breaks over the years, I decided to wait till I retired before getting the repairs done properly by a specialist. In the meantime, I'm a fairly audible breather. Darth Vader, they call me. When Denis Fogarty does his impression of me at the top of the bus, he spends the first thirty seconds just doing heavy breathing into the mic.

What else? The gym monkeys get a giggle from some of my test scores, also from the fact that I can do a forty-minute weights session in twenty. Most of all, though, they slag me for being grumpy, especially in the morning, a trait inherited by my three-year-old son, Tony. I once had to give Barry Murphy an early-morning lift to Dublin and when he got into the car, I told him to say what he had to say there and then because there wasn't going to be any conversation after that. And I was true to my word. Sorry, Baz. And sorry to any of you who had doors slammed in your faces over the years. You know I'll miss you all, dearly.

I'm sure they'll miss me too, but not right now. I've already wished each of them good luck. Now it's time to grab Payney and go. We walk out the door and down the corridor but instead of turning into the tunnel leading to the pitch, we turn left and into the elevator. Only then does it really hit me. I'm leaving a lot behind.

1

EARLY DOORS – KILLALOE

Keith Wood always said I was bitter. 'Jesus, Foley,' he once announced, 'you must be the bitterest bastard in Ireland.' There's no truth in this of course, though I did have some acidic problems early on. I was an awful colicky baby. Apparently, I didn't stop yelling for the first seven months of my existence. Yelled for seven months and then barely opened my mouth for the next twenty years except to eat, says my mother. I must have given her and my father a terrible time. Seven sleepless months. They now joke they would have thrown me out the window but for the fact that we lived in a bungalow.

That was in Murroe, a village eight miles outside Limerick where my mother grew up as Sheila Collins. One day in 1970, a friend persuaded her to go on a boat-trip social organised by Shannon RFC, and that's how she met Brendan Foley. Six months later, they were married. My dad is pure Limerick city, born and bred in the parish of St Mary, but my mother persuaded him they should build a house on a plot beside her parents' place. She's a persuasive woman.

Murroe was home for me till I was seven. First there was just Mam, Dad, me and Rosie, my older sister by a year and my first real competitor. Orla came along three years after me. One of my earliest memories is of Mam coming home from the hospital with our baby sister and how I was sulking up in the palm tree at the side of the house when they got back. I'm still not sure if this was a) because I was fed up with all the attention Rosie was getting from Granny – she got away with all sorts – or b) because I sensed a new addition to the family could only be bad from my point of view. So I stayed up the tree, looking down on Rosie and Granny as they poked about in the rain barrels trying to find me.

I was a quiet kid but capable of throwing the odd strop. One thing that can't have been too good for my general disposition was the time I took a glug out of some weedkiller. It was there in a can on the kitchen table where Granddad had been mixing it. How was I to know any better? I was only four. It was straight off to St John's Hospital in the old Renault 4 to be pumped out. You can imagine the fright for my folks, though.

I gave them quite a few scares over the years. My childhood memories are punctuated by accidents and emergencies. On my Holy Communion, it was my knee, blood seeping through my best pants after I fell on a piece of glass while playing football with the lads in the square in Killaloe. On the day of my Confirmation, it was a whack of a hurley to the head. Dad soon gave up on summer holidays after I had a fit on the beach at Spanish Point, aged five or six – fortunately, they found a local who had a car and who knew where the GP lived, although we're still not sure what was wrong with me. Even more serious was the bout of meningitis I had when I was ten, which kept me in hospital for a couple of weeks. This was another scare for my parents and a pretty serious issue for me too – it put my participation in the annual Shannon Swim in jeopardy.

By this stage, we had moved to Killaloe, a picturesque town on the River Shannon about a mile from Lough Derg, which has been my home for the past twenty-eight years. My dad was working as a sales rep for the drinks company Dwans, so in some respects buying a pub was a natural development. Mattie Hayes' bar needed a good bit of work but the location, looking down on the Shannon from Church Street, was spectacular. He sold our bungalow for £30,000 and bought Mattie Hayes' for £29,000 – a good deal all round. Dad got builders in to knock out a few walls and make the interior more spacious – spacious enough for a pool table, I recall. Brendan Foley's did a tidy trade for the ten years he kept it, a mixture of local regulars and day-trippers from Limerick and farther afield during the summer. We lived upstairs.

Being so close to the water – and with my record on personal safety – it was vital that the Foley kids learned to swim. Peter Lacey taught us in the Shannon, using a rope or a hoop, as he did with hundreds of local kids. Only later did we find out that Peter couldn't swim himself, so we were rightly goosed if we slipped through the rope. Thankfully, it never happened and we all became strong swimmers – Rosie, Orla and I are all qualified pool lifeguards. The best way to prove it was with the Shannon Swim, an annual event usually contested over the half-mile from the Pier Head to the old bridge that links Killaloe with Ballina. It's a serious business – very serious when you're stuck in hospital with meningitis, one of the symptoms of which is general irritability, and your sister is favourite to win the bloody thing. I remember hassling the old man non-stop to get me out of hospital in time, and even though I was discharged on the day of the race, I forced him to let me swim. Fortunately, the race was postponed for a week because of rain – don't ask. Rosie did win the following week, of course, but finishing first in my age grade was some consolation.

We competed in schoolwork and in sport. This, remember, is a girl who has won thirty-nine international rugby caps and played county camogie and football for Clare. She'll gladly tell you about all her victories over me. She'll tell you about the hole in one at the pitch-and-putt course in Killaloe, where we had niggly contests – Dad and Orla against the two of us. What she probably won't mention is that we spent twenty minutes searching for her ball before someone decided to look in the cup. She's one of the more competitive people I've come across – but she's not as competitive as Keith Wood.

I first came across Woody shortly after we arrived in Killaloe. Dad had already played a few times for Ireland at this stage and, as a rugby person, he knew Gordon Wood, the former international and Lion, who lived with Pauline and their seven children a short hop up Main Street. Seeing as the roof on the pub needed some serious work, it seemed to make perfect sense that the Foleys would take over the top floor of the Wood house for the couple of weeks we were homeless. So began a long friendship that has been based mainly on a mutual determination to outdo one another in sporting endeavour.

We played a lot of sport with and against each other. Sometimes, it just boiled down to leathering a sliotar at each other from short range in the Woods' backyard. It wasn't a big yard – we were maybe fifteen yards apart – and when this missile was coming at you, it sharpened up your evasion skills in no time. Strangely enough, the tennis matches we played against each other over the years were even more ferocious in their way. Now it's just golf, but there's still an edge to our contests.

We made an odd couple. I was a quiet, shy kid, big for my age – I really shot up between the ages of eleven and thirteen. Woody was a year older but tiny, too small to make the junior cup team in St Munchin's, a scut with a mop of black hair. And he was confident – not cocky, but as outgoing as you'd get in a small, country town. He'd hold his own, whether it was up at Smith O'Briens GAA Club at the top of the town or hanging around in Crowe's playing Pac-Man and pool. I suppose it was a help to have two older brothers who'd beaten a path for him. It was only after his Inter Cert that he sprouted and really began to devote himself to rugby. When he was twelve or thirteen, he was a nifty hurling midfielder, skilful and brave enough to play with the Under-16s. And he never went through a game without smashing at least one hurley. He always backed himself, and never held back.

Woody was two years ahead of me in national school and in Munchin's but there were stages in our growing up when we were inseparable. Even when I was stuck in hospital with meningitis, he used to come in and keep me company over a game of cards – anything, as long as it was competitive. He seemed to like coming down to the pub, where we'd go upstairs and have marathon video-game sessions on our prehistoric Atari 2600. He also knew that going to Foley's meant he'd get free bottles of Lucozade – and chips. We did pub grub, so chips were always available in abundance. Years later, Noel Murphy, the Ireland team manager, used to look at the body–fat ratio scores of K. Wood and A. Foley and ask, 'Is there fat in the water in Killaloe?' I always reckon it must have had something to do with the mountains of chips we ate as young fellas.

My mother never fed us rubbish, quite the opposite. There'd usually be half a maiden heifer in the massive thirteen-foot square freezer out the back. We'd go through some amount of food. She was big into home-made soups – it was the only way she'd get vegetables into me. I was a bit scrawny as a youngster so she determined to build me up. Years before rugby players were guzzling protein shakes, my mother was concocting her own – usually, it was three raw eggs whisked up in a glass with some Lucozade and down the hatch. She was big into vitamins, too. If she read somewhere that such-and-such was good for you, that was it. I must have had the most expensive pee in Munster. When I started going on away trips with schoolboy teams, she'd ring up the hotel and ask my room-mate if I'd taken my vitamins. The mortification of it! Alan Quinlan's mother likes to sprinkle holy water on you as you're leaving her house. With my mam, it's vitamins. Stay any length of time in her company and she'll get a few Cs and B pluses into you.

She has always been a generous host. It seemed that if anyone spent more than a few hours in the pub, they wouldn't be let go without a feed. People often stayed over. My folks were very friendly with Moss and Anne Keane – not surprising since Moss and my dad soldiered together for so many years –

and they were regular guests. Often it was impromptu. I have this late-night image of Mossie shuffling down Main Street with Woody's old cot up on his shoulder – a makeshift bed for young Sarah Keane who'd been brought on a visit.

People used to ask me if I was in awe of Mick Galwey when I first started playing senior rugby in Shannon. Not really, to be honest. International rugby players lose some of their mystique when you're used to seeing the massive frame of Moss Keane – another second row from Currow – coming down the stairs for breakfast after a late night in the pub, his hair sticking up at the back and his shirt hanging out. My folks and their friends enjoyed themselves. Mam and Dad always had bags of get up and go. They got married young, had kids young and have remained young. They manage to have their own lives and at the same time have been incredibly supportive to their kids in everything. We have always done things as a family.

Killaloe was a brilliant place to grow up. It's a lovely little spot, a heritage town of higgledy-piggledy streets on a hill that slopes down to the broad and beautiful Shannon. It's a pity the way it's gone, with houses sprouting up but no infrastructure to deal with the increase in population. Killaloe is now a bottleneck. There were no traffic lights when I was a kid. We had the freedom of the town and its surrounds. We'd wander up the hills or out to Brian Boru's fort with bows and arrows – as we learned in national school, Brian Boru was High King of Ireland in the eleventh century and came a cropper at the Battle of Clontarf. On warm days, it was straight down to the Pier Head or the stone bridge across to Ballina. The older lads used to stop trucks, climb up on top and dive into the river, as if the bridge wasn't high enough as it was.

We played sport, and lots of it. I was naturally keen on rugby but Dad wasn't at all pushy about which sports we played. We had plenty of options. There were tennis courts over in Ballina and also beside the pitch-and-putt course, where I worked for a while and first got into golf. We played soccer wherever we could, but mainly for Star Rovers, and ran plenty of cross country with St Lua's Athletics Club. It took me a while to get over losing the St Munchin's First Year Mile to Tony Nolan, a lad from Kilkee, especially as the medals were being presented by Frank O'Mara, a three-time Olympian and former pupil of the school. And I'd led all the way.

But the centre of our universe was Smith O'Briens. It's an unspectacular patch of land up the back of the town beside the boys' national school. You could easily pass its iron gates without noticing it, but it was special to us. Named after William Smith O'Brien, one of the leaders of the 1848 Rebellion, it has plenty of history – the club won the first Clare senior hurling championship final in 1887, beating Ogonnelloe at the Mill Field, Broadford, on 17 July. Impressed by the historical detail? I got it from the club's official history, written by my old national school principal, Sean Kierse. Unfortunately, the club can't claim to have lived up to such an auspicious beginning. By the time I joined, it was on intermediate level, and suitably chippy about it – only recently did it regain senior status. Very few club players went on to represent Clare at senior level, which contributed to the general sense of being hard done by, although, in reality, it was simply because so many good underage players went away to work or to college.

We were pretty tribal as youngsters, our bond strengthened by constant disappointments – we were good enough to make finals, never good enough to finish off the job. We played together all the way up – the Needhams, the McLeishes, the Scanlans, the Gleesons, the McCarthys, the Moriartys, Brian Lenihan, Liam Kelly, Finbarr Ward, Enda Keane, Sean O'Sullivan, Woody and myself. Because of my height, I often played with Woody's age group. He'd describe me as an awkward hurler but I reckon I was nifty enough. We had good coaches, including the late John 'Tar' McCarthy, Charlie O'Connor and the late Bernard 'Bomber' Carroll, who were probably a little ahead of their time in the way they worked hard on our skills – we'd spend entire sessions when we were allowed to hit off our weaker side only. I could break a hurley off a fella, though. I was good enough to play minor for Clare, once against Galway in Tubber. Seeing as the selectors didn't get in touch again, it can't have gone particularly well – I was actually reluctant to play as I hadn't hurled for months beforehand – but at least I have represented my adopted county. Woody and I also played for an East Clare Under-16s side that was beaten by Waterford in the Munster final at the Gaelic Grounds. There were only a couple of points in it.

Woody was a brilliant hurler, very skilful and incredibly aggressive, one of our key players until he fell in love with rugby at around the age of sixteen. He started as a corner-forward but ended up in midfield, probably so he could get more of a swing at the ball. The number of hurleys he broke. He'd literally go through five or six a game. It's just the way he is. They used to have fundraisers purely to stock him with sticks.

Hurling's a character-building sport. You're there with weapons after all, and the thing is you can't shy away. I learned that quickly enough. Step back a small bit, that's when you get split. You really have to be in the thick of the action, and it's such a quick game, so intense. There are so many obvious ways in which it's different from rugby, yet I reckon hurling for your parish is pretty good preparation for any professional team sportsman. That parish mentality is something I share with Marcus Horan, John Hayes, Mick Galwey and Denis Leamy, and I don't think it has done us any harm. You're playing with your neighbours, who rely on you as you rely on them. You go out and play for your friends and your family, you wear your jersey for the parish. We did that an awful lot and had great pride in what we did.

Sometimes we came up short. In fact, a lot of the time we did. It seemed like we were always looking at someone else receiving the trophy. At one stage, I blamed it all on my mother and wouldn't allow her to come to watch – it was obvious, any time she came, we lost. So one game in Newport – East Clare against North Tipp as I recall – I made sure she watched from outside the gate. We won, so that proved the point.

I have an Under-16 county hurling medal at home somewhere, but it hardly counts – I was only twelve, about fifth sub, never even close to getting on. Mostly, I remember the defeats in semi-finals and finals and how hard I took them. In particular, there was a Minor B final up in Tulla against Scariff, who are just up the road from us. We never got on with them. There was always a bit of bite and a bit of niggle. Anyway, we drew with them in Cusack Park and felt we were unlucky to do so. It went to a replay and then another before they pipped us. As if that wasn't bad enough, the following week my opposite number, Pat Minogue, turns up at our front door looking for

Rosie. One week, we're breaking hurleys off each other, the next he's coming to take my sister out. I wasn't impressed. I answered the door and when he asked for Rosie, I just grunted and left him there. I may even have closed the door before going inside and saying, 'That bollocks is here for you.' I've never been a good loser. I eventually forgave Pat but only when it became obvious he was going to marry Rosie.

Mostly, my way of coping with disappointment at losing was to move on to another sport. Basically, we played whatever was on the television at that particular time. If it was the US Masters, we were up at the pitch-and-putt course, trying to get up and down like Seve. For the Tour de France, we were Stephen Roche or Seán Kelly on our BMXs. Come Wimbledon, I was Lendl to Woody's McEnroe.

When it came to soccer in the early 1980s, you basically had two choices, Liverpool or Manchester United, and I went for Man U. I particularly liked Frank Stapleton and Bryan Robson, no-nonsense pros who got the job done. Closer to home, there was Tony Ward, who not only played on the Munster side that beat the All Blacks at Thomond Park but also played at the Market's Field for Limerick United against a Southampton side including Kevin Keegan. We saw Spurs at Thomond Park too, saw Glenn Hoddle score four goals in a 6–2 win, and then we went back to Killaloe and replayed everything.

Sport has always dominated my life. When I look back now, though, I realise I had only one true hero. And he's still my hero. My old man.

2

DAD

One of my favourite photos is of my son Tony, looking slightly nervous after a certain game in the Millennium Stadium in 2006. He was still a few days short of his first birthday, far too young to know what all the noise and flashbulbs were about, but at least he'll be able to look at the photos for the rest of his life. Unfortunately, I wasn't there for what was probably my dad's biggest sporting day – when Munster beat the All Blacks 12–0 at Thomond Park in 1978 – and I wasn't happy about it, either.

The day before the game was my fifth birthday. There wasn't much point trying to explain to me that this was an all-ticket match and the Munster Branch didn't give players free tickets, or that it was midweek and therefore Dad would be working up until lunchtime and not home beforehand. All I knew was that there was a game at Thomond Park, and when Dad was playing at Thomond Park, I went with him. Why should this day be any different? The toys really came out of the cot.

I was something of a fixture in the Shannon changing room from the age of four or five. This wasn't part of some plan to indoctrinate me in all the ways of the club, just some shrewd thinking on my mother's part. Sending me along was a means of getting me out of her hair for a few hours every Saturday – more than a few hours if Shannon happened to be playing outside of Limerick. On top of that, it was one sure way of knowing that my father would be home at a half-respectable hour that night.

So that I'd be safe, he'd take me into the home changing room and there I'd stay until kick-off. Even if they went outside for a few lineouts, I'd stay in Dad's corner to mind his spot. Not that anyone was about to take it – you had to die or be dropped before anyone took your spot in the Shannon changing room. One day, Ger McMahon threw his coat up on Dad's hook, just to get a rise out of me. Sure enough, I let out my best growl, 'That's my father's place.'

Most days, I'd just sit there, taking it all in, listening to the chat and wondering at the strange practices of Gerry 'Locky' McLoughlin. He'd take spoonfuls of honey before the game, or glucose, or bananas, whatever his craze was at the time. I'd inhale the fumes off the Deep Heat and soak up the banter, which would gradually give way to louder, angrier tones as kick-off approached. It was quite interesting for a young fella to watch men warming up, all the old routines – pick the spuds, pull the chains, shouting one to ten. I'd just stand up on the bench with my back to the wall, making sure I wasn't punched or stood on.

Shannon psych-ups probably weren't suitable for a five, six or seven year old but I wasn't complaining. No doubt there was plenty of chip-on-the-shoulder stuff, especially if Con or Garryowen were the opponents. Shannon had been a senior club for a quarter-century at this stage but were still fuelled by memories of their struggle for acceptance – either that or there was bitterness that so few of our players had been capped. There was always a cause of one sort or another. Listen to this stuff for long enough and it's bound to have some effect on you.

In the early days of the club, everybody in the Shannon team came from the historic island parish of St Mary in the heart of Limerick. In the 1970s, the parish started to expand in size to allow in the McLoughlins and Colm Tucker, who were born just outside, and it had positively mushroomed by the time Mick Moylett arrived from far-flung Ballina.

Dad had moved to the parish when he was two years of age, in tragic circumstances – his mother, Rosaleen, had died a matter of hours after losing a baby in childbirth. Dad and his brother Gerard were raised by their aunt and uncle, Madgie and Freddie McNamara, who lived in St Mary's Park. It wasn't a large house and Madgie and Freddie had four kids of their own, and not a lot of money, but Dad has happy, warm, loving memories of childhood. He was ten before he realised Madgie wasn't his real mother.

Soccer was probably his first sporting love. Limerick had a decent team back then and the Market's Field was a popular spot. He remembers games involving forty or fifty men and boys, kicking a ball up the street. It wasn't until he was fourteen, the year before he left the Christian Brothers School in Creagh Lane, that he happened across St Mary's RFC, a nomadic club, who trained and played wherever they could before finally settling in Corbally. Three years later as a stringy seventeen-year-old, he was on the Saints team that won the Munster Junior Cup for the first and only time, against Waterford City. This was in May 1967, just coming into the Summer of Love. I'm not sure the Summer of Love happened in Limerick, though. That final had to be scheduled for a 7 p.m. kick-off because the afternoon was closed for sport, reserved for the celebrations to honour the centenary of the Redemptorists Confraternity.

We have the Saints team photo somewhere. Dad's the lanky kid with a full head of hair in the back row. There wasn't much meat on him at that time, but he soon learned how to look after himself – you had to take it and give it to survive in Limerick junior rugby. By twenty, he had joined Shannon, the senior club in the parish, made special in Dad's eyes by winning the Munster Senior Cup in 1960 under the captaincy of Michael Noel Ryan. Ryan was the local scout leader and he used to keep the trophy on his hall table, so Dad would catch a glimpse of it every time he'd call to collect the keys to the scout hall. It's a massive trophy. There's a picture of Dad raising it above his head in 1977, after the first of Shannon's two-in-a-rows under his captaincy, club legend Frankie Flynn is alongside him singing 'The Isle'. There's another picture of me standing beside it the following year. I don't look so happy about the fact, but maybe that has something to do with the short pants Mam had me got up in.

I would have barely watched Dad play in those days – too busy with other kids playing our own games along the dead-ball line. All I knew was the obvious stuff. He was good enough to play for Ireland and the only reason he didn't win more than his eleven caps was that there was a bias against Shannon players. At least, that was what I heard repeatedly over the years. Guys were capped in his position who had less ability but came from farther up the country, or were favoured by the Dublin press. The Dublin media had a lot to answer for, of course, protecting the players they liked by not mentioning them if they made a mistake. I was told they never gave Dad a fair shake because of where he was from. I didn't hear it from him, I should hasten to add, but I heard it from Mam and people in Shannon. Again, when you hear it often enough, it becomes part of the way you view the world.

I've watched videos of his games and you can see he was hard and honest as the day is long. He was an old-school second row who jumped two in the line, the hooker firing it in low, hard and crooked. Back then, to tell a second row he hadn't been seen all day was probably the biggest compliment you could pay him. He was in the thick of everything. Moss Keane says he was great to follow around a field, 'mainly due to his economic use of yards travelled'. I like to think I picked up a bit of that off him. I also like the description of him by Alan English in *Stand Up and Fight*, the story of the 1978 game against the All Blacks: 'Among Limerick rugby people, those drawn from the city's working-class strongholds and beyond, Foley was loved … People knew when his time was over he would be there alongside them, supporting the next generation. He was all heart, the soul of Limerick rugby …

Brendan Foley was the player the ordinary supporter identified with more than any other.'

By then, he was the senior figure in a serious Shannon pack, and, judging by the stories you hear, they could be a fairly cranky bunch. The current Munster team see themselves as being self-critical and demanding of high standards from each other but the Shannon side of thirty years ago wasn't much different. The old man wasn't slow to slip his bind and give Locky's balls a good squeeze if he felt Locky was scrummaging for his own benefit and not the entire unit's. He also had an edgy relationship with Locky's brother Mick, known as Bungalow, despite packing down alongside him for thousands of scrums over the years. On one occasion, they even came to blows during a game, when Mick took exception to being told how to go about his business at a ruck. That edginess probably had something to do with their success.

For three of the pack to get capped – Dad, Locky and Colm Tucker – certainly says something. Before Dad was capped against France in 1976, Brian O'Brien was the club's sole international. You always hear them talking about how, if there was a player being watched by the national selectors, he always seemed to be the one who was credited with the try at the bottom of the maul. It didn't matter who actually scored. They all got up off the ground, hugging the fella who was on show. That's the way they were.

They say there should have been a fourth cap from that pack – Noel Ryan, who didn't play for Munster until he was in his thirties yet was a fearsome scrummager. The story goes that at one Irish squad scrummaging session the week before a Five Nations game, he did a job on Mick Fitzpatrick, the incumbent Irish tight-head, with some help from Dad and Tucker. Fitzpatrick couldn't play the following week as a result and so Locky got in, with Noel on the bench. Locky apparently needed treatment about five times during that game but he never left the field and Noel, the man mainly responsible for getting Locky back in the side as it happened, remained uncapped. There were no easy caps back then.

Shannon were pretty mean with the ball, too. They didn't play ten-man rugby. That would have been too expansive. Paul O'Shea was the scrum-half and the only time he passed was to Eddie Price, the number eight, if he had stood off the scrum. Niall O'Donovan and Sonny Kiely eventually took over at eight and nine and, on one occasion, Sonny made the mistake of giving the ball to the backs. The Shannon pack had the unfamiliar experience of trudging back thirty metres for a scrum and as they packed down, Niallo got a warning from the second row. 'Any more of that messing and it's the last you'll see of the ball.'

It was serious on the pitch but they knew how to enjoy a few drinks after the match. As professionals, we envied the old schoolers and their long trips back from away matches. I got to see some of it first hand. Shannon particularly liked games in Galwegians because that meant a visit to Moran's of the Weir, the ancient seafood bar in Kilcolgan, after the game. This was one of just a few stops on the way home.

People were reluctant to travel in the same car with me after I puked all over Seanie Moynihan on one trip to Galway. I got my head out of the passenger window but, unfortunately, Seanie's window was also open, so he got a faceful. A general nuisance, I was. On one trip to Old Wesley's ground in

Kilgobbin, I had to watch the game from an alickadoo's brand-new Saab to shelter from the snow and when I got bored, I built a snowman inside the car, which wasn't the best for his electrically heated seats. Either I was too shy to join in with Portadown Under-10s when they were a man short and keen to have me, or I was too bold for my own good and dislocated my shoulder by taking on some bigger boys in Thomond Park. I don't think Dad had planned on another evening in hospital with me.

More likely, he would have planned on ending up in Angela Cowhey's pub in 'the parish'. By the end of most match days, I'd be knackered, sprawled on a seat under a few coats and deaf to the singing, until Dad would throw me up on his shoulders and bring me home. I suppose I should be happy that he remembered me. Brian O'Brien went all the way home one night before realising he'd forgotten his son Padraig, who now plays second row for the Shannon Firsts. He was still asleep under the coats when Briano got back into Angela's.

There were times when Mam would go to the games and take me home afterwards – big occasions, like those cup wins, when there was serious celebrating to be done. One skite lasted until the Monday, but Dad was too clever to come home empty-handed. Just as he was coming through the door and Mam was about to let fly, he produced a puppy from behind his back, a gift. God knows where he got it from but the idea was inspired. That was typical of Dad's sense of mischief. One night, I woke to find him standing over me alongside Susie Hickey, the local seamstress, and Jerry Moriarty, the local detective and my football coach, the three of them giggling. Dad had a pair of scissors in his hand and said he just wanted to straighten out my fringe for me. I was having none of that. I spent the remainder of the night with a hurley in the bed for self-defence.

He has a good sense of humour and knows how to tell a story. There's the one about the phone call he got from Noel Murphy in Greystones late one boozy Saturday night after a Shannon game, to tell him he'd been called into the Irish team to play in Paris the following weekend and that he needed to be in Lansdowne Road for training at 10 o'clock in the morning.

'Brendan, I want you to promise me one more thing.'

'What's that, Noel?'

'Promise me you won't drink any more tonight.'

'Noel, I can't.'

'What do you mean? You've been selected to play for your country!'

'No, I meant I can't possibly drink any more, Noel.'

My mother says Moss Keane has been living off Brendan Foley stories for the past thirty-odd years. It was certainly Dad who said before one game, 'Moss, you'd better play well today or I'll be dropped.' He was dropped plenty of times – maybe not in the same league as Mick Galwey, but often enough. There was a long line of willing second rows waiting to replace Willie John McBride when he retired in 1975, and Dad was just one of them. Ronnie Hakin, Harry Steele, Jim Glennon and Donal Spring all took turns to partner Mossie and then waited nervously to see if they'd passed the test. Once, Dad learned on RTÉ Radio that he'd been chopped, as he was driving a van over a bridge in Portumna. I don't know why that detail has gone down in Foley lore, but it has.

He won his eleven caps in the space of six seasons and only

got a run of five games in his final year, 1981, when he was thirty-one, and then along came Donal Lenihan. End of story. No doubt Dad used all the conspiracy theories about various selectors and their anti-Munster, anti-Shannon bias as motivation. Before any trial matches I played in, he always advised me to wear something that would help me stand out, such as white shorts if I was supposed to wear black. At the same time, he's not a bitter individual by nature. The way he looks at it, he'd have liked a few more caps but there was compensation in the fact that he went on three major summer tours – to New Zealand in 1976, Australia in 1979 and South Africa in 1981 – and to tour the southern hemisphere was an especially big deal in those days.

He has a pile of happy memories from those tours, and some crazy ones – such as the time after a test in Loftus Versfeld when they 'borrowed' a penguin from Pretoria Zoo and smuggled it back to the team hotel, put it in the lift and pressed the button for the penthouse floor, where the South African and Irish committee men were in their own penguin suits, sipping gin and tonics before the official post-match function. Out waddled the petrified penguin and proceeded to foul itself all over the carpet in front of some shocked officials. That was very cruel but very funny, too, by all accounts. Another time, Terry Kennedy was lowered out of a hotel window, suspended from bedsheets tied around his ankles, in order to pinch a flag, or maybe he was just hung out of the window by his ankles to give him a fright. It happened. You wonder how Peter Stringer would fancy that.

Most of the incidents that happened on those tours will stay on tour. I'm just happy that I got to see Dad play for Ireland.

The first time was the best – the 21–7 win over Wales in 1980, which was only the second time we'd beaten them in a decade. I had a grand view from the West Upper, perched on Willie Duggan's knee! Willie was out of favour at the time, despite being a key character in the Irish pack that had won two tests in Australia the previous summer – Ireland were the first of the home countries to win a series south of the equator. Donal Spring had replaced him at number eight but he was still determined to go to the match, so there he was loping around the Shelbourne Hotel on the morning of the game in search of a ticket. When he spotted my mother sitting with me having a pre-match drink, he had an idea.

'Any spare tickets, Sheila?'

'Sorry, Willie, all I have is the two, for me and himself here.'

'Sure, he doesn't need a ticket.'

Soon, we were wading through the crowd outside the stadium, me up on his shoulders with a fine view of proceedings, Mam trying to keep up with us. The IRFU steward saw Willie coming and was ready with a forbidding glare, but there was no arguing with Willie in this mood.

'Don't think you're getting in with the kid on your shoulders,' says the steward.

'And who the fuck is going to stop me?' responds Willie. Argument over.

There were more problems with stewards after the game but, again, solutions were found. My mother tried to get me in under the West Stand to see my dad but the jobsworth wasn't letting me through. Fortunately, word reached my dad and, soon enough, I had been smuggled down the corridor into the changing room, where I was perfectly at home. I even got to travel back to the Shelbourne on the team bus with a police motorcycle escort, this time perched on Dad's knee and staring down at the crowds as they cheered and waved. Maybe I got a taste for it then.

Back at the hotel, I ended up in a room along with Tommy Kiernan's kids, watching *Match of the Day*. Before that, though, I got to hang around Dad's room while he got spruced up for the official post-match dinner. No doubt Mam was downstairs with the wives and girlfriends, who had to keep their distance until the speeches were over – amazing when you think of it. Anyway, at one stage, along comes Ollie Campbell, asking my dad if he'd a spare pair of cuff-links. They'd been presented with hundreds of the things on tour in Australia the previous year but I wasn't to know that. As far as I was concerned, my dad was being taken for a ride by one of the backs. The next time I saw Ollie was the following season, after the first Five Nations game, at home to France. Immediately, I was nudging my father in the ribs and whispering, 'Did he ever give you back those cuff-links?' Ollie makes a point of sending me a set most years.

All things considered, Dad had a pretty good time out of playing rugby – plenty of trophies with Shannon, a victory over the All Blacks with Munster, eleven caps for his country and three tours to the southern hemisphere, thousands of memories and hundreds of friends. The only thing that left him feeling bitter was the way his senior career ended, with a suspension for foul play, which was a complete travesty of justice.

The irony was he had retired from playing at the end of the previous season, 1981–1982. He'd given it heart and soul for fifteen or sixteen seasons and now he had a pub to run and three young children, who were demanding more and more of his time. But Shannon were struggling with injuries the following season and he wasn't the sort to turn the club down, especially when they turned up at the pub one Saturday morning coming up to cup time, begging him for a dig-out. It was just a friendly game in Terenure, but there were no such things as friendlies in those days, and Terenure were going well.

As I understand it, one of their tactics was to collapse the Shannon rolling maul and they were being allowed get away with it. Apparently, Dad told referee Gordon Black that someone was going to get hurt if the maul kept collapsing but he was told to concentrate on his own job. Sure enough, minutes later, Terenure collapsed the maul again and one of their players was trodden on, a head injury, blood everywhere, and Dad gets sent off for the crime – even though he had nothing to do with it. I know he had nothing to do with it for two reasons. First, he told me so. Second, so did a group of Terenure alickadoos I met years later after an Ireland game in Twickenham. They were still embarrassed that Dad had got the blame and did what they could to clear his name but without success. Gordon Black was convinced Dad was the culprit and his testimony ensured the Munster Branch banned him till the end of the following season.

I know who did kick the Terenure player, but that's by the by. There were no videos in those days to prove anything, certainly not for club games. At the hearing in the Royal George Hotel, it was reported that the Terenure player needed twenty-two stitches to the wound, which sounds improbable given that he finished the game. In any case, Shannon appealed the decision to the IRFU but to no avail. The referee's word was final. What a way for a fantastic career to end.

Terenure wasn't Dad's last game of rugby, as it turned out. Typically, he ended up going back to where he started, St Mary's, for a couple of seasons. As well as giving him the chance to 'put something back in', it kept him in some sort of nick for the annual golden oldies trips to Bermuda. He was never one to turn down a trip or a reunion. I've also been an excuse for him to stay involved in the game, either as a coach or as a supporter.

It's not my style to get too emotional, but we are very close. He worked hard, running the pub and starting up a bus-hire company, which is still going strong, yet he took me everywhere with him. He was a relatively young dad, so we've been able to play plenty of team sport together. We played a bit of Gaelic football for Smith O'Briens and, for a few summers, we played soccer for the Mall Bar in the Limerick inter-pub competition. It was basically a Shannon team, including old stalwarts John Pearse, Terry Fitzgerald and John Deegan. You had to have someone in the team who was over thirty-five and that was Dad, casting a large shadow as goalkeeper. We played out in Grove Island, beside St Mary's rugby club. I used it as part of my pre-season training but it was always competitive. We won it one year.

Dad was my first rugby coach. Over the years, he and I have spent hours together watching rugby videos and talking about them. Dad's other passion is watching westerns, classic films – *The Searchers*, *Rio Bravo*, *The Magnificent Seven* and anything starring John Wayne. He got a John Wayne boxed set recently and likes *The Alamo* in particular – what else would you expect from a Limerick man but a film about a siege?

Mainly, we would watch rugby matches, though, played and replayed, a lot of videos of the great Welsh teams of the 1970s, or the history of rugby presented by Nigel Starmer-Smith. I assumed everyone else was doing the same thing. Now I'm at it with Tony. He's only three but he knows old Heineken Cup matches so well he can predict what's coming. Must be in the blood.

3

BOARDER RULES

I sometimes find it amusing when people tell me how much my parents love me. If I was so special to them, how come they sent me to a boarding school just thirteen miles from home? I suppose they had good reason. Living above a pub was hardly the ideal studying environment. As a result, all three Foley children did time as boarders – Rosie in Bruff, Orla in Thurles and me, for all of six years, in St Munchin's College in Corbally, two miles outside Limerick on the Killaloe side. I've been asked if this was good preparation for a life in professional sport. It certainly did my rugby no harm – Munchin's is a bit of a rugby factory and has produced many Ireland internationals – and as Gordon D'Arcy and Simon Easterby will tell you, the boarding experience sharpens your survival instincts.

Going to Munchin's in the first place was flukey enough. My

friend Sean O'Sullivan was sitting the entrance exam one Saturday afternoon, which was to be followed by an evening in the cinema and the newly opened Burgerland in town. I was due to go along for the fun part of the trip but my folks reckoned I might as well sit the exam while I was at it. At least, that's the way it was presented to me. It was probably all part of some elaborate set-up to get me into the exam hall.

Munchin's in itself was an attractive proposition, mainly because of its rugby tradition. I was just reluctant about the idea of boarding. My folks had already suggested boarding in Roscrea, but I was dead set against that. I would have been perfectly happy to do what Woody did from the age of thirteen – head off on the Limerick road every morning on foot with his thumb outstretched, then thumb home again in the evening. Different times.

Anyway, I passed the exam, was offered a place and my folks insisted I became a boarder. I hardly had a choice in the matter. The first year was a tough experience for a twelve-year-old. I was used to small-town Killaloe and being spoiled by my mother. Suddenly, I was being driven up a 200-metre tree-lined avenue to a 200-year-old academic institution. The vast three-storey building housed 800 boys, around 250 of whom were boarders. It was busy and it was noisy but it was my new home. I got to visit my real home every second weekend from Friday evening till Sunday evening, while every other Sunday we were allowed home for six hours or so. That's not as bad as some boarders have it, but it still took some getting used to.

One thing I figured out pretty quickly was that the boarders ruled the school. They were there all the time, so if something needed sorting, the inmates usually took it upon themselves to get it done. It goes without saying that first years were at the bottom of the food chain, but just in case there was any doubt, early in the autumn term your dorm would be raided in the middle of the night and suddenly you'd be on the floor with your mattress on top of you – nothing more frightening than that in my experience but it kept you on your toes.

I also quickly learned that the name of the game was not getting caught. The priests had leather straps, and if you were ever found doing anything against the rules, they'd wear them out off your hands. Years later, I was told that corporal punishment was abolished in Ireland in 1982 by the Department of Education. I didn't enter Munchin's until 1987 and it was still thriving then.

One incident from my first year sticks in my mind. It was a Sunday, the day the seniors played a Munster Schools Cup game against Crescent. The senior boarders returned to the school at around eight with a few beers on them. When Fr Garry Bluett, the school president, caught a whiff of their breaths, he hauled them all out to the hall and let rip with the strap. It kind of set the tone. When you're twelve years of age, sitting down to study, and all you can hear is seventeen- and eighteen-year-olds screaming outside the door, it makes a lasting impression.

I got the strap plenty of times over the years. You'd raid another dorm at three or four in the morning, destroy the place and then try to get back undetected, which wasn't easy. There were only certain routes you could take, and the priests had them well covered. If you got caught, you took your punishment. I had no complaints, to be honest. It taught you some respect and a few manners. Above all, it taught you not to get caught. There was no brutality, as such. Garry Bluett would give you a kick up the arse as quick as look at you – he wouldn't stand for any messing – but if you got a kick up the arse or a whack of the strap, the likelihood was you deserved it. I can't have minded too much because the family have remained on good terms with Fr Garry. Seven years after I left the school, he officiated when Olive and I got married.

We got plenty of religion in Munchin's. Every Tuesday, Thursday and Sunday, we were at mass in the chapel at 7.30; every other day, we had morning prayers at 7.45. We also had to attend evening prayers every day, as much to calm us down before three hours of study as for spiritual reasons. The routine was definitely good preparation for one aspect of rugby – time spent in camp or on tour. Sometimes, professional rugby is unhealthy because you can be away from your family and normal life for up to two months, with every hour of every day mapped out on a schedule that is slipped under your bedroom door every evening. You're in each other's faces most of the day, and it can be stressful. At least Munchin's prepared me for that. It didn't make me as neat and tidy as the Easterby brothers, who learned their habits at Ampleforth, a real blue-blood public school. It didn't turn me into a brilliant time-keeper – I used to tell the Munster players I'd been delayed by the bridge in Killaloe if ever I was late for a training session. But boarding school did prepare me for long periods spent exclusively in male company and taught me how to survive in that environment.

Watch a rugby team having dinner together and you can usually spot the ex-boarders. Food is the most important currency in any boarding school. We had two major complaints. We always said the food was horrible in Munchin's, awful muck. The other complaint was there wasn't enough of it. A lot of trading went on, a lot of bartering. You'd usually get two sausages for one fish finger, although values did tend to fluctuate, depending on availability. The eating habits of boarders were strange, but amusing at the same time. Again, there was one golden rule – don't leave your plate unattended.

I had a big enough appetite – there was plenty of me to feed. I was one of the tallest in my class, and physical bulk can be an asset in the jungle. At the same time, I was still fairly shy, which probably had something to do with having a lisp. Woody christened me 'Slurpy' almost as soon as I joined him in Munchin's. I didn't mind it too much – Slurpy was better than Woody's nickname, Uncle Fester, after the ugly bald butler from *The Munsters*. I was the quiet kid in the corner, never one for saying something if it didn't need to be said. Orla and her friends called me 'Mono' for a while, because of the monosyllabic responses they'd get any time I answered the phone at home. Languages weren't my favourite subjects. I didn't fancy Irish or French, and Latin definitely didn't do it for me. I was more a numbers person.

At one stage, Mam signed me up for elocution lessons at the school. One afternoon every week, my sports time was put on hold as I sat in a classroom with a few other unfortunates, going through the time-honoured drills.

She sells seashells by the seashore. The shells she sells are surely seashells. So if she sells shells on the seashore, I'm sure she sells seashore shells.

or

*Thirty thousand thoughtful boys thought they'd make a
thundering noise so with thirty thousand thumbs, they
thumped on thirty thousand drums.*

A few months later, Mam rang up the school and demanded
her money back. Rather than pronouncing his t-aitches, her
son was coming back to Killaloe at the weekends with a broad
Limerick accent – too much time spent in the company of
those rough city boys. The same happened to Marcus Horan,
another country boy, from the village of Clonlara, who picked
up a city accent just months after arriving in Munchin's. Mam
got her money back, by the way.

I was more articulate playing rugby, or hurling, or Gaelic
football, or handball. Sport was big in Munchin's and this was
where I got my confidence and found my voice. There were
four pitches behind the school – three rugby, one GAA –
handball alleys, indoor and outdoor basketball courts and an
indoor swimming pool. There was something to be done every
day after school, which was just as well given you'd be sitting
down studying for two or three hours each evening. I had
energy to burn, and I burned it playing whatever was going.

Mostly it was rugby. Dad had got me to play some minis
with St Mary's and with Shannon Under-14s, and I'd played the
odd game for Ballina/Killaloe, but you could be thirteen
playing against sixteen-year-olds. It was the same thing with St
Mary's. The schools game was a better set-up, to be honest,
because of the junior and senior cups. I was involved in one or
the other for five straight years, and they provided a major focal
point for every school year.

The other attraction of rugby was that Dad was quickly

asked, and quickly agreed, to get involved in coaching. His rationale was simple. He'd be going along to watch the games anyway, so he might as well be making himself useful. He didn't realise what he was signing himself up for. I'd barely arrived at the school and he was coaching the senior team. From my second year till I left St Munchin's, my dad was my coach.

Some kids might have been self-conscious about this but I didn't mind in the slightest. Dad made me captain and played me at number eight, which is the most important position in any schools team, because he's usually the main ball-carrier. As I've said, I was a big kid. Dad remembers one day when he was coaching the seniors, he spotted a kid in the distance wearing a Leinster jersey, then realised it was one of his swaps and the kid was me. At thirteen, I was filling one of his old shirts. Naturally, I could do a bit of damage with the ball stuffed under my arm. Sometimes, I'd take the kicks, too, if the mood took me.

Dad didn't do any coaching courses or get any badges but he didn't need to. He had played on successful teams with great players and under great coaches. He knew what he was at. He knew how to set a standard of performance that fellas were capable of maintaining, and if you didn't reach those standards, he would tell you, no doubt about it. He was great for little skill-drills as well – tackling, passing, off-loading – rather than just picking two teams and letting them knock lumps off each other for an hour.

You could learn about the confrontational aspect of rugby from him as well, how every game is first and foremost a battle. I learned about various ways to get at an opponent and intimidate him legitimately. He told me punching was an easy option and one that would more than likely result in a penalty to the opposing side. A punch doesn't really hurt anyway, not when the adrenalin is flowing. You'd often be punched and wonder why the fella bothered. 'Hit him hard in the tackle, or in the ruck,' Dad used to tell me. 'You can do more damage to him that way, and it's legal.' There were areas within the laws of the game where you could use your size and strength to the best effect. He was always big on discipline and not getting involved in silly stuff. There were always other ways of making your mark.

We'd talk tactics after training, coach and captain, father and son. In part, that was because I was already addicted to the idea of winning – or allergic to the idea of losing. Also, it meant I could be fifteen minutes late back after training and not get into any trouble with the priests. Some Sundays, I'd be a bit late signing back in after Dad had taken me to Donkey Ford's, a lovely little chipper near St John's Cathedral, where they fry everything in lard and wrap your one'n'one in old newspaper. Dad's presence ensured I could bend the rules a small bit.

Looking back, it's as if, in every sense, I was following the trail he had left for me. In my second year, when a few of us Under-14s were drafted up to the Munchin's junior cup team (JCT), our first-round game was against Glenstal at Thomond Park and I togged out in my dad's old spot in the corner of the home changing room, the spot I had protected so carefully years earlier. We won, too, only to be knocked out by Pres Cork in the semi at Musgrave Park – not the first time Pres beat us, which is a sore point.

Hurling still dominated my summers but at some stage along the way, I realised that rugby would be my number-one sport. It probably had something to do with the excitement and intensity you felt at schools cup matches. From this distance, they seem quaint affairs; back then, it was life or death, with actual crowds watching you, noisy, committed, chanting crowds. Match reports appeared in the newspapers the following day – every time I got a mention, it was as 'son of former international, Brendan'. Sometimes, photographers even showed up from the *Limerick Leader*, *Cork Examiner* or *Evening Echo*. Rugby promised trips abroad – my first experience was a Munster Schools trip to Wales when I was an extremely naïve fifteen-year-old. It also presented a greater chance of winning trophies. With Smith O'Briens, we were always nearly men. In my second year on the Munchin's JCT, we won the cup and I was captain, beating Christians in the semi and then Crescent in the decider. That was the first time I lifted a trophy. It's an intoxicating feeling. I experienced it again the following season, when we won the Bowen Shield for Under-16s.

From there, you'd imagine we were set up as favourites to win the senior cup but there was a complication. Munchin's do a five-year senior cycle, unlike Pres and Christians, who do six. As far as I'm concerned, this is the main reason those schools have won the senior cup so many times over the years. Am I bitter? Of course I'm bitter. I had the experience of losing a cup final to Pres and it sticks in my craw to this day. Pres were coached by a career guidance teacher by the name of Declan Kidney who'd already enjoyed a fair amount of success with Pres teams – they'd won the cup the previous year, beating us 4–3 in the quarter-final at Thomond Park. Deccie was a bit lighter back then and had more hair but already he had a reputation for being organised and knowing how to push the right motivational buttons.

We reckoned we'd done the hard work by beating Christians down in Cork in the semi-final. Our record that season was pretty decent and we had Pres in Limerick again. But they did a number on us, fair play to them. Deccie had them well wound up, telling them we had already booked a hotel for the victory dinner and had kegs of beer ordered. There was no truth in any of it, of course, but why let the truth get in the way of a good psych-up? The Pres boys came out all guns blazing. They were tactically well prepared. Brian O'Meara, their scrum-half and a future international, swapped with flanker Jerry Murray when it was our put-in to the scrum, and every time I picked from the base, he was all over me like a rash. Looking back, I probably took too much on myself that day, tried to beat them single-handedly. It's a long time ago but I haven't been allowed to forget it. Deccie still has the golf bag the Pres boys gave him as a thank-you present at the end of the season, in the Pres colours, black and white. Some day, I'm going to get some petrol and a lighter and torch that feckin' bag.

That was 1991–1992, the year I repeated the Leaving Cert – not for academic reasons. I'd actually done okay first time around, getting the couple of honours I needed to be accepted on a course in marketing at what is now the Limerick Institute of Technology. I've no decent explanation why I wanted to do marketing. Perhaps it was because so many of the All Blacks who toured Ireland in 1989 seemed to be in marketing jobs for sportswear companies. It said so in their pen pictures in the match programmes. Anyway, I knuckled down to the studies that year and got the points I needed. We had three and a quarter hours study as standard every evening, plus a desk in your room in case you wanted to burn some midnight oil, which I did. As I recall it, the Leaving Cert was more about memorising and regurgitation than using your imagination.

I was even awarded Student of the Year, an academic prize – the first rugby player and the first boarder to be chosen. No doubt my former team-mates will get a right giggle out of that. My old man was just shocked. He came to the school with Rosie to pick me up and as we were driving down the tree-lined avenue, I chucked my parchment over into his lap with the words, 'They gave me that.' When he saw 'Student of the Year', he nearly crashed the car. I remember Rosie was pretty quiet all the way home.

The main reason I repeated my exams was rugby – specifically, the small matter of an Irish Schools trip to New Zealand, scheduled for July and August 1992. I'd have been a relatively young school-leaver in 1991, only seventeen, with the prospect of playing with the Shannon eighteen and twenty-year-olds. Dad had toured New Zealand himself with Ireland in 1976 and knew how much I'd enjoy the country and how much I'd learn. I'm sure another reason he was keen on me going was because he fancied going on the tour himself! So he advised me to repeat just a couple of subjects, have a crack at winning the schools senior cup and go on the tour. I'd played for the Irish Schools side the previous season, so it was reasonable to assume I'd be in the shake-up again.

My first experience of international rugby was against Australia Schools in January 1991 in a gale at Thomond Park. I remember a few things vividly – the sense of pride at being the only Limerick representative on the Irish team, the wretched conditions, but, most of all, the size of the Aussies. They were enormous, bronzed and some of them bearded. Having beaten New Zealand Schools before departure, they arrived here in their snazzy tracksuits after walloping Welsh Schools 44–0 in Cardiff. To our eyes, they were exotic beings. We'd heard how some of them had already 'signed forms' for rugby league sides – their captain, Craig Polla-Mounter, went to the Canterbury Raiders. They had other future pros in Stu Pinkerton, Jacob Rauluni, Peter Jorgensen, Scotty Bowen and Matt Burke. As it turned out, from our team only David Corkery and myself went on to make a living from the game.

The Aussies didn't seem quite so exotic once they were exposed to the icy wind and rain of Thomond Park in January, however. We led 9–0 at the break and had them rattled, but they rallied well, and their superior physical strength – and one dodgy enough try, as I recall it – proved too much for us. They eventually won 13–9. To have given them their toughest game on an unbeaten tour was small consolation, especially as Munster should have beaten them in Cork a few days later, again in foul conditions. Some of the Aussies got to see snow for the first time. They nearly turned blue with the cold – but still escaped with a win.

If the Aussies seemed big boys, they were puny compared to England, who arrived in Limerick in March with plenty of advance warnings about a pack that was bigger and heavier than the forwards in the senior England team. This seemed unlikely – until we got living proof at a pre-match reception where they strolled in wearing their impressive navy blazers (we were in standard issue v-neck pullovers). To give one example, Simon Shaw, a future England international and Lion, was already six foot eight inches and eighteen and a half stone, to my relatively spindly fifteen stone. Weights training was still pretty much a foreign concept for schools rugby players at that stage. When we scanned the pen-pictures in the official match programme, we could see they were nearly two stone a man heavier in the pack. Look back at some of the names in their team and you realise we did well to compete – Tim Stimpson, Daren O'Leary, Paul Burke, Matt Dawson, Steve Thompson, Tony Diprose, Richard Hill and Shaw. We knew there were four or five in their team who were Irish-qualified and used this as motivation. We gave it everything but there was only so much tackling you could do against that pack and we were eventually submerged 15–0.

Wales beat us 14–11 at St Helen's but we avoided the wooden spoon by defeating the Scots 17–9 in Kelso. I thought it was amazing that we were getting the opportunity to play at grounds I'd previously only seen and heard about on *Rugby Special*. (I thought it was even more amazing that we had to toast the Queen before the post-match dinner in Scotland.) This was nothing, however, to the prospect of playing in such places as Athletic Park, Wellington, or Lancaster Park, Canterbury – grounds you read about in books by John Reason about Lions tours, names that cropped up in overheard conversations between Dad and Moss Keane. Repeating the Leaving Cert was a small price to pay for a crack at a free trip to the greatest rugby country in the world.

New Zealand was home to Buck Shelford, All Blacks captain and an obvious role model for any aspiring number eight around that time. I was a Dean Richards fan, too, but Shelford was special. He was an almost mythical character, hard as nails and a real warrior figure. We'd heard the story about how he'd had a testicle almost ripped off by a stud in one game but played on till the end. In a country where hard, uncompromising back-row forwards are considered royalty, he was king.

Munster may have beaten them in 1978 but the All Blacks still had a special aura. If anything, the wonder of that story only added to their mystique. When Shelford's tourists came here in 1989, I travelled to Cork on the train to see them play Munster. The talk in Shannon beforehand was all about how Sonny Kiely, our scrum-half, had been done out of a place by Michael Bradley – another injustice against our club. Once the game started, I was more interested in the running battle between Shelford and Ken O'Connell, who took every opportunity available to fling himself at the All Blacks' captain. I remember thinking how I would have loved a cut off him myself.

So you could say that trip to New Zealand held a certain attraction for me. The Ireland senior team were due to tour there the month before us but the players didn't share the same enthusiasm. All you heard about was the number of them crying off for business reasons. There must have been nearly twenty players who were unavailable. Not surprisingly, they had a tough time of it against the provincial sides but then nearly pulled off a shock victory in the first test. I remember getting up in the early hours to watch those tests, seeing Neville Furlong hopping around John Kirwan to score early in the second test, before the All Blacks began to pile on the points. But as a team, we didn't read too much into those games because we had a different agenda and, as we saw it, a different mentality. We weren't going to keep the score down. We were going out there to win.

On the face of it, we had no reason to be overconfident. For the second year in a row, we'd lost to England and Wales and had beaten Scotland. I knew we'd a better team than the previous season, however. We had Jonny Bell, Brian Begley, Conor McGuinness, Clem Boyd, skipper James Blaney, Jeremy Davidson and an open-side flanker, Conor Davis from Belfast Royal Academy, who I'm convinced would have played for Ireland if injury hadn't intervened. We also had one D. Kidney as a coach, and he knew how to create competition for places and instil belief.

If I had one reservation before departure, it concerned the accommodation arrangements. Apparently, we were to be billeted with our opposite numbers for all eight games leading up to the one test match against New Zealand Schools in New Plymouth. God knows what it would be like staying with complete strangers the length and breadth of the country. As it turned out, this was one of the best parts of what was a brilliant tour. Not only did you get to see how people lived on the other side of the world – every time we reassembled there were stories to be swapped, notes to be compared about food and sleeping arrangements – it actually helped bring us closer together. I remember eating pumpkin soup for the first time, going bungee jumping in Taupo and being chased by the local traffic police one night in Invercargill and giving them the slip. One time I was taken possum shooting on a farm up around Napier. You shone the torch into a tree, saw the reflection of their eyes, took aim and fired. That was the first time I'd had a rifle in my hands. Brilliant crack. When we were in Gisborne playing Tairawhiti, I stayed with Anton Oliver, whose dad Frank had jumped opposite my dad at Thomond Park in 1978. Strangely enough, no mention was made of 1978 when we were there. Kiwis don't tend to dwell on defeats.

Another great thing about the tour was that we travelled the length of the country by bus – from Invercargill on the bottom tip of the south island, through Dunedin to Canterbury, Blenheim and all the way up to the north island, to sulphurous Rotorua, where we were given a traditional Maori welcome. We got to see what is an amazingly beautiful country, unlike so many modern tours, where players are sealed off inside hotels and departure lounges. It also helped that we were successful.

In the lead-up to the test, we won seven games out of eight and the one we lost – to Hawke's Bay, 13–15 – was due to a late intercept try. We set high standards for ourselves, trained hard and backed ourselves to win. Anyone who got an opportunity gave it their all. Deccie made sure of that. You knew from early on that he was boss. Nobody messed with him. He had us well organised and every time we were going out on the pitch, we were going out to prove a point, whether it was to the locals or to each other. I remember going into a huddle before the second-last game and him telling us, there's one guy guaranteed a place and he's not even playing today – that was Conor Davis. We were just chomping at each other to get into the side. At the same time, he knew when to release the tension. In the week leading up to the test match, we did no video analysis of the All Blacks side and knew very little about who was in or out of their team. The day before the game, we actually played a game of rounders.

It was reported locally that we took New Zealand Schools by surprise but I'm not so sure. Our first liaison officer doubled up as their team manager, so he had plenty of opportunity to see us play and train. He wasn't the only one. When we trained on the eve of the Canterbury game, we noticed a young fella at the side of the pitch on a lawnmower, cutting the same piece of grass over and over. Turned out it was the Canterbury captain masquerading as a groundsman. It was a bit of an eye-opener to see what lengths the Kiwis would go to in order to gain an edge on their opponents.

The test was on a Saturday afternoon and served as the warm-up act for one of Taranaki's NPC games, so by the final quarter, we were playing in front of a pretty decent crowd. They got some good entertainment and the right result – just. They had some side – Jeff Wilson, Trevor Leota and a kid called Jonah Lomu playing opposite me at number eight. We weren't remotely in awe of them, however, and it showed as we got off to a flyer, leading 13–0 midway through the first half – this was the first game we'd played where tries were worth five points each. They rallied but we still led 19–17 at half-time, and 25–17 with fifteen minutes left. That was when it got a bit annoying. Lomu scored off a quick tap under the posts to bring them within a point. Into injury time, they had us under enormous pressure but we defended like lunatics. One of their players knocked on but the ref – a local ref, of course – allowed play to develop. Someone went off-side at the next ruck and the ref ignored the knock-on but awarded the penalty for off-side. Wilson kicked the points. What a kick in the guts.

I was lucky to have Dad there because you need someone to put an arm around your shoulder at times like that. We were drained, physically and emotionally. I remember going to dump my bag on the team bus an hour after the final whistle and around eight or nine guys were sprawled over the seats, fast asleep. We'd put that much into it, only to come up short. We rallied for our last night on tour, naturally, but only numbed the disappointment rather than removed it. In the local papers, we were, predictably, the plucky Irish, which was a bit hard to take.

At least our efforts weren't completely in vain. On the back of that tour, the IRFU was encouraged to set up the Rugby Foundation, which, in turn, became the Academy, a means of fast-tracking talented young players and giving them guidance on fitness, strength and skills, so we'd be on a par with our counterparts in the southern hemisphere. The following March, I received a letter from its chairman, Ken Reid, inviting me on board. There were around twenty of us and we'd come together for intensive training weekends in boarding schools, including Clongowes and Blackrock, slipping out for pints in the local pub in the evening if we'd the energy left after long days. The schoolboys squad was invited along as the union's special guests to the November test against Australia in Lansdowne Road. We sat behind the committee box in giggly form, having had a few reunion pints before the game. I was now a marketing student and on the loose. No more rushing back to Munchin's to beat Garry Bluett's curfew.

4

CLUBBING IT

Now that my playing days are over, I can finally admit it. I once considered joining Garryowen – for about two seconds. It's amusing to think what would have happened at home if I'd actually mentioned it as a genuine possibility. While my parents have been incredibly supportive of their kids over the years, this would have been a bit different. Brendan Foley's one and only son wearing that sky-blue jersey? We're talking excommunication at best.

I can't deny that it's flattering to be approached by a club when you're only eighteen years of age. Shortly before I went on the schools tour to New Zealand, an invitation popped through the letter box from the Garryowen Executive Committee, who wished to make a presentation to honour my selection – I still have the letter, on headed notepaper. I went along because it was the decent thing to do. Mam and Dad, clearly feeling protective, came along too. There were also a few phone conversations with Murray Kidd, the future Ireland coach, who had guided the club to the All Ireland League title the previous season. But all along, I made it clear – I'd practically been born into Shannon RFC and there was no looking beyond that.

The fact that Murray had even approached me shows the effect that the AIL had on the club landscape in such a short time. A load of clubs had been opposed to the idea of a national league, saying it would never work. Now, after two seasons of huge crowds and massive media interest, they were all clambering to get on board, begging the IRFU to expand from two divisions to four. As time went on, the flaws in the competition became obvious. Back in 1991–1992, with just eight games a season, there was no continuity. And while those eight games were unbelievably intense, they weren't of a high enough standard to prepare players for international rugby. For a young player coming into it, though, that didn't matter. The AIL was a really big deal – especially if you played for a Munster club.

The league was the ultimate vindication of Munster club rugby. When it all kicked off in 1990, the media were convinced that clubs such as Wanderers, Malone and Ballymena would be top of the pile – I remember that Malone flew down to Limerick to play Shannon on the opening weekend of the league. As it turned out, Munster clubs won the first nine league titles, with Limerick clubs winning seven of those in a row. The Limerick derbies were mad, manic affairs. When Garryowen came to play Shannon in that 1991–1992 season, the day that Woody really made a name for himself, there was an estimated crowd of 18,000 at Thomond Park. This was before the days of terracing at either end, so people piled onto the grassy banks, anywhere they could get a view.

When Limerick teams travelled up-country, the trains were packed with supporters, who drank and sang their way home, usually as winners. Everybody bought in to the idea that this was our opportunity to prove a few points after years of being looked down upon – even now, with the gap between the professional and amateur games widening every year, Munster players take pride in the fact that our clubs have been dominating the AIL. Back in the early 1990s, the Dublin and Belfast clubs weren't prepared for the invasions, either on the pitch or in the clubhouse bar. The whole thing affected the make-up of the Irish team. If you look at the team that nearly beat Australia in the quarter-final of the 1991 World Cup, it had no Limerick players, but in the following Five Nations, you had Phil Danaher and Richie Wallace from Garryowen, with Woody on the bench and Paul Hogan getting a run in Paris. Gaillimh (Mick Galwey) was back in the frame, along with Shannon club-mate, Mick Fitzgibbon. By the time Young Munster won the AIL in 1993, Peter 'The Claw' Clohessy had become their third capped player.

At this stage, the provinces didn't really count for a whole hill of beans. Interpros were trial matches of sorts but you'd get just a few hundred punters going along. Obviously, there was a big crowd at Musgrave Park when the touring Wallabies turned up in 1992, and beating them was a big deal, but there was as much interest in seeing fellas from Garryowen having to get on with the fellas from Shannon, or seeing anyone having to get on with fellas from Cork Con. The one man I knew for whom Munster still meant a whole heap was Dan Mooney, who coached the Munster Under-20s team I was on. Dan is pure Young Munsters, and probably drinks in Charlie St George's across from the train station in Limerick, but when he was in charge of that 20s team, he was just pure Munster. His big thing was bitterness and pride. He always felt you should be proud of where you come from and who you represent, but have that bit of bitterness, a bit of dog in you, a chip on the shoulder. You have to want something more than the opposition want it, and be ruthless in how you go about getting it.

This all came out in a team talk before we played Ulster in Ravenhill. It was the first time I'd come across someone who believed so passionately and intensely in what he was saying about Them and Us. Ulster were a decent side and had stocked their team with quite a few fellas who had played for their senior side. Dan told us they didn't rate us. No one in Ulster rated us. No one rated us full stop. The media didn't give us a snowball's chance in hell. We believed him. At least, we wanted to believe him. We wanted the world against us, anything to get the hatred levels soaring. We wanted to come out seething with anger at the injustice of it all. We did, and we won. We won the interpro title that year, in fact, and Dan Mooney's words have stayed with me.

My main ambition that first season out of school was to play senior rugby as soon as possible. I won't forget the first night I turned up at Shannon training because it was also the first night I met Eddie Halvey. He was sitting in his car when I walked in by the old Shannon clubhouse at Thomond Park, and he opened the door and told me to hop in for a chat. So began a long friendship. We wouldn't always see eye to eye over the years. We'd argue about what happened Saturday night, about women, about him not passing me the ball, about him not shutting up yapping at referees, about anything, but he was good crack and an unbelievably talented athlete. At that stage, he already had a reputation as someone who could play soccer and Gaelic football almost as well as he could play rugby. Imagine if he'd ever trained properly. Still, back then, you knew he was capable of going places and it was exciting to think you might be playing alongside him.

Eddie looked and acted young, but for all his tight T-shirts, he is actually a few years older than I am. That said, he was still a relative youngster in the Shannon team of 1992. The club had made a reasonable start to the AIL, coming fourth in its first season, then finishing runners-up to Garryowen, but this was the same team that had won three consecutive Munster senior cups in the late 1980s and it was now running out of legs. Some of the old characters, and some of the old traits of Shannon teams Dad played in, were still there. Training sessions could often be narky, violent affairs. You wanted to avoid certain guys in contact sessions. Mick Fitzgibbon had no respect for his body whatsoever and would go through you for a short-cut. Kieran Maher was one of the hardest men I've come across on a rugby pitch. One night at training, there was a mass brawl. Paddy O'Grady had announced he was making himself unavailable for selection because guys who had missed the odd session were getting picked – he was referring to Gaillimh, who was in the Ireland squad at the time. Gaillimh got wind of this and it all exploded at the next session. I remember one of the props, a fella called Alan Supple from Abbeyfeale, just turning on his heels and saying he was off home. He wasn't travelling all that way to get his head knocked off. But that was the way things got sorted out in Shannon – on the training pitch.

I wanted to be as close to everything as possible, so I was delighted when Denis O'Sullivan, the First XV coach, asked if I'd tag along for the first AIL game at home to Greystones, to give bag-man Jack Kiely a hand. At eighteen, I was obviously a bit green for the AIL front-line, but it was good that he wanted me involved. Once again, I found myself in the position of an observer in the Shannon dressing room, only, this time, I had a better idea of what all the shouting was about. As it turned out, my career as assistant bag-man didn't last long. Third game in the 1992–1993 season, we had Young Munsters at Thomond Park. Mick Fitzgibbon couldn't play because of a broken finger, so I was told I was on the bench. Twenty minutes in, Paddy O'Grady went down injured and I heard a shout, 'Tell Anthony Foley he's on.' I nearly fell over in the rush to get my tracksuit off.

So I made my AIL debut against Young Munsters, or the Cookies as we called them. They were a frightening bunch, including the Clohessy brothers, Peter and Ger, Paco Fitzgerald, Ger Earls and so on. If there had been a television match official (TMO) or citing commissioner in Thomond that day, he would have been kept busy by both sides. As someone coming with a bit of a reputation from the schools game, I was an obvious target for roughing up, and the Cookies didn't disappoint. I took a raking early on and before I could get back on my feet, one of them was in my ear with, 'You'll get nothing easy here today.' Just because you were eighteen, they didn't treat you any differently. One time when I was on the ground and vulnerable, I remember feeling the thud of an opposition boot on the turf between my legs, dangerously close to my groin. I was back on my feet fairly quickly after that. They were so aggressive, so abrasive. If you got in their way, they'd run over you. Basically, the Cookies bullied their way to an AIL title that year and fair play to them. There are a few ways to win a league and that's as good as any.

I was happy just to survive the Cookies experience. As it turned out, I didn't miss an AIL game for Shannon for the next six seasons. There were times when I had injuries that needed rest, and maybe I should have taken a day off – in particular, I should have had a gammy ankle taken care of a lot earlier than I did – but there was always a short-term cure to get me through games and my instinct told me to play. I think I just liked the regularity of a game of rugby every Saturday afternoon.

That 1992–1993 season was tough as we struggled to keep pace with some ambitious clubs. Kiwis and South Africans were popping up everywhere and it was hard to imagine they were coming purely for the scenery. Similarly, high-profile Irish players were suddenly changing clubs where previously there had been practically no movement at all. Shannon refused steadfastly to pay players, even when professionalism came a few years later, but that season, as we slipped down the table, was a worrying time. Our recruitment effort was all at Under-20s level, and resulted in, among others, Alan 'Quinny' Quinlan joining us from Clanwilliam and John Hayes from Bruff. We had a successful team, coached by my old man, but we couldn't grow up quickly enough. Coming into the final two league weekends, we found ourselves with the grand total of one point from six games. Basically, we needed to win away to Dungannon and Garryowen in order to avoid the dreaded drop to Division Two.

This was one of those sliding doors moments when you wonder what might have become of the club, and of various individuals, if the result had gone against us – things were so competitive back then that it would have been hard to hold on to players if we'd been relegated. On the face of it, we didn't give ourselves the best chance of survival, for the night before the Dungannon game, the entire team had five or six pints each. That was the problem with travelling the day before the game in those days. It all looked very professional, having the team meeting in the hotel up north, followed by the team meal, but then it's still only nine o'clock and you can hear a band warming up in the bar and a few locals walk into the foyer in their glad rags. Sure, one or two pints wouldn't hurt. Fellas in the club still talk about it – mainly because it worked. We weren't looking too clever when Dungannon scored first but we just about got home, thanks to Billy O'Shea's place kicking and a drop-goal from Jim Galvin.

It was strange back in Limerick that night – the Cookies celebrating their league title after beating St Mary's in Lansdowne Road, ourselves knowing that we had one more shot at staying up at Dooradoyle the following Saturday. Garryowen were already safe and could have done us a favour by rolling over – it was between ourselves and Ballymena to see who got relegated and Ballymena had played all their games. It didn't feel like Garryowen did us that favour but we did win, 27–11, and survived.

That year's Shannon AGM was more like a crisis meeting. There was even talk of doing what Garryowen had done and hiring a foreign coach, which would have gone completely against the club ethos of developing from within. Niall

O'Donovan ended up getting elected, despite the fact that he was young enough to play a few games the following season. It turned out to be a brilliant appointment for Shannon, and indeed for Irish rugby, but Niallo had to endure a few scary moments in his first season. A good half-dozen of that Under-20s team were blooded and, come springtime, we found ourselves scrapping for survival again.

On a personal level, I was really enjoying the opportunity to play highly competitive games against decent players every week. You learned how to look after yourself pretty quickly. There was a good buzz about the league as well. In the past, the only club rugby you'd see on the telly was *Rugby Special* on a Sunday and that was all Hawick and Kelso, Bath and Leicester, with letters on their backs. Now, by the time you'd showered, got into your blazer, wolfed down some stew and been handed a pint, RTÉ were showing highlights from the other games around the country.

The drill for most AIL Saturdays was the same. If you weren't heading into Angela's from the Shannon clubhouse, you were on a bus coming back from Dublin, Cork or Belfast, drinking cans and on the way to Angela's. The Garryowen and Munsters lads would be in their respective pubs and at some stage we'd all end up in the Brazen Head – or Ted's as it was known. There'd be good crack and plenty of banter but you had to mind what you said, because there was always the chance that it would be repeated, with a few embellishments, in some team meeting the following week.

Socially, then, it was all great. I was still living with the folks in Killaloe but on AIL weekends I'd stay in the apartment Woody was sharing with Garryowen club-mates Stephen McIvor and

Paul Cunningham in town. During the week, I'd go into college most days – or rather, I'd head into Bobby Byrne's, the pub across the road, to watch MTV, play pool and drink coffee. I knew from early on that a marketing career wasn't for me and my attendance at lectures and tutorials was poor, at best. The subject held no interest for me and I left after a year to do a business administration course at the Mid-West Business Institute. Rugby was already the focal point of my week – training Tuesday and Thursday evenings, matches every Saturday. The only problem was we weren't winning very often. In fact, we only avoided relegation that season on points differential.

The real turning point came in a pub in Portlaoise, on the day when Garryowen won their second title in three years. Our game away to St Mary's had been called off late because of a waterlogged pitch and we were on a magical mystery tour back to Limerick. We watched Garryowen beat Blackrock on TV and it was like a switch being flicked in our heads. This was the same Garryowen we had beaten 6–0 a few weeks previously, yet here they were lifting the trophy, while we were busy trying to avoid relegation. We just needed to get organised. So we did.

First, we needed a couple of experienced players to balance the youngsters coming through. Gaillimh convinced Brian Rigney, a massive man with international experience, that it was worth his while travelling from Portlaoise on Tuesdays and Thursdays, even though he'd only be paid petrol expenses for his trouble. Someone else persuaded Conor McDermott to join from Bohemians.

Then we needed to get fit. That summer of 1994 was murder. Niallo got Dave Mahedy from the University of Limerick involved and he worked us hard, making us run up the hills in Cratloe Woods and around the track at UL. We even had Sunday sessions of tip rugby – to run the drink out of us from the previous night and prepare us for the Monday night fitness sessions, which were hell. I thought I was in reasonable shape at the time. Steve Aboud and Willie Anderson of the IRFU had given us programmes to stick to, and paid for membership of Lakeside Leisure Centre in Killaloe. But this was the first time I'd done what we'd now call a proper pre-season. I couldn't wait for the games to start. It turned out to be quite a season.

5

CAPPED WITH THE UNDER-14S

I didn't sleep a wink the night before my first Ireland squad session. Nerves? Not really. Alcohol, more like. I'm not sure what time it was when I stumbled back from Leeson Street to the Berkeley Court Hotel that Saturday night in November 1994. All I know is that it was late and Niall Malone, who was supposed to be my room-mate and therefore my alternative alarm call, wouldn't be arriving from the UK until the morning. I was sober enough to know this was a problem. If I put my head down, there was the danger I'd sleep it out and be late for my first engagement with the national squad, set for 9.30 a.m. on the back pitch at Lansdowne Road. Not good. Not good at all.

In my dazed state, I reckoned the best thing to do was stay awake, so I made some coffee and turned on MTV, but every time I sat down, my eyelids started to droop. There was only one thing for it, so out of the door I went, down the corridor and into Terry Kingston and Paco Fitzgerald's room. They wouldn't be happy, naturally, but once I got them talking, I'd make it through to breakfast and last the day on adrenalin. There'd be plenty of that in my system. I was determined to make an impression. I can hear you thinking, if he was so determined to make an impression, what was the twenty-one-year-old new boy doing out on the lash till all hours the night before? Easy. That's what you did in those days, especially if you wanted to become accepted as a member of the group known as 'The Under-14s'.

The name was coined by Willie Anderson, who had been forwards coach of the international team for the previous few years. He used it to describe the behaviour of a group of players within the squad, all of whom just happened to come from Munster. Come to think of it, the hardcore members all came from Limerick, and thanks largely to results in the AIL, membership was growing – Gaillimh, Claw, Philip Danaher, Paco, Woody, Halvey and now me. The idea was to play hard on and off the pitch. We liked playing practical jokes and having a few beers. I suppose the justification was that we were bringing a sense of fun to what had become a serious business, and helping to create some team spirit – not that I felt the need to justify anything. I was just happy to be on board.

Admittedly, I was late joining the Under-14s. The concept had really been born on Ireland's tour to Australia the previous summer, which has gone down in history as the Last ⟨ Drinking Tour. I was actually disappointed to miss out ⟨ tour. In the Under-21s, we'd been told that nationa⟨

Gerry Murphy was planning to blood a few kids in Australia, and he took Corks (David Corkery), Jonny Bell and Jeremy Davidson. By the sounds of it, they had some crack.

Most of it was fairly juvenile stuff. They made sure they got Neil Francis, for instance, and got him good. By this stage of his career, Franno was a senior player, and fairly sensible, so whenever a kangaroo court was set up on tour, he was appointed judge. He came up with some pretty heavy punishments for the Under-14s but they got him back on the Saturday of the test against the Wallabies in Sydney. When he went up to his room to grab his kitbag on match day, the door handle came away when he turned it – the lads had unscrewed everything but left the door locked. So here's an international second row locked out of his room a couple of hours before kick-off, with the bus waiting outside reception and a few jokers sniggering down the back.

As a former boarder, I knew to have my wits about me. Check inside your shoe before putting it on – there could be some mashed banana in there. Always pull the duvet right back to check for foreign bodies before hopping into bed. It still goes on. Alan Quinlan and John Hayes called into Gaillimh's after an AIL game a few years ago and when they opened their kitbags at training the following Tuesday, a couple of Neasa Galwey's dirty nappies were in there. The stink! You don't leave your stuff hanging around. Fellas get bored easily and when they're bored, they can be dangerous. Back in the old days, if you were reading a paper in the back seat on a car journey, one of the others would set it alight with a cigarette lighter. There were still smokers in the team back then. Come to think of it, if you fell asleep in the back of the car, there was a good chance one of them would tip cigarette ash into your open mouth.

We'd had a long trip up from Cork that Saturday evening before my first squad session, but it was a happy trip. Munster had just beaten Ulster for the first time in fourteen years, so there were plenty of stops along the way for liquid refreshments. There was a set routine for these squad Sundays, as I quickly learned – get to Dublin after your game, get checked in to the Berkeley Court, get fed and then get to the pub. We'd hop in a taxi up to Kiely's in Donnybrook and, a few hours later, move on to Leeson Street. A strange way to prepare? Not when you remember that this was traditional behaviour from rugby players. Drink was part of the game. We'd grown up hearing stories about the English prop Colin Smart downing a pint of aftershave, and John Jeffrey and Dean Richards kicking the Calcutta Cup up Prince's Street. Certain Irish forwards were legendary for their capacity to hold drink and still perform on the rugby pitch.

Tell Paul O'Connell these stories about the Under-14s and he stares at you goggle-eyed. 'How did you expect to win?' he asks, and I suppose he has a point. I just explain to him this was the way things were done. We were amateurs. He still shakes his head. He can't believe our attitude towards nutrition, for example. After that sleepless night, I tucked into a nice greasy fry-up a couple of hours before heading down to the back pitch at Lansdowne Road to train with the other élite rugby players. Pre-hydration? I had a glass of breakfast juice with me fry, thanks. Recovery and rehab from the bumps and bruises sustained the previous afternoon, or even the previous night? Rehab hadn't been heard of yet, at least not in a sporting context. It seems incredible now that the best players in the country would be put through a full-on contact situation twenty-four hours after they had played a serious game of rugby. These days, you'd do a pool recovery session the next day and that would be it. Back then, we were all amateurs with day jobs, and those Sundays on the back pitch were a rare opportunity for the coach to get some work done.

So we shrugged off the bumps, strains and niggles as best we could. A long queue would form outside Dr Mick Molloy's hotel room on the Sunday morning but by mid-afternoon, when we finished off the session with a full-on game, you'd have to be pretty badly injured to opt out. These were effectively trial matches where you'd be going toe-to-toe with your direct competition. There was carnage. You'd be practically guaranteed a scrap at some stage of the proceedings.

Corks, Halvey and myself were already a threesome and we were smart enough to realise that we'd all benefit if we worked together. If there was one player we picked on, it was Ulster flanker, Denis McBride. It wasn't just that he was another back row doing his damnedest to get picked, it was his attitude. He was virtually professional a good twelve months before the game went pro. He didn't drink, he watched what he ate and, because he wasn't physically the biggest of blokes, he ate weights for breakfast. All of the Ulster guys were into physical conditioning, and had been since Jimmy Davidson's time in charge during the 1980s, but McBride took it particularly seriously, and we were uncomfortable with his seriousness. We heard he did press-ups and sit-ups while watching TV and reckoned he didn't have a life. He was no crack. So if one or other of us saw an opportunity to give him a dunt in those training games, we took it. I now realise, of course, that in taking their physical preparation seriously, McBride and his Ulster team-mates may have been on to something. At the time, all I could see was that whatever I was doing, it was working.

In representative terms, I hadn't been mapped at the start of the season. To give an idea of just how far down the list I was, when a Munster preliminary squad of thirty-eight players was announced in August, the three number eights were Ben Cronin, Brian Toland and Len Dinneen. I was still shy of my twenty-first birthday and thought maybe I'd have to wait another season to get a crack at interpro rugby. But I got an unexpected break when Munster played Edinburgh Districts at Thomond Park, which went well for me. And then Shannon just took off.

The AIL was strangely structured – what's changed? says you. The first five games were played on straight weekends in September and October, while the second group of games were slotted in where possible between January and April. The only positive spin you could put on such crazy scheduling was that whoever won the league did it in all conditions. We proved ourselves to be a side that could play in good weather and bad – despite having a reputation to the contrary. The joke went that the last time our wingers received an attacking pass, it was so long ago that the ball had a lace. Very funny, but totally misleading. In fact, if you look at videos of some of our rugby that year, we scored some cracking tries. Sure, we had a strong pack, and if we sensed an advantage up front, we would ram it home. But our top two try-scorers that season were Billy O'Shea and Andrew Thompson, wingers both. Just thought I'd put that one to bed.

What made the difference for Shannon compared to the

previous couple of seasons? Obviously, the fitness work we did during the summer was a massive boost, physically and mentally. We also had a better balance between youth and experience. We were captained by Pat Murray, who was great to play in front of because you knew if the ball went skyward he'd gobble it up. It's a shame Pat was never capped. He was a better footballer than he was given credit for.

We had other strong characters in key positions, including Gavin Russell and Jim Galvin at half-back, Paddy Kenny at hooker, plus two beefy boys in the second row in Gaillimh and Riggers (Brian Rigney). A sprinkling of up-and-comers included Halvey and me in the back row, along with Andrew Thompson on the wing. Thommy made quite an impression after arriving from Wilson's Hospital – not one of our usual nurseries. First, he starts going out with the club PRO's daughter, Sinead O'Loughlin. Then he takes over the place kicking from Billy O'Shea and ends up the most consistent and prolific points-scorer in the history of the AIL.

We built up early momentum by beating Mary's fairly handily at home and then Garryowen, the champions, 15–10 at Dooradoyle – a sweet result. We ran riot against Lansdowne and finished up the first stretch of games with two tight wins over Old Wesley and Sunday's Well. I remember the Wesley game mainly for the stud I took to the side of the head, which opened up an artery. Very messy. I knew it was serious when I had to be stretchered off with a blood wound. My mother was beside herself, and had to be restrained from going after the culprit. My team-mates were almost as bad, and nearly lost the game in trying to exact retribution, or so I'm told. Dad was giving me running reports while I was being stitched up in the medical room. The following week I was available for the 10–6 away win against Ken O'Connell's Sunday's Well side, which was one of the toughest games of the league campaign.

With Shannon five from five in the league, it wasn't too surprising that we had a decent representation in the Munster side for the interpros. As I've said already, playing for Munster came a distant second to playing for your club in terms of intensity. We came together for a couple of sessions before each game, and on the day before that aforementioned game against Ulster, a few of the lads got a bollocking for going out on the lash on the Thursday night in Kinsale. The games were serious enough, though. There was the small matter of a Rugby World Cup in South Africa at the end of the season, and Munster doing well would be good for all of us. I was quietly aware of the possibilities in the back row. Brian Robinson's knee had given up on him and Pat O'Hara injured himself in the one November test, against the USA. Paddy Johns had had a run of games at number eight but seeing as Corks was being viewed as a seven, there were definitely possibilities at six – given the laws back then allowed loose forwards to break off the scrum early, the roles of the back rowers were less clearly defined than they are now. I had already played there for the Under-21s.

I did myself no harm by being part of the Irish Under-21 team that beat England 12–8 at Ravenhill in November – it was two days later I learned that I'd been included in that twenty-eight-man Ireland squad for Sunday training.

Munster beat Ulster 17–16, then we walloped the Exiles in London before demolishing Leinster 36–14 in Donnybrook, which clearly called for another long night in Kiely's. We wrapped up the 'grand slam' by beating Connacht in Galway. I did nothing earth-shattering but it all helped the cause, as did a positive outing in a trial match on the back pitch at Lansdowne Road on New Year's Eve, when I had a run at six. The Five Nations opener against England was just three weeks away and Ireland were going for their third win in a row against the Old Enemy. They wouldn't chance a nipper against Dean Richards and his mates. Would they?

We were at Shannon airport when I got the call from Noel 'Noisy' Murphy, team manager and chairman of selectors. By now, Noisy and Gerry Murphy, the national coach, had figured out it was healthier to have squad sessions on a Monday evening, so the IRFU shelled out for flights from Cork, Limerick and Belfast to Dublin and taxis to Clontarf FC, which had floodlights. Naturally, I thought it was a wind-up by Gaillimh when I heard the announcement for Anthony Foley to pick up the nearest courtesy phone – this was in the days before everyone had mobiles. I found a phone just in case and the voice at the other end of the line wasn't Gaillimh's. It was Noisy, a man for whom I will always have enormous affection, and not just because of what he had to tell me then. I'd be making my Ireland debut against England at Lansdowne Road the following week, at blind-side flanker. Holy shit. Ring home. Quick.

I was a jumble of emotions – proud, naturally, and giddy at the prospect of standing for the national anthem at Lansdowne as Dad had done. Against England. Dean Richards. Will Carling. Brian Moore. Christ! It was a lot to take in and I didn't have much time. There were twelve days to go but in that time we'd have maybe only three or four field sessions – because of work commitments and the regulations on amateurism, we wouldn't be assembling until the Wednesday before the game. So I had a lot to learn, even allowing for the fact that I'd have Gaillimh, Claw, Woody and Corks with me in the pack. Woody had been made pack leader aged twenty-two, which says a fair bit about the impact he'd made in the space of three caps. 'He does so much talking anyway, we decided we might as well make it official,' explained Gerry Murphy.

I'm sure Woody talked as much as usual that evening in Clontarf but I can't have been taking much of it in. My head was buzzing and my fingers were numb from all the handshakes. Meanwhile, the phone was hopping back in Killaloe. Mam kept a list of all the people who rang over the next twenty-four hours and it ran to five or six foolscap pages. When I emerged from the dressing room in Clontarf after training, press, radio and television were all looking for a word – mostly from Paul Burke, however, seeing as he had played for England at just about every underage level imaginable, often partnering Kyran Bracken at half-back, but was now making his debut for Ireland and taking Eric Elwood's place in the process. 'Cause for Much Celebration in Killaloe and Teddington' ran the headline in *The Irish Times* the next day above a report that went through both our backgrounds in detail, although it was only discovered the following week that we are related on my mother's side. We answered the questions and bolted for the airport. There were late flights for Limerick and Cork to be caught, and pints to be had.

It was late enough on that Monday evening when we reconvened in Angela's, but the Limerick branch of the Under-14s put on a decent show for me. Woody, Danser, Claw, Paco, Halvey and Gaillimh were all there. It could have been a scene from *Goodfellas* and I was becoming a 'made guy'. Happy memories. The only complication was the fact that Shannon, now six out of six in the AIL after beating the Cookies, were away to Blackrock the following Saturday. I wanted to play yet this was seven days before my international debut and tradition had it that, in these circumstances, you took the day off. I argued that this was different. This was the AIL. Previously, players had merely skipped a friendly – as I recall, Gaillimh missed a game against Ballymena before his Ireland debut but it was a fairly meaningless fixture. Shannon's game in Blackrock was far from meaningless. So I played. The papers made it out to be some heroic gesture on my part but it would have killed me not to play.

We had a score to settle with Rock for one thing – they'd given us a licking at Thomond Park the previous year. In Brennie Mullin, Niall Woods and David Beggy, they had a backline that had done a number on plenty of sides, but their coach – a certain Eddie O'Sullivan – had also put together a decent pack. They had Paul Wallace and Shane Byrne in the front row and Dean Oswald, a Kiwi back-rower who was good enough to play for Leinster. They were in the running for the league for the second season in succession.

It turned out to be one of those memorable AIL occasions. Steady rain all morning ensured the Stradbrook pitch was like glue – and this was no harm, I'll admit, given the pace they had out wide. The Shannon supporters travelled in large numbers and made their presence felt. Their moment came during the second half when Billy O'Shea fly-hacked a block-down half the length of the pitch and, with Mullin and Woods breathing down his neck, got a fingertip of downward pressure. Blackrock people will still dispute this but Billy was only doing what we're brought up to do in Shannon – chase like hell, dive for the ball and wave your hand in the air afterwards no matter what. It was good enough for the ref so it was good enough for us. With a 10–3 lead in those conditions, there was no catching us, and that was another night of celebrations on the road home.

I took it fairly easy, for obvious reasons. My main concern now was in making the minutes, hours and days pass as quickly as possible. I went into college on Monday and Tuesday, then up to Dublin on the Wednesday. One player who didn't join us was Michael Bradley – tragically, he and his wife Gillian had just lost a baby to illness. Brennie took over as captain and Niall Hogan of Terenure came in at scrum-half. It was now a baby-faced middle five with Niall, Burkey and myself all making our debuts, and Paddy Johns was easily the most experienced player. Then we had another disruption when Jonny Bell cried off injured, to be replaced by another debutant, Niall Woods. England had just one first cap – full-back Mike Catt, who was an obvious target for some early Lansdowne Road hospitality.

I assumed Catt was suffering from nerves because I know I certainly was. I was glad of any diversion – getting fitted out for my blazer and slacks, hiring a dress suit for the post-match banquet at the Berkeley Court – but there was no escaping. When we trained in the mud at Trinity College on Friday morning, we were aware of English supporters' accents in the background. They were all heading to Donnybrook later in the afternoon to watch the A game, but it was decided we wouldn't go along – better to avoid the crowds if possible. I wouldn't have minded the distraction. Anything to stop the waves of nausea building up.

6

NOTES ON A DEBUT

10.30 a.m., Saturday, 21 January 1995

Room 303, Berkeley Court Hotel

I'm awoken by the sound of footsteps in the corridor outside –
not ordinary footsteps but the mad, frantic thump-thump-
thump-THUMP-THUMP-THUMP-thump-thump of some-
one sprinting past your door. Then I hear the same thing a few
seconds later going in the other direction, then back again.
What the fuck? I look over at Corks in the other bed and he just
shrugs his shoulders. So I peel myself off the bed, pad across the
carpet, open the door, pop my head out – and nearly have it
ripped off by a blond-haired lunatic lashing down the corridor
at 100 mph. It's Geoghegan.

I'd been brought up to think of wingers as peripheral figures
who didn't have any real influence on the game. Certainly, in

Shannon, they were there to chase kicks and tackle, or to catch kicks and put them into touch. My heroes were all forwards, naturally enough – Shelford, Duggan, Keane, Tucker and Foley B. But Simon Geoghegan was an inspiration, first when, as a teenager, I watched him turning scraps of possession into tries or tackling like a madman, but especially when I got to see him up close. I always felt it was a shame his career ended prematurely through injury, or that he wasn't born about ten years later. He was made for professional rugby. It was a serious business for him. He was an incredible athlete and an unbelievable competitor, who spoke his mind – I seem to remember him getting into hot water for complaining about the quality of preparation a few years before I was on the scene. He was good fun, and quick-witted. He'd be there in Kiely's on Saturday nights during those squad training weekends, giving as good as he got, but also looking after himself. You got the impression he wasn't going to fly over from the UK at weekends just to piss about. Instead, you find him pissing up and down a corridor in the Berkeley Court in shorts, T-shirt and socks four and a half hours before we're due to play England.

For me, this actually isn't the best start to the day. Seeing Geoghegan's intensity only raises my heart rate a beat or two and that, in turn, makes me feel queasy again. The good news is that it's 10.30 a.m., which means I've had a decent night's kip – even if it's with the assistance of one of Doc Molloy's sleeping tablets. Corks took one. This isn't his international debut – that was in Australia the previous summer – but it's his first game at home and he's shitting himself too. It's good to be sharing with someone you played alongside at schools level. That's some comfort. I think.

Time for a shower, then maybe some breakfast, if I can stomach any food. I consider a shave but decide against it. I look young enough as it is compared with Deano and the boys. Dean Richards. Holy Christ! I look out of the window. At least it's dry and bright. Off to the right, I can see the back of the West Stand, Lansdowne Road. Holy fuck!

10.45 a.m., Breakfast

It's really an early lunch. A 2.45 p.m. kick-off means this is getting close to the last opportunity to load up on fuel, but no can do. Torn between the nausea that comes with trying to get food down your throat and the fear of taking on England for eighty minutes on an empty stomach, I manage to nibble my way through a banana, then another. Better than nothing, I suppose.

11.15 a.m., Team meeting

I had a soft spot for Gerry Murphy. He wasn't what I was used to. He was Trinity College, Wanderers, old establishment clubs, and he'd played as a back. He had a gentle manner and didn't go in for roaring and shouting. I suppose I liked him most of all because I reckoned he must have had faith in me to select me in the first place. He was also helpful with video work, often driving down to Limerick to go through tapes with me on the strengths and weaknesses of guys I'd be up against.

However, this close to kick-off I'm in need of someone who knows what I'm going through. I'm lucky in some respects. I've spoken to Dad and Gaillimh's here to guide me. Brennie Mullin's helpful, too. But in this situation, there's no one thing anyone can say that will take away the horrible feeling in the pit of my stomach.

It's funny looking back at the old newspaper cuttings. The week after the England game, I did a blow-by-blow account of the day with Liam Hayes for the *Sunday Press* – yes, it's so long ago that the *Sunday Press* was still going. I did my best to give the impression of a confident young fella. 'We'd watched the Five Nations preview on BBC,' I told Hayes. 'Corkery and myself. Eddie Butler's preview. We felt good. We felt we were going to win. The previous two Irish teams had beaten England. We felt our team was good enough to beat them as well.'

We felt good? Horseshit. We were in bits.

All you're hearing from people who'd been there is, 'Enjoy it because you're not going to remember it. It's going to fly by you.' How can you enjoy it if it's going to fly by? You're asking a lot of questions, trying to figure out what you've signed yourself up for, and of course you're doubting yourself some of the time. You're wondering whether you should be there at all.

You try to think what Dan Mooney might say in a situation like this. It shouldn't be hard to build up a bit of hatred when it's England you're playing – Will Carling, Brian Moore. The problem is that some people have us going into the game as marginal favourites. Two years previously, when Gaillimh had scored his famous try at the Havelock Square end, our lads had been able to feed off a few disrespectful pre-match comments of England coach Geoff Cooke. In Twickenham the year after that, they had the presence of Kyran Bracken, born in Skerries but declared for England, as their source of motivation. Another victory. When you think about 1995, though, it was England who had all the motivation. They faced the unthinkable prospect of losing to the Paddies for three years in a row. And you can be sure Moore and his mates had been lapping up all the media talk about how, in Nick Popplewell, Woody and Claw, we had the best front row in world rugby.

They weren't so shabby themselves. Our shock one-point victory in Twickenham the previous season had been their only championship defeat. They still had the bones of the pack that got them to the World Cup final in 1991, with Martin Johnson a more than adequate replacement for Paul Ackford, and they were massive. Johnson, at six foot seven inches and seventeen and a half stone, was the titch in their second row alongside the six foot ten inch Martin Bayfield. At blind-side, you had my opposite number Tim Rodber, the army boy, a mere six foot six inches and also over seventeen stone. Ben Clarke, only an inch shorter, must have been one of the biggest open-sides in the history of the game. Then holding them all together at the back was Deano – only six foot three inches but eighteen stones of granite. We'd decided we were best moving them around by playing a quick, rucking game, with Burkey getting it wide where possible, but that was before we saw the conditions at the ground.

12.00 noon, Lineout practice, Lansdowne Road

We walk down to the stadium, past the touts, the burger and hot-dog stands. It's almost empty inside apart from a few TV people, and it's like a wind tunnel. The lineouts will be a lottery. Back up at the hotel, the lobby is now packed, full of cigar smoke, beery breaths, slaps on the back and a general feeling of claustrophobia. (You can see why the team stays a bit farther out of town these days, away from distractions.) When we escape to our own floor, I manage to squeeze another banana into me and try to think of ways to kill time.

1.45 p.m., Pre-match walkabout

I'm uncomfortable in blazer and tie, and stick close to Woody, Gaillimh and Corks. There are no practical jokes today. In the stiflingly warm changing room, my number six jersey hangs on its hook, in between Franno's and Corks'. I get strapped and taped but when I go to put my gumshield in, I gag. Going back outside in the fresh air for the warm-up doesn't help much either – it comes as a shock to see the terraces, virtually empty twenty minutes ago, now almost full. I keep returning to the mantra – back yourself. You wouldn't be here unless you were good enough to be here. But back in the dressing room, with fifteen minutes to go, I'm still struggling to keep the gumshield in. I'm not the only one on the verge of puking – quite a few players are making sudden bolts for the jacks. You just try not to look for fear it will set you off. Jesus, just let's get outside. Just let's get on with it.

2.44 p.m., Seconds before kick-off

While Burkey waits for the nod from the referee, Monsieur Thomas, I'm standing between Woody and Gaillimh, preparing to chase, and they are both roaring, 'HIT THE FUCKERS!'

Working with Steve Aboud and Willie Anderson of the IRFU Foundation, I had done a fair bit on the psychology of rugby, especially on the importance of clear thought and accurate execution at moments of intense pressure, but in this moment, the culmination of everything I'd ever done on a rugby pitch, what I had to do was make the biggest collision possible, inflict the most pain.

I take great pleasure in piling into Rodber as he receives

Burkey's kick. Wallop! I've hit one of them. I'm into the game.

It would be dishonest of me to try to describe the match as a neat sequence of key moments and scores, because that's not how you experience it. There is nothing neat about your first experience of international rugby. The normal rules of time and space don't apply. It's a blur, a violent ordeal that's a million miles from Blackrock v. Shannon in Stradbrook. Enjoy it? This is not about enjoyment. It's about survival. Certain moments are lodged in the memory, obviously, such as a grapple with Dean Richards at the first lineout, after he threw an elbow at me. Suddenly, we're rolling on the ground, tearing lumps out of each other. There is no option but to stand up for yourself. Put up with his messing and you'll be his bitch all day. It's one of the basic laws of competitive sport. He keeps mouthing off at me when the lineout re-forms but I can't hear what he's saying and don't want to hear anyway. I'd been told by Gerry Murphy not to respond to any lip, even to avoid eye contact if possible, and that's fine by me.

It would also be hard to forget Carling's cheesy grin as he ran past after scoring, with the game seemingly seconds old. That's the one thing everyone I spoke to was right about. Everything happens ridiculously quickly. One second I'm standing behind Franno at a lineout five metres from our line, our throw. Next, they've pinched Woody's throw and Rob Andrew is running hard at Burkey and they've scored. You have no reaction time. Nothing is as you tried to visualise it. Their forwards are tapping and charging from deep, staying upright in contact, transferring cleverly, playing keep-ball into the gale but doing everything at a pace that fries your lungs. You fling every ounce of your being at a white shirt, the one you think has the ball, but it is always a split-second too late, so you drag yourself up off the turf, run back a few metres and do the same thing again, but it's never enough. Soon Ben Clarke has peeled off one of these mini-mauls to score England's second try and they're 12–3 ahead when it's us that needed to be two scores up on the strength of the gale. And then, just like that, it's half-time.

Whether through fear or desperation, or maybe because England reckoned they had the job done, we avoided a complete rout in the second half. I even got my hands on the ball, got the chance to run, which presumably was the main reason for me being there in the first place. It seemed every time I was put to ground, England came away with the ball and Andrew was banging it back downfield. But at least I got to experience the wave of positive energy that comes from the crowd when you bounce a tackler and surge forward. That's one of my very few memories from a second half that went even quicker than the first.

There is just one sequence that I can recall almost frame by frame and it came well into injury time. Niall Woods is haring down the left, kicking ahead, catching Catt in possession in the corner. Then Gabriel Fulcher, on for Franno, almost scores, only for the ref to award us the penalty. I'm running frantically to get there and just as Burkey tosses the ball to Brennie, I grab it, tap it to myself, run at Tony Underwood, a soft target if ever there was one, and I score. It makes no difference to the result but 8–20 looks a bit better than 3–20 and I've scored on my international debut. It takes an age for me to scrape myself off the turf but I'm not milking the moment, believe me. I'm just shattered.

6.00 p.m., Medical room under the West Stand

The game has been over for nearly two hours and I'm still struggling to produce a sample. What a pain in the arse. Things kept moving quickly after the game. Just as Rodber came into the changing room to swap jerseys – and kindly told me to keep my own because the first is special – I felt a tap on the shoulder. RTÉ wanted a word. Then came another tap on the shoulder – the drug-testers have drawn your name out of the hat along with Gaillimh, Underwood and Catt. That was another novelty. But now, nearly two hours later, I'm the only one left in this small concrete room with an empty plastic container in my hand and a stomach bloated with water while the international weekend carries on without me. Finally, Gaillimh walks in with a solution – a pint of Heineken from the post-match reception. Bingo!

My body needs food, rest and a massage. Instead, I have to walk back to the team hotel because the bus is long gone. Then I'm squeezing through the mill at the Berkeley Court to find my folks. After a few pints with them, it's up to my room, into my tux and down to the dinner, where I am the evening's entertainment for Messrs Rodber, Johnson, Richards, Danaher, Ubogu and whoever else is on my table. Gaillimh is there, too, definitely, because I remember he was supposed to be looking after me. Judging by the state I ended up in, he didn't do a very good job.

I should explain. One of the things that goes with making your international debut is that every one of your team-mates, and every one of your opponents, is obliged not only to buy you a celebratory drink but also to make sure that you drink it. Basic arithmetic says that's a lot of alcohol. As post-match routines have changed, it's a custom that's becoming harder to enforce. Some countries, recognising that élite athletes shouldn't be made to sit in stuffy rooms eating rich food and listening to long speeches shortly after they have played high-intensity games, now hold much shorter, less formal post-match affairs. The IRFU committee take the post-match entertainment seriously, however, and at the dinner on the night of my debut, a stag affair, the players on my table were taking things seriously too.

I think that was the night when the nickname Axel was born. It might have been Dean Richards who came up with it, but I can't be sure. I can't be sure of anything apart from the fact that at some stage fairly early in the evening, I had to go up and collect my international cap from the IRFU President Ken Reid, and that my friends were determined I would puke before so doing – just like England's Steve Ojomoh after the corresponding fixture the previous year. Only seconds before Ojomoh was called up before the top table, he'd been emptying his stomach into an ice-bucket. Somehow, despite being forced to down full glasses of red wine in one, followed by obscure cocktails, I avoided this fate. Maybe it was because I had nothing solid in my stomach to throw up. I now wonder if I ate anything apart from those three bananas that day and night. It was the port that finished me off. I don't know if it was instinct or a kind, guiding spirit that pointed me in the direction of my bedroom when the dinner was over. I just have this vague recollection of stumbling around the foyer of the Berkeley Court, not knowing my arse from my elbow, trying to figure where they'd put the lifts. In one sense, it was a fitting end to what had been a disorienting day.

No need for sleeping tablets that night. The only thing that woke me was hunger. The custom in those days was to meet in Kitty O'Shea's for brunch, then head home in time for BBC's *Rugby Special*. The hardest bit was walking to Kitty's. There was no part of me that didn't ache horribly. Then, along with the poisonous pain of the hangover and the depressing memory of defeat, came the awful realisation that I had a week of exams coming up at the Business Institute. At least the newspapers were reasonably kind to me, and over the next few days, interview requests arrived from the Sundays, which I took as a positive sign. At the end of our chat, Liam Hayes asked me whether I could live with ten years of international rugby. 'It's a hard life,' I responded, 'but it'd be nice.'

Dad, Mam, Rosie and me, 1976.

Dad captains Shannon to win the Munster Senior Cup

As children at home in Murroe.

Always the one with the ball! Me with Rosie.

Underage hurling with Smith O'Briens, Killaloe.

Senior Cup for St Munchin's v. Rockwell, 1990.

 Irish Schools, 1991–1992

New Zealand Schools Boys tour 1992 with coach Deccie.

Shannon 1995, a week before my Irish call up,
leaving pitch with Kieran Maher.

Drinks in the Mall Bar, celebrating my Irish call up.

Keith Wood, Mick Galwey, Phillip Danaher and Peter Clohessy – the Under 14s! Pictured at St Munchin's College.

I caught my prize.
Myself and Olive on our wedding day, July 1999.

7

A HEAVY FALL

'I didn't like losing to England. Losing is not something I accept.' So I told Brendan Fanning in *The Sunday Times* the week after my debut. Well, I was going to have to get used to losing, with Ireland at least. It was a strange contrast. Shannon had unity of purpose, consistency of selection and a winning culture. Ireland had none of these things. We'd had two consecutive wins over England and a couple of decent performances on tour against Australia, where the lads had benefited from having an extended period training together without the distractions of day jobs or exams. This had helped to promote the idea that we were heading in the right direction. In truth, we were all over the place. When you consider rugby was only a few months away from being declared professional, it's frightening to think how amateur we were.

The selection system was a joke, for example. Just as had been the case in my dad's era, there were as many as five selectors, all of whom had their own agendas and their favourite players, which meant it was virtually impossible for Gerry Murphy to be given the team that he actually wanted. There was certainly no chance he would get the same team for two games in a row. After the defeat by England, there was carnage. Conor O'Shea, Niall Woods, Niall Hogan, Gaillimh and Corks all got the bullet for the trip to Edinburgh two weeks later, with Franno dropping out injured. I was the only member of the back five to wear the same jersey for the two games running.

Now, I'm all in favour of competition for places, but the sort of chopping and changing that went on back then can't be good for confidence or cohesion. It certainly didn't work against Scotland. I remember being told beforehand that the forwards weren't allowed to carry the ball – a strange instruction. Clearly, it was felt our strength was out wide. Sure enough, Brennie Mullin and Jonny Bell both scored nice tries but we were beaten 26–13, which increased the pressure on everyone – players, management and IRFU.

A lot of that pressure was coming from an increasingly aggressive media. Leading the charge was the late Mick Doyle, who used to let fly in a column in the *Sunday Independent* and also on RTÉ's late-night chat show *Rugby After Dark*. Doyler was a former coach of the Irish team, which made it even harder for some of the older players to take. He was giving Franno a particularly hard time, although he didn't refer to him by name – he was either 'Yer man' or 'the Belvederean', a reference to Franno's controversial change of club from

Blackrock to Old Belvedere. I had time for Franno. We were close alphabetically, which meant we roomed together a bit. He was a senior player, so I'd have to make him cups of tea, but we got on grand. I certainly didn't think he should have to put up with some of the shite he was getting from Doyler. The senior players had agreed there would be no co-operation with the *Sunday Independent* – we would even refuse to talk to RTÉ during the World Cup because of what he was saying about us. That didn't stop the newspaper finding things to write about though, as we discovered the week after the Scotland defeat.

Under the headline 'This Is A Team Without A Soul', David Walsh revealed that several of the squad had been out on the lash in Dublin during a two-day squad get-together the weekend before the Scotland game.

'The weekend before the Scotland game was set aside for the squad and the players trained twice on Saturday and again on Sunday morning,' Walsh wrote. 'The players worked long and hard on the Saturday. That Saturday evening, at least seven of the players hit the town. Two of them were at the over-21 disco in Bective, another group finished the night at The Frog Café on Baggot Street. It was around 4 a.m. when they left. The majority of the seven were part of the team which played in Edinburgh. Training was due to begin at 9.15 on Sunday morning.'

There were no prizes for guessing that the Bective Two were Woody and me, the two sprogs. Staying in our hotel room to rest up for the following day's training wouldn't have been high on our list of options for that Saturday night. We were up in the smoke and there was socialising to be done. When this got into the papers, we weren't concerned with the rights and wrongs of going out the night before an Ireland training session. We just wanted to know who had leaked the story. It definitely wasn't good for Woody, who was chopped for the next game, against France.

Naturally, he wasn't the only one. Burkey was replaced by Eric Elwood and there were more musical chairs in the pack, albeit caused by illness and injury to Ben Cronin and Paddy Johns. I had the pleasure of playing alongside Davy Tweed, the man with the UVF tattoo on his ankle but who'd throw a dig for you if you were on his side, especially during those Sunday morning matches on the back pitch at Lansdowne.

The other good news was that Halvey was called up for his first cap when Paddy pulled out with suspected appendicitis. It was brilliant to be playing a test match alongside someone who had become a good mate. It was a tough gig for us, though. We were up against a serious French back row in Philippe Benetton, Marc Cécillon and Abdel Benazzi. They had around a hundred caps between them, and ran the show. We were happy to trail just 3–0 after playing the first half into another Lansdowne Road gale, but we barely saw the ball in the second half and lost 7–25.

That gave us zero wins from three games, one away from a whitewash, and the sense of desperation was clear from what Noisy and Gerry were saying to the media afterwards – we had to have a forty-man élite squad; we needed to look at what Australia were doing; we didn't need to be professional to have a professional attitude; we needed professional help. All of it was true.

As a means of preparing us for international rugby, the AIL was totally inadequate and the schedule was too spread out.

The best players weren't getting enough guidance, week in, week out, on how to prepare physically to compete with the big teams. In terms of individual player development, I felt I'd benefited from the IRFU Foundation but that could only take you so far. After that, it was pretty much all down to Gerry Murphy, and he was under enough pressure as it was. There had been a development tour to southern Africa in 1993, which had positive aspects, but it seemed like nothing was done on the back of it. The same was true of the tour to Australia the following summer. It was all very haphazard, and meanwhile, the union was happily turning a blind eye to the fact that other countries were tooling up for full-blown professionalism. For the committee men, professionalism remained a dirty word.

I see all that now, and I probably read a bit about it at the time, but it washed over me. When you're twenty-one, you don't think of the big picture. You're too excited by the fact that you're playing international rugby, and surviving. I was one of five players to appear in all four championship matches (there were more axeings for the final game in Cardiff). Even Doyler was saying reasonably nice things about me. After the France game, his assessment was: 'Anthony Foley started well, but was overcome with the malaise that affected the senior pros in the pack and was running around like a blue-assed fly in the end. He kept going though.' From Doyler, this amounted to glowing praise.

I was quietly chuffed with the way things were going. I was getting phone calls asking me to play for the Barbarians, which was a big deal back then. As long as I stayed fit, I was odds-on to go to the Rugby World Cup. In South Africa! At the start of that season, I hadn't even been capped by Munster. You don't ponder the amateur–professional debate when your next game is at the old Arms Park on Paddy's weekend. What a stadium! What an anthem! We even won, squeezing home 16–12 against a side that was in the same World Cup group as us. We celebrated like we'd won the title.

I had plenty to celebrate around that time. The Saturday before the Wales game, Shannon got good news – Garryowen had beaten St Mary's and handed us the AIL title with one game still to play. The league had been spluttering along all the while at a rate of around one game a month but this didn't halt our momentum. Win number eight was an 8–6 mud-fest away to Cork Con and then came what was effectively the clincher – another wet, two-point win on the road, away to Dungannon. We effectively won it on place-kicking. Two of their penalties rebounded off uprights, whereas Andrew Thompson kicked four out of four. Maybe it was something to do with the fact that on the morning of the match, he'd gone up to Stevenson Park to practise with the Gilbert ball we'd be using that afternoon – we preferred the slippery Mitre ball in Shannon, the one no one else seemed to be able to hold in the wet.

Having Garryowen seal the deal wasn't the perfect way for us to win our first league but did we let it spoil our night? Besides, we'd get another chance to celebrate after the final league game, against Instonians at Thomond Park. I remember it was played on a sunny day in early April and we got a big crowd, including the Taoiseach, John Bruton – like I said, the AIL was a big deal back then. All that was at stake was whether we could become the first club to win the league with a 100 per cent record. Instonians made us sweat for it – they scored a try, and we'd only conceded two tries in nine games up until that point – but we led all the way and won 16–13. Gaillimh had a huge match – a timely response to the fact that he'd been left out of the World Cup squad, which had been announced the previous day. I remember that Noel 'Buddha' Healy was first out of the traps when we needed a blood replacement in the second half. Buddha was our replacement prop, and well into his late thirties at this stage. He wasn't the temporary replacement that Niall O'Donovan had nominated but Buddha wasn't going to let that interfere with him getting an AIL medal. He was there in the thick of it as we sang 'The Isle', led by Frankie Flynn.

This is the same Frankie Flynn who sang the same song after my old man lifted the Munster Senior Cup in 1977 and 1978. We celebrated just as hard as they had back in the 1970s, basically going on a three-day bender. That Saturday night, we brought the trophy around the pubs in town before finishing back at the clubhouse. The following day, we met in Cowhey's at lunchtime, eventually moving on to The Office, another Shannon pub. Then on Monday, it was Flannery's for breakfast and off we went again. So we got the bones of three good days on the beer – madness when you think back on it, but great crack. I suppose the way we thought about it was, we'd put in so much work since the previous August we deserved a decent blow-out. There were still nearly two months before we'd be heading to South Africa. Besides, I felt bullet-proof.

I got shot down in Treviso. If I had to give back one international cap, I'd probably choose the 'friendly' we played against Italy shortly before departure for the World Cup. It was probably planned as a nice warm-weather preparation opportunity but it turned out to be an ambush. The only blessing was that there was no television coverage of the game back home and only a few newspapers sent reporters. There were still casualties, however, and I was one of them.

Treviso will go down as one of the great disaster stories in Irish rugby history. The warning signs were there before the game, when the management foolishly trusted the locals to arrange transport from the hotel to the stadium. We waited for the bus to arrive but it never came. For maybe half an hour of a beautifully sunny afternoon, we were sat on bags in the forecourt of the hotel, waiting and watching Noisy working himself into a lather. Eventually, after numerous frantic phone calls, he realised desperate measures were called for and ran out onto the road to try to flag down a few taxis. It was hilarious. So that's how we got to the Stadio Monigo, in convoy, arriving with about twenty minutes to go before kick-off. Noisy pleaded with the referee, Tony Spreadbury, to delay the start but he was having none of it. We basically had time to get togged out, strapped up and on to the pitch.

Compare this with the Italian preparation. They'd been lobbying for years for inclusion in an extended Six Nations, so every game against one of the established countries was a massive opportunity for them. I read afterwards that they'd been in camp for over a week before this test. They certainly played like they meant it, whereas we were all over the place. Maybe some of us were subconsciously minding ourselves because it was so close to the World Cup. Italy weren't minding themselves. They were a bloody good side, too. They had a serious pack of forwards, all big men who could scrummage and maul you off the park, and brilliant half-backs in Alessandro Troncon and Diego Dominguez. Dominguez really killed us with his tactical kicking. Every time we thought we were getting somewhere, he'd knock us back downfield. They won 22–12 and probably should have won by more. They certainly got full value for their first victory over a top-tier country. Their lap of honour must have been embarrassing for our union committee men, quite a few of whom had made the trip – Venice is only a short hop from Treviso, so that would have been an added attraction. Only the previous week, the union had reaffirmed its commitment to amateurism and, boy, had we been made to look amateur.

That wasn't the end of it, either. Come check-out time at the hotel the following morning, Noisy was presented with a monumental bar bill that had been run up the previous night, for which union secretary Philip Browne had to write a cheque. Then, there was the matter of the laundry bags that some of us had taken with us from the rooms – not the sort of thing you'd imagine a hotel would value that highly. Well, this hotel must have valued them highly, because the manager demanded they be handed back, even if it meant luggage being taken off the team bus (which had finally arrived) and opened. Luckily, I avoided the public embarrassment of being branded as a petty thief – I'd checked out early to catch a flight for Rosie and Pat's wedding, so I wasn't on the bus. I did subsequently get a bollocking over the laundry bag issue, however, which made it an even worse trip in terms of my place in the pecking order. It seemed like the management had a stick with which to beat a few of us and they were going to beat us hard.

I was still pretty confident I'd have a significant part to play in the World Cup pool matches against New Zealand, Japan and Wales, especially considering they were scheduled to take place within an eight-day period, and all of them at altitude.

Recognising the extra physical stress caused by playing several thousand feet above sea level in Johannesburg and Bloemfontein, the management had been given permission to hire a fitness expert, Giles Warrington, who started getting us into shape during a two-week camp in Kilkenny – not exactly a high-altitude location, but at least we had a specialist on board. Still, nothing could prepare me for the land I'd get in Jo'burg, when Noisy threatened to send me home from the World Cup.

The Tuesday before the All Blacks game, a few of us broke curfew. The team had been announced that day and, as I expected, I was on the bench – the back row was Corks, Denis McBride and Paddy Johns. That evening, I met Rosie and Pat, who were on honeymoon and, on the way back, I popped in to a bar to meet the dirt-trackers (players not in the twenty-two), who were out with a few of the backroom staff. We weren't out all night but we were definitely late getting back to the hotel, and given the goings-on in Treviso, we had to be on our best behaviour. So it wasn't good to hear that Noisy was on the prowl back at the hotel. I liked Noisy a lot. In Edinburgh earlier that season, when Conor O'Shea was the only unaccompanied player for the post-match banquet, Noisy had convinced one of the waitresses to be Conor's date. If you had forgotten a pair of black shoes, he'd lend you his. He'd look out for you. But in the team hotel in Jo'burg that night, he was looking out for us in a different sense.

I was a few seconds behind the other curfew-breakers, walking up the stairs when I bumped into John Martin, our physio, who advised going back down to the lobby – he'd just seen Noisy on the players' corridor. This was like trying to avoid Garry Bluett in Munchin's. I tiptoed back downstairs, into the lobby, turned the corner and bumped into Noisy, coming out of the lift. He wasn't happy.

'What time do you call this, Anthony?'

'I was jush meeting my—'

'And we have a game against New Zealand on Saturday! That's why we have a curfew.'

'I'm sorry, Noel. I was jush …'

'You're slurring your words, Anthony.'

'I always slur my words, Noel …'

That last line is usually guaranteed a laugh. It didn't seem so clever at the time, or the following morning when Noisy rang me to summon me to a meeting in his room before training. As far as I could make out, I was the only one who'd been nabbed. My room-mate, Paul Wallace, had just walked straight into the room, no hassle. I was even more worried when I went to Noisy's room at the appointed time and found George Spotswood, the IRFU's Rugby Administrator, also in attendance. This all looked very official. Sure enough, Noisy tells me they are considering sending me home. If this was designed to give me a fright, it worked. I was barely able to speak. Eventually, they told me they were reprieving me but that I was on a final warning. Also, I had to apologise to my room-mate, Paul Wallace, for coming in so late and disturbing him. I managed not to smile.

The relief. My World Cup was still on track – or so I thought. In reality, it was already over. I sat on the bench for the All Blacks game, watched my old opposite number Jonah wreak havoc on the wing, but played no part. I benched in Bloemfontein and got on for a few minutes as a blood replacement. Big deal. Halvey replaced me on the bench for the game against Wales back at Ellis Park, came on and scored the winning try. I enjoyed our trip up to Sun City, and had a laugh down in Durban, where we lost the quarter-final to France. I acted as cannon fodder in training in the mornings and then found some entertainment for the rest of the day. I freewheeled. I experienced the 1995 World Cup as a passenger.

Looking back, I see it as a huge missed opportunity. I see how naïve I was, but I don't think I lost any sleep over it at the time. Other distractions lay ahead. A few weeks after we returned from the World Cup, Shannon were off on a pre-season tour to Canada. I remember being told to meet at the clubhouse where there would be a coach to take us to Shannon airport. When I got there, fellas were propping up the bar on their second or third pint. It would be some tour, and it had been some year. The way I figured it, when I'd sat down with Dad to set targets for the season and he'd suggested I aim high – a place in the World Cup squad, for example – I'd thought why not? And here I was ten months on, just back from the World Cup. I'd played on a Munster team that had won an interprovincial grand slam; Shannon had won the AIL for the first time and not lost a game; I'd played every game in the Five Nations, and all at twenty-one. Not bad really. It certainly didn't occur to me that I was already on a downward slope.

8

ARRESTED DEVELOPMENT

Thursday, 29 May 1997, Rotorua National Stadium
Twenty-five minutes have been played and the scoreboard
reads: Bay of Plenty 45 Ireland Development XV 3. I have just
been called ashore by Ireland coach, Brian Ashton. No injury
issues here, just 'Come in, your time is up' – *after twenty-five
minutes*. In a representative career that lasts over a decade, there
are always going to be times when you feel anger, frustration
and disappointment, but it's hard to think of any experience to
match the sheer humiliation of Rotorua – 12,000 miles from
home with no place to hide.

Officially, we are an Ireland Development squad but as far
as the New Zealanders are concerned, we are just plain Ireland
and we're a joke. This is our second week on tour and already
we've been hammered 69–16 by Northland and walloped 74–17

by a New Zealand Academy XV. Now, against second division Bay of Plenty, a team of amateurs and semi-pros who are jumping out of their socks for a crack at an international side, we have conceded six tries in twenty-five minutes of the most disastrous rugby imaginable, a nightmare sequence of dropped passes and missed tackles that has the locals hooting abuse at us as we form another post-try huddle behind our try-line. Brian Ashton, the recently appointed national coach, decides drastic action is required.

As we jog towards halfway to prepare for Richie Governey's next restart, I'm a little puzzled by what I see on the touchline. Rob Henderson, Steve McIvor, Dave Erskine and the tour sprog, David Wallace, all have their tracksuits off and look ready for action. Then comes the sickening realisation. Tactical substitutions had only been introduced that season, to a mixed reaction from players – fellas were uncomfortable with the idea of being hauled off in the final quarter, but there is no one who knows what it feels like to be subbed before half-time. Until now. There are four of us – Justin Bishop, Rory Sheriff, Andy Matchett and me – and Shane Byrne will join us in a few minutes. We become known as the Rotorua Five. I am the only member who is already a capped international. As we take our place on the all-too-exposed bench near the touchline, I can hear mocking laughter from the stands.

It gets worse. The lads who replace us make a real difference. Scivor is full of energy, full of yap, Hendo is punching holes in midfield. As half-time approaches, they have clawed back a couple of tries and the game is on again. We can hear Ashton and Pa Whelan, sitting behind us, becoming animated. I'm just sitting there bewildered. I've been to Rotorua before. Five years ago, I was one of the main men on that Irish Schools side that won here. Sweet memories. On the way down here, I was able to warn the lads about the constant smell of sulphur from the geothermal activity in the area, which has earned the town the nickname 'Rotting Rua'. Now, sitting on this bench, it just smells like my career is going down the toilet. I'm sitting there, thinking, 'Maybe I'm not cut out for this professional rugby crap.'

Professional rugby was two years old by the time we toured New Zealand but we were still coming to terms with what professionalism really meant. It seemed like no one in Ireland had been ready for the announcement that came from the International Rugby Board in late August 1995 – rugby union was 'open'. I certainly wasn't prepared, mentally or physically. I was in Toronto when the news filtered through, on tour with Shannon. It was a great tour, rugby-wise and socially, and it set the club up for another crack at the league. There was just one small personal drawback when I went over on my ankle in the first game. Although it sounds hard to believe, it would be more than four years before I got it fixed properly. I'd have physio on it and strap it up before games but there never seemed to be a good time to stop, take time out and get it sorted. Almost as soon as we came back from that tour, a Munster selector rang me about playing in a friendly. I told him I could barely walk on the ankle.

'Tog out anyway, have a run around and see how it feels,' he responded. When I said the ankle needed rest, he made it pretty clear I was putting my place in jeopardy. As a twenty-one-year-old, what do you do? You play. During the first few years of professionalism, mis-management of players was a recurring theme.

By the start of the 1995–1996 season, Murray Kidd had taken over from Gerry Murphy as Ireland coach, with Pa, who had been forwards coach, taking over from Noisy in the highly influential role of manager. I was happy enough with Murray getting the gig, seeing as I knew him from the AIL. With Pa, you could never be quite so sure where you stood. He was uncompromising. I knew that from the stories Dad had told me about Shannon v. Garryowen in the old days, and from playing with him for Munster and against him in final Irish trials. He was also hard to read. When he'd been forwards coach, he'd take what looked like the test pack off to one side during a training session and tell the rest of us, 'Don't read anything into this.' Then that eight would be selected for the test. But you knew from the amount of time he spent in the changing room talking to players that he cared.

You wouldn't get any mollycoddling from him. Once, in the lead-up to the 1995 World Cup, he offered me a lift home from a training session in Dublin and then dropped me at Birdhill and told me to thumb a lift the ten miles to Killaloe. He was running a little late for his tee-time. Standing there weighed down with bags, watching his Merc zoom into the distance, I smiled at the notion of being surely the first player of the modern era to thumb his way home from a national training session.

As players, our relationship with the union clearly changed once we became employees. I can't honestly remember when I first received a pay cheque because payments were fairly haphazard that first season, and mainly came in the form of match fees. As I recall it, we were to be paid IR£3,000 for a test match with a £1,000 win bonus, although after a while the union got clever and turned it the other way around – £1,000 appearance and £3,000 for the win. There were match fees for Heineken Cup games but these seemed to vary from province to province. In truth, the players were as disorganised as the union and the provincial branches. Briefly, we had a sports agency, ProActive, negotiating with the union on such issues as insurance and payment for squad training sessions, but we were playing catch-up, just like our employers.

On the playing front, I'd a bit of catching up to do myself. Any hope that my fall from grace at the World Cup was just a short-term disciplinary issue was erased when I heard the team to play Ireland's first test as a professional side, against Fiji at Lansdowne Road. Jeremy Davidson was brought in at number six to beef up the lineout, alongside Corks and Paddy Johns, with Denis McBride on the bench. I got on to the larger squad for the USA game in Atlanta only because Halvey pulled out, and even then, I didn't get a run. It was the same in the Five Nations, when Jeremy, Paddy, Victor Costello, Corks and Denis McBride took turns. I had to be content with A team games. The A circuit had its attractions. Playing on a Friday afternoon meant you got full value out of international week-ends, especially the away trips – two nights on the town, drinking away the uneasiness of not being involved in the main event. When you've had a season centre stage, it's not a nice feeling to be on the fringe.

I knew my ankle still wasn't right. Dad suggested that wearing high-top boots would provide extra support but I couldn't bring myself to wear them. It wasn't so much the slagging you'd get as the fact that they were uncomfortable. Besides, it felt as though they were slowing me down, and I didn't feel that speed off the mark was one of my strengths as it was. I just strapped the ankle and half-hobbled my way through the season. Munster's involvement in the Heineken Cup, all two games, was an interesting diversion but didn't seem very significant – the English and Scottish teams didn't even take part and there was no way of knowing what the tournament would become. The only positive to come from that season was another AIL title for Shannon, and even that was fortunate to some extent – we relied on an unlikely Cookies victory at Dooradoyle to clinch the league on points difference over Garryowen. We had the satisfaction of knowing that we'd beaten Garryowen earlier in the year but as league titles go, this one was fairly poxy.

A pretty crappy season all round – Shannon's success apart – ended with the Students' World Cup in Johannesburg. I was looking forward to it. I thought we had potentially a very good side if the Jonny Bells and Jeremy Davidsons travelled, but they didn't. I had the impression the IRFU didn't really rate the tournament. Anyway, it went pear-shaped. We didn't even get out of our group and ended up squeezing past Uruguay in one of those plate competitions. Everything about the trip was crap, from the awful food down to the student accommodation. Our manager, Andy Crawford, took out his credit card so we could stay in a hotel. Even so, from my point of view, it had been hard to miss the symbolism. Twelve months after being in Jo'burg for rugby's showpiece event, you're back in town but sleeping in student dorms.

*

Of course, the option of going to England occurred to me. Everyone else was doing it – Woody (Harlequins), Corks and Burkey (both Bristol), Paddy Johns, Darragh O'Mahony, Paul and Richie Wallace (all Saracens), Jeremy, David Humphreys, Malcolm O'Kelly, Victor, Niall Woods, Fulch, Mark McCall, Conor O'Shea and various others (London Irish) and so on. It was a case of last one out, please turn off the lights. I thought it was a joke when, years later after they had sorted out the provincial set-up, the IRFU described the way they had centrally contracted most of the top players as a 'master-stroke'. What about the way they let everybody head off to English clubs in the first place? Was that part of the master-plan? At one stage, I think we had the grand total of five full-time pros in Munster. At least we got to know each other pretty well.

I wouldn't say I had clubs beating down the door, chasing my signature, but I did have options. Woody, Corks and I were all invited along to the Westbury Hotel in Dublin to meet Harlequins coach Dick Best. Woody took what was on offer, while Corks ended up with Bristol. I didn't fancy the 'Quins package. This is coming into the 1996–1997 season, when there was talk of the union offering IR£30,000 and a Ford Mondeo, which was a decent enough deal back then, especially for a home-bird such as myself. I kept my options open, though. John Mitchell, forwards coach under Kidd, was playing for Sale at the time, and I took a quick trip over there on his recommendation. I also remember Dad and I talking terms with Derek Eaves of Coventry at the Dublin Airport Hotel.

In the end, Munster's attitude, as much as anything else,

convinced me to stay. While some UK-based players were being flown home to play for their provinces in the Heineken Cup that season, Munster coach Jerry Holland said he wouldn't pick me unless I was based at home. That was what I needed – a decisive pull in one direction. This was another sliding doors moment. Who knows what might have become of me if I'd ended up in Coventry? I stayed at home, and was rewarded with one of those £30K contracts and new wheels.

To justify the deal, I needed a break, and missing Ireland's defeat by Western Samoa in a floodlit, midweek game at Lansdowne Road was just the piece of luck I required. I watched that game in Kiely's after taking part in a great win with the A team over the Junior Springboks in Donnybrook that afternoon. This, on top of Munster's Heineken Cup win over Wasps at Thomond Park, earned a few of us an international recall against Australia at Lansdowne Road. I was picked at eight, too, which was a bonus. Things were looking up.

It says a lot about our view of ourselves in 1996 that we were pretty chuffed to lose 22–12 to what was a pretty ordinary Wallabies team. The general consensus afterwards was that they had just been stronger and fitter than we were, especially in the final quarter, which was when their out-half David Knox, playing in one of his few test matches, struggled over the try-line off what looked suspiciously like a forward pass from George Gregan. It was a gammy enough old try and the Aussies celebrated like men who knew they'd got off the hook.

The southern hemisphere teams were all fitter and stronger than we were, it's true. This was a time when 'upper-body strength' was one of the buzz phrases, and some of us were only just getting used to the idea of proper weights training. The team management and the IRFU's fitness consultant, Andy Clarke, were determined to do something about it, but it was a battle for them, and us. A lot of the players still associated extra fitness work with punishment for playing poorly, such as the old-style 'puke sessions' you'd do on a Tuesday night after losing the previous Saturday. We were naïve. We had no idea about what was required if we were to match the top sides for fitness and conditioning. The management's attitude was pretty old-fashioned, too. It was like they were saying, 'Okay, if you want to get paid for playing, you're going to work bloody hard for your cash.' It was all quantity and no quality.

Admittedly, professional rugby was in its infancy and everyone was stumbling around in the dark. We hadn't yet figured out the importance of rest and a proper diet. If you took an afternoon nap back then, you were considered a bit of a slob rather than someone who might be taking steps to improve the quality of his training that evening. As for food, we ate pasta by the bucketload because someone said it was better for you than spuds. There were no individualised diets, no monitoring of quantity or quality. During squad sessions in Dublin, fellas would be ordering breakfast in bed, all sorts. If you felt peckish, you ordered something on room service and it would go on the tab. That might be okay for the greyhounds, the fellas who burn off everything. I was never one of those. In 1999, I was up to 115 kilograms, which is a good five kilos above my fighting weight.

We hadn't a clue. At one stage, we used to have Jaffa Cakes and wine gums beside the trays of isotonic drinks at Ireland training, on the misguided notion that we'd benefit from the jolt of sugar, which we would for ten minutes. Then you'd get the post-sugar low and feel knackered. Probably the best example of how ignorance could affect performance came in the lead-up to Murray Kidd's last game in charge, against Italy. I'm not sure whose bright idea it was to have a fitness camp the week before a test match but that, believe it or not, is what we did. A trip down to the Algarve in early January sounded like a nice idea on one level. Unfortunately, it lashed rain for most of the week. The pitch where we trained was just below a driving range, under about two inches of water, so as we'd be doing our press-ups, all we could hear was 'plop'. Anyway, we did a full battery of fitness tests on the Wednesday and then travelled home the next day for a test against the Italians who were coming, as usual, with a point to prove. It was an appalling way to prepare for a test match – shocking – and it showed. To be fair, the Italians were good, again – we were blown away by Cristian Stoica, their brute of a centre – but some of us were walking around the pitch by the end, clearly knackered, and we lost 29–37. Murray paid with his job, and he wasn't the only casualty. It would be three years before I next started a test match.

I never felt it was anything personal with Brian Ashton. He was always a gentleman, always said hello, but I could tell from his first training session that he had pretty radical ideas about the way he wanted to take us, and I suspected I wasn't the sort of number eight he wanted on board. His first drill, involving forwards and backs, was a fairly straightforward test of our ability to throw a skip pass off the left hand. He didn't look too impressed with our efforts. Probably the one forward who looked most comfortable doing it was Eric Miller – you may remember Eric hitting Jim Staples with just such a pass off the base of a scrum in the lead-up to Denis Hickie's try in Cardiff in 1997. It was a great try, and a good win, but Brian's only win against a top-tier country. His problem was that he was an idealist. He had admirable ideas about the way we'd play the game but they bore no relation to the talent at his disposal. We'd work on skills but never to such a level where we'd have been comfortable using them in an international game. Put under pressure, you revert to what you are comfortable with, and most of us weren't very comfortable with left-handed skip passes.

That first training session took place in Limerick, probably on Pa's say-so. From then on, though, everything seemed to happen at the ALSAA complex beside Dublin airport to accommodate those players who, like the coach, were flying in from England. Every session, it seemed a couple of new accents could be heard, fellas playing in the English Premiership who had an Irish relation somewhere. It felt like you were a second-class citizen if you were based at home. Certainly, if you look at the Ireland teams from around that time, the vast majority of players were with Premiership clubs. This was a pretty nervous time for a lot of us – there was even talk of having Ireland training sessions in London to save the union the cost of flying everyone home. It didn't matter how well we were rattling along at Shannon because Ashton didn't watch the AIL. He just didn't rate it. To a degree, you could understand his attitude but it wasn't good for the confidence of the Ireland-based players.

I got one chance in the Five Nations, against England at Lansdowne Road, coming off the bench after eleven minutes when Eric was concussed. I would have been better off staying put. We were demolished 46–6, Ireland's biggest championship defeat. For some reason, I was singled out for heavy criticism in the video review the following week. Mike Brewer, the former All Black who was filling in as Ashton's forwards coach, went through me for a short-cut for something I did or didn't do at a restart – I can't remember the point, only the feeling of humiliation. I thought it was over the top and some of the senior players said the same thing to me afterwards. Brewer was an awesome player and I rated him as a coach, but we weren't at the stage where we could handle this sort of honesty. Brewer was still playing for Blackrock, and Shannon played them a few weeks later in the league. I'd say he woke up pretty stiff and sore the morning after that game.

This was some consolation for missing the final Five Nations match against Scotland – Eric's concussion ruled him out but Ashton brought in Ben Cronin at eight. Ireland lost 38–10, another record margin. I was rated a 'development' player, which meant I'd be going to New Zealand and I was excited at the prospect. As I said earlier, I had happy memories of the place and the travelling party were a good crew. Gary Halpin had been made captain, Halvey was going, Fulch, Crow (Niall Woods), Scivor, Hendo. We'd have the crack. There was the usual pre-tour giddiness around the Castletroy Park Hotel as we prepared for departure. If only we knew what lay ahead. Some day, someone will write the book of the tour. It will read a bit like *Alive*, the story of the South American players who crashed in the Andes and ate the bodies of their dead team-mates to survive. There were no actual casualties from our tour but it wouldn't surprise me if a few people are still receiving psychotherapy. We were paid a tour fee of just £2,000, with match fees of £500 for the games against the NZ Academy, the Maori and Samoa. Looking back, I would have paid a few grand not to go.

One lucky bastard who avoided the trip was Paul Wallace. He had his bags packed for New Zealand when he got news that Claw had pulled out of the Lions tour to South Africa due to injury. So Wally got to go on what is generally regarded as the best tour in modern times, and was picked for the test team that won the series. Meanwhile, we were getting flogged around training pitches in crap weather in one-horse towns. For we were flogged, in every sense – physically, in training, every day, then by our opponents and ultimately in terms of our confidence. Just flogged. It was a vicious circle. We weren't remotely prepared for the physical intensity of the matches – even the second-division sides we played, such as Bay of Plenty and King Country, had guys who were wanting to make an impression, maybe earn a contract with one of the big teams, and they played like they meant it. Our results were poor – we won just one match out of seven – so the management's response was to beast us in training. Guys picked up niggles because they weren't getting proper rest and that in turn affected performance.

The only good thing about getting injured was that it offered the possibility of being sent home – Halvey got lucky, so too did David Humphreys. It was like a race to get out of there. That sounds terrible – to be on tour representing your country and hope you'd get sent home – but any means of escape would have done. It was miserable. You'd train twice a day, and some of the places we were staying had very few distractions. One evening we ended up playing charades – I remember struggling with 'Othello'. Everything would shut up in the late afternoon in places like Lower Hutt. Just saying the name gives me the shivers. Time passed so slowly. I'm not sure how long the tour lasted but it felt like around five years. So we envied Halvey when he picked up some bacterial infection and was shipped home. 'How do you get that? What do you have to drink?' we asked. Mikey Lynch's favourite memory of the tour is when he got a blood infection and had the luxury of an entire week in hospital, with team-mates bringing him fruit. Meanwhile, one player was rumoured to be kicking a ball as hard as he could without warming up in the hope of ripping his hamstring.

I know Ashton was frustrated – by then, he realised what he'd let himself in for – but that doesn't excuse the way he treated some people, bawling them out for making mistakes. We nicknamed him 'Shat-on'. I felt sorry for Rory Sheriff and Alan McGrath, club-mates of mine who were really only kids. With Shannon, they had Gaillimh to guide them. On that tour, it seemed like there was no guidance at all, only bollockings, and it was supposedly a development tour. Fellas were still trying to find their way in professional rugby and this experience just turned them off the idea. In terms of productivity, it was a disaster.

I was in a strange position – a capped player but still only twenty-three, and being rapidly drained of confidence. After the Rotorua experience, Ashton made it pretty clear to me that he was giving me one last chance, in the next game, against Thames Valley. Unfortunately, I took a bang in the first half and ripped a bicep muscle – a pity, because the game had been going well and there was definitely a feeling of turning a corner in terms of the ball-in-hand, no-kicking game that Ashton was trying to instil. Thames Valley were probably the worst team we played but any positive sign helped. So I was very disappointed at having to come off, and further pissed off at the way the injury was managed after that. The X-ray showed no break and no dislocation but from the amount of internal bleeding, it was clear something was not right. The management's reaction? Train tomorrow and see how it goes. I well remember bumping into Andy Matchett during a cross-over drill because I have never felt pain like it. What next? I was taken away to get injected with something. That was the type of crap you had to put up with. Denise Fanagan, the tour physio, actually took a photograph of the injury as evidence, but I never had the balls to complain.

In part, this was because of the old rugby ethos – show no pain, get on with it. The difference was this was our careers that were being messed with. By the end of the tour, guys with genuinely serious injuries were being told to train anyway. In one freak injury Barry McConnell, the Bristol hooker, rammed his knee against a goalpost in training. The poor lad was in agony. Shat-on's response was to bollock him for his awkwardness. 'Those bloody posts were there all day. Did you not see them?' It was something along those lines. Barry was twenty-one, a talented player with real promise, but we barely heard of him after that.

In circumstances like this, you felt the best thing to do was grin and bear your pain. I was picked on the bench for the final game, against Samoa in Apia, and in the lead-up Fulch, who by then had taken over as captain, came up and asked me, on the

QT, 'Are you actually fit enough to be on the bench?' He knew I was having difficulty lifting my arm above my head, but I said nothing to the management. It was as though pulling out would have given them another stick to beat me with.

My happiest memory of the tour? Boarding the flight out of Samoa. I'd never been so happy to get home, even if it meant reading some of the newspaper reports. *The Sunday Times* had player ratings for all of us and mine read as follows: 'Anthony Foley – a big fish in Limerick, he drowned in New Zealand. Unfortunate to get injured against Thames Valley but the tour was an unpleasant experience for him.' Cruel, but not a million miles from the truth. The annoying thing was I felt my problems weren't all of my own making. Two years previously, I had wasted a World Cup through complacency and indiscipline. This was different. I was trying hard but being treated like shit.

So, when Shannon asked me to captain them for the coming season, I was delighted. It probably wasn't the best thing for my body – my ankle still needed proper rehab and I wouldn't be getting it if I was playing every week – but at least someone was showing me some love, and I needed a bit of that. The other development was with Munster. Word had it we were getting a full-time director of rugby. We'd been told on tour by IRFU president Bobby Deacy that it would be Andy Leslie, the former All Black – or at least that Leslie was '80 per cent certain' to take the job. He ended up turning it down, like John Bevan before him, but at least there were signs that Munster were getting themselves organised, which I thought was interesting. I didn't know the half of it.

9

HARD YARDS

Not only have I the dubious pleasure of being one of the Rotorua Five, I am also a life member of the gang of nightclub outlaws known within the Munster set-up as the Pod Four. The only reason you haven't heard of us before now is because Princess Diana died. Confused? Perhaps I should explain.

The Pod Four – Gaillimh, Claw, Buddha Healy and me – landed ourselves in a small bit of bother on the way back from an interpro match in Belfast at the end of August 1997. To call it an incident is overstating things. We'd had a few pints in the Harcourt Hotel and then went in search of a few more. I knew at the time we weren't suitably attired for the Pod – you don't get many blazers and ties in there – but we tried our luck anyway. Sure enough, we were told the place was full and they weren't letting anyone else in that night. That was grand, until four other lads breezed past us into the club. When one of us asked for an explanation, it got narky very quickly. One of the bouncers was pretty decent – I think he was a rugby player from Greystones and recognised us – but the other lads got a bit aggressive, especially a member of the nightclub management, who started hurling insults from the other side of a railing. It was probably just as well we had Buddha with us because he was a bouncer in Limerick at the time and knew we were best just moving on. Basically, that was that – until the following Monday, when a story appeared in the *Star* newspaper, turning our small dispute into a mass brawl involving four international rugby players, two of whom – Gaillimh and Claw – were pictured. Clearly, someone had seen an opportunity for the nightclub to get some publicity.

The only one of us who was in any way disappointed by the story was Buddha – because he wasn't named as one of the 'four international rugby players'. The Munster Branch found out pretty quickly who was involved, though, and the powers that be weren't very amused. We got a right bollocking for our troubles, and there was even talk of us losing our contracts, and over nothing. In the end, we were just fortunate that we'd been knocked off the front page by Princess Diana, who had died in Paris that very night. She took up so much space that we were pushed well inside, to around page thirteen. As Claw said at the time, he'll never forget her for it.

The Pod incident was typical of the way things were going for me at the time. Before touring New Zealand and Samoa, I had been offered a renewal of that £30K contract but didn't sign. Around ten days after we returned, I received a letter from Pa telling me I was not being offered a national squad contract 'at this point in time' but that my form would be 'carefully monitored from the season's commencement'. Looking back, I wonder how this would have stood up to legal scrutiny. Anyway, four days later, on 30 June, the IRFU's Administrative Officer Martin Murphy wrote to tell me to return my Ford Mondeo to the union's offices in Lansdowne Road. In the end, I was offered £25K and no car. Being docked the five grand was rough but to lose the car really made me feel like a second-class citizen.

It was clear I was now viewed as a provincial player. Soon, I wasn't even guaranteed that. Our first European Cup pool game was against Harlequins at The Stoop, eight days after the Pod incident. On the Tuesday, as I was walking out to train at Thomond Park, David Wallace told me our coaches, Declan Kidney and Niall O'Donovan, wanted a word with me over in the corner of the pitch. I kind of knew what was coming. Greg Tuohy, who'd barely featured for Munster and never featured subsequently, was going to start at number eight. I wasn't even on the bench. I was being 'rested', or so Deccie said, anyway. Somehow it felt more like another almighty kick in the arse. Things were not good.

This was our third year of the European Cup and, to be honest, the tournament was a bit of a slow burner at first. There was a fair bit of interest when Swansea came to Thomond Park to kick it off in November 1995 and we were delighted to beat a side we considered more professional than ourselves. I'm just not so sure as many as 6,000 spectators were there that Wednesday afternoon as the ERC website suggests. The atmosphere didn't feel as intense as at some AIL games in those days – and it's worth remembering that certain ambitious clubs, including Shannon, were adamant that they, and not the provinces, should be representing Ireland in the new competition. Just a couple of Munster supporters made the trip to the southern French town of Mazamet the following week when we blew a promising position against Castres and ended up losing 19–12. The noise and hostility of the French crowd was an eye-opener but for us the tournament was over as soon as it started – two games in the space of eight days and that was our lot.

It got a bit more interesting the following season when English and Scottish teams decided they wanted in. There was definitely something a bit different about having Wasps coming to Limerick – very English, yet very international with Inga Tuigamala and Gareth Rees in their team. And there was definitely something nice about beating them 49–22, even if a couple of our tries were a bit fortunate. When that same Wasps side put 77 on Toulouse, the tournament favourites, we realised we were in with a chance of actually qualifying from the pool if we could beat Toulouse over there. As if. They beat us 60–19 and played some scary rugby in the process – yes, that was the famous occasion when Pat Murray gathered us into a huddle and urged us not to let them score more than fifty points.

We still managed to enjoy ourselves, though. In fact, that trip was great crack. On the night after the game, we had a good few beers and a singsong in the bar across from the hotel. I remember Buddha getting an unmerciful slagging from Scivor for the fact that he'd lasted just fifteen minutes against Christian Califano. Buddha had come off with a ripped bicep muscle yet was still able for an arm-wrestling contest with one of the locals that night.

For all the hard work Buddha put into his rugby, he was a bouncer first and foremost, just as Pat Murray, Munster's full-back spent his working week in the TSB office in Limerick. Eventually, after a fair bit of encouragement from Brian Ashton and others, the IRFU realised it needed to professionalise the provinces, especially as the European Cup was moving to a home-and-away format for the 1997–1998 season. First, they had to get professional coaches. I remember John Bevan, the former Wales and Lions winger, attending a meeting at Thomond Park before the development tour to New Zealand, at which he set out his vision for Munster. He was an impressive enough individual, with a good playing CV – Wales, British and Irish Lions and Warrington, the rugby league club – but he got cold feet when he learned that only a handful of players were contracted for the following season. Andy Leslie didn't fancy the job either, and you could hardly blame him – how can you be expected to produce results in a professional tournament if you don't have a professional squad of players?

It's funny to think the only reason Deccie and Niallo got the gig was because no one else wanted it. I was happy enough with their appointment because I knew both of them well and rated them. Granted, I did wonder how Deccie would get along with Gaillimh and Claw. He was prescriptive, well prepared, a stickler for detail but he'd coached at schools level and with Dolphin. He was used to running teams on the basis that everyone was equal. Gaillimh and Claw were a law unto themselves. There was bound to be friction.

Gaillimh and Claw were even more inseparable than in the old days because they'd had to endure time apart when Claw went off to spend a Super 12 season with Queensland – a direct result of a lengthy suspension for foul play. We wondered if Claw would come back from Brisbane armed with information on, and insights into, a professional set-up that was a good bit farther down the road than ours. All he came back with was a suntan and a million stories, none of which are repeatable here. He was still worshipped by the players, however, which was the awkward thing for Deccie in particular. If Deccie was the schoolteacher, then Claw was the smart arse at the back of the class.

As anyone who's played with or against him will tell you, the thing about Claw is his unpredictability. You never knew what he'd come out with next. At a team meeting, he could say, 'Not naming names, like, but Dominic Crotty, what the fuck were you doing back there?' and get away with it. On the pitch, he was a great man for striking bargains with his opposing prop and then finding a way of 'sickening' him, as he'd say himself. He once sickened Gary Halpin at a time when they were both competing for the Ireland tight-head spot. It was during a supervised bleep test – one of those continuous shuttle runs where the pace increases with every bleep. As soon as they were both feeling the pace, Claw quietly suggested they pull out at the end of the next length. Halpin was happy to go along with the plan and duly stopped – only to be sickened by Claw, who ran another length.

Claw was a messer and a reluctant trainer but he was also someone you'd want on your side going into war. He'd already had plenty of setbacks in his career but he gave the impression of having no regrets. He was fearless, and incredibly resilient. Gaillimh was the same. Here was someone who'd been on tour with the Lions yet was dropped from the Ireland team a record number of times, so he was used to adversity. He was, and is, a great man for giving advice. Like Claw, he was irreverent and, also like Claw, he was never the greatest trainer, but the two of them were worth their weight in gold for a team. So if Deccie pulled rank, he ran the danger of alienating two players who were hugely influential within the squad.

There was awkwardness for a while, definitely. I can't remember any specific incident, just a mutual suspicion that gradually eased as Deccie made subtle compromises without letting the lads walk all over him. He knew they were irreplaceable so he let them do some of their training on their own, for example. People talk about us being a team with two training centres, in Cork and Limerick, but for a while there, we had four centres – Cork, Limerick, Kilkenny (where Gaillimh lives) and Kilkee (where Claw has his holiday home). Deccie kept them happy and, by managing them this way, probably helped prolong their careers. They, in turn, grew to respect his way of doing things.

In fairness, everybody was still finding their way with this professionalism lark. It didn't help that our competitive season was over by the second weekend in October. That was the way things were structured – three interpros, followed by six straight European pool weekends, end of story. Having lost away to Harlequins and Cardiff, we squeezed past Bourgoin at Thomond Park but then lost to Cardiff in Cork, which put an end to our hopes of qualification. To be honest, this was pretty much in keeping with our expectations. We hadn't yet built a tight culture, and part of that was to do with some of the old suspicions between the Limerick and Cork contingents. Woody copped a fair bit of grief for highlighting it in a newspaper interview around this time but there were cliques, certainly, and you could sense the Cork fellas were unhappy about having to stay at least one night a week away from home as we began to train more and more at the University of Limerick.

It wasn't just a Cork–Limerick thing, though. Inter-club rivalry was thriving, even though we were all contracted to Munster. You saw it especially in the lead-up to the 1998 AIL final between Garryowen and Shannon. The Garryowen lads wouldn't come into the weights room in UL while we were there, preferring to do speed work on the track outside. We were work-mates, yet for a few weeks, we barely acknowledged each other.

If there was one game that started the bonding process, it was our victory over Harlequins in the final pool game of that 1997–1998 season. It was a big occasion, with Woody, fresh from his Lions success in South Africa, leading a side that included Will Carling, Thierry Lacroix, Laurent Cabannes and Jason Leonard back to his home patch. I was just glad to be involved. I'd been dropped for the game over at The Stoop, of course, and since it wasn't televised, I'd had to arrange a beer with Rhys Ellison, Shannon and Munster's new Kiwi recruit, so he could give me the lowdown on how the game had gone and who had played well. I got back in for the Cardiff trip only because of an injury to Shane Leahy, the Garryowen second row, with Ultan O'Callaghan moving to the second row to accommodate me. I'm glad to say I got a fair old run of Heineken Cup games from then on.

On the face of it, only Harlequins had something to play for that Sunday in Thomond Park, since we were well out of the qualification race. But looking back, the game seems like the start of something special – not Munster as a real force in Europe, but certainly Thomond as a real fortress. There was a buzz around town that night, a sense of something that people wanted to be part of. Woody took the 'Quins boys to Nancy Blake's and we had the crack. I remember my old man having to have words with one of the 'Quins players for showing an unhealthy interest in my baby sister, Orla – for the second time that day, he was repelled in Limerick.

I enjoyed that game. With unerring accuracy, every one of Lacroix's restarts went directly to me, allowing me a good gallop with the ball. It was good to play well on a big occasion – not that it did me any good in international terms. By now, I wasn't even featuring in the A team squads, so with Munster in cold storage until the following season, I had to devote myself to leading Shannon. At least that was going well. Pat Murray had taken over as coach from Niallo and we'd recruited well. Mark McDermott, Johnny Lacey and Paul McMahon had all come in and we'd been fortunate that our name came out of the hat when Rhys was being allocated a club. Christ, did that man know how to make a tackle.

I enjoyed captaincy, too. Sometimes it was hard making yourself heard out on the pitch – playing in the middle of a back row with Alan Quinlan and Halvey was like playing in stereo – but it was a good experience, thinking and planning for an entire squad. You noticed more about the different characters who go to make a team. After the game, in the changing room, while the young fellas were on the hunt for extra drink vouchers, Jim Galvin, our out-half and a bit of a legend in the club, would be slipping away to his farm in Kilfinnan with a quiet, 'Cows need milking.' A few minutes later, Rhys would be launching into one of his famous one-man hakas.

As we went in search of our fourth straight AIL title, the very fact that our success was being almost completely ignored by the national selectors allowed us to build up a bank of bitterness to sustain us through the winter. After every win, Pat seemed to be giving out to the press about the fact that Gaillimh or Halvey or myself had been overlooked.

Fuelled by anger, we topped the table with twelve wins out of thirteen, and headed into the league's first play-offs. We squeezed past Mary's in the semi – they were the one Dublin side that we always struggled against – before beating Garryowen 15–9 in the league's first official final, a tense, dour, try-less, all-Limerick affair at Lansdowne Road.

My main memories are of Andrew Thompson's place-kicking and Gaillimh's playing a full eighty minutes despite having torn his bicep during the warm-up. That just about summed up the man. I was incredibly proud to lead him and the team to the title. Just for good measure, we also won the Munster Senior Cup, beating the Cookies 19–18 at Thomond Park. I still have a picture of me raising the trophy above my head and letting out a roar. I'm not sure what words came out but it could have been something along the lines of, 'FUCK 'EM!'

I hadn't lost all hope of an international recall. Brian Ashton resigned as national coach after the first game in the 1998 Five Nations and the sight of Warren Gatland, his replacement, at one of Shannon's home games was a real boost. He got a warm welcome from Tommy Creamer, the man on the PA, and an ovation from the crowd, which says a fair bit about how Ashton had been viewed in Limerick. This wasn't just a PR stunt by Gatland. By bringing Eric Elwood, Victor Costello, Gaillimh and Claw into the Ireland squad for his first test in charge, he made it clear he was going to acknowledge his home-based players. God bless him, he even picked A.G. Foley on the bench for the final A game of the season, against England in Richmond. I was also included in the touring party for South Africa that summer. I didn't need a second invitation.

Based on results alone – two fairly scabby victories out of five provincial games and two heavy defeats in the tests – Ireland's tour to South Africa in summer 1998 looks a bit of a disaster. In fact, it was a very happy and, in some senses, productive tour. Compared with the development tour the previous summer, it was heaven. Gatty, as he quickly became known to us, was a players' coach. He was only thirty-four, so he had barely stopped playing – Gaillimh, Claw and Paddy Johns played club rugby against him when he was with Galwegians. He was approachable. At times, he was almost too pally, drinking pints and playing cards with us and bumming fags off Claw and Hendo, but he knew where to draw the line and we respected him. Unlike Ashton, he was a pragmatist. This was life before Brian O'Driscoll and Gordon D'Arcy. He set about getting the basics right. As a forward, he understood the importance of the set-pieces and worked us hard on them. He tightened up our defence and he set about making us fitter. He tried to make us hard to beat.

As a former All Black, Gatty came from a winning culture,

and as a former Connacht coach, he had a good feel for what made Irish people tick, talking about loyalty, trust and gaining respect. He treated us like adults and made allowances for Woody and Wally, who had barely had a rest since the Lions tour the previous summer and so joined the tour late. He understood the importance of consistency of selection – up to that point, there were so many changes from game to game that it had encouraged almost a mé féin attitude among players – and he was smart enough to see the potential in Hayes. Most of all, he and Donal Lenihan, who'd been appointed manager after Pa resigned, brought us closer together as a group. There would be no leaks to the press, unlike during the previous regime, when fellas spilled their guts off the record if they were unhappy with the management. We would stick up for each other when the going got tough.

Our solidarity was well tested in South Africa, and not just on the pitch. The locals took every opportunity to tell us how we'd be wiped by their beloved Boks, and generally to make things difficult for us. Before the first test in Bloemfontein, our bus was blocked at the gate of the stadium for what seemed like an age, with Bok supporters rocking it from side to side, pelting it with pebbles and shouting in Afrikaans – the only words we could recognise were 'Keith Woods'. Woody was virtually a hate figure in South Africa because of his part in the Lions success, and the Boks themselves seemed on a mission to take revenge, cheap-shotting him at every opportunity. He soaked it all up, kept sledging them back with lines about South Africa's record on human rights and then, after the second test in Pretoria, leading the entire squad in a defiant rendition of 'From Clare to Here' at the post-match function.

Personally, I took more positives than negatives from the tour. Granted, I didn't make it into the twenty-two for the tests and another obstacle had appeared in the shape of Dion O'Cuinneagain, a South African-born, Irish-qualified back row, who made his debut in Bloemfontein. But I had taken a step back from the international wilderness. The management picked me as captain of the midweek team – Axel's Angels – choosing me ahead of Gaillimh. What's more, Gatty came out with the encouraging line that I was 'a player who could lead us in the future' – I was still only twenty-four, after all.

The Angels managed to win just one of our three games and were on the end of an embarrassing 52–13 hammering by Griqualand West in Kimberley. I scored one of our two tries that day, but playing on a bone-hard pitch was a reminder that all was still not right with my ankle. Still, we were just over a year from the World Cup and I took encouragement from the fact that I was back in the picture – too much encouragement. Not for the first time, I was deluding myself.

10

HELPING HANDS

When Declan Kidney is doing his psychoanalysis thing with us, one of his favourite analogies is about your life being like the four legs of a chair. Each leg represents a different aspect of your day-to-day existence as a professional rugby player – your skills, your fitness, your psychological life and your social life. Pay too much or too little attention to one of the legs and you lose stability. It was pretty corny the first time we heard it and he's rolled it out a few times since then, but like most Kidneyisms, it's actually very true. And it just so happens that an upswing in my love-life coincided with a significant improvement in my professional life. Come on down, Olive Hogan.

Olive comes from Scariff, a village a few miles up the road from Killaloe, but I got to know her when she was in boarding school with Orla at the Presentation Convent in Thurles. She says her earliest image of me is of this enormous rugby player draped over a sofa in my folks' house, staring at the TV and eating large plates of sandwiches served by my mother, while she sat squeezed on the other sofa with Orla and a couple of other class-mates, waiting for Dad to give them a lift back to school. Orla, on the other hand, insists I was positively animated whenever Olive was in the house, almost to the point of being chatty. All I remember was being smitten from the start.

Being naturally shy, I needed some assistance and it was willingly provided by Mam and Orla. It turns out my folks had known Mary and Eddie Hogan for years – Eddie was a butcher in Scariff and Mary was a primary-school teacher. Mam was very keen on the match. So she and Orla set about bringing the two of us together – even if it required that Olive be hijacked. For this, effectively, is what happened that fateful day when Shannon played Con in Cork in the Munster Senior Cup, January 1998. Mam and Orla invited Olive on a shopping trip to Cork but took her to Musgrave Park instead – her first ever rugby match. Then, having bought her cider in the Dolphin bar, they neatly made themselves scarce for my post-match entrance, whereupon I produced the immortal chat-up line, 'Are you coming back on the bus?' Somehow she agreed, not knowing we'd be making quite a few pit-stops on the way. By the time we rolled back into Limerick, she'd been bullied up the front of the bus to give us her rendition of Kate Bush's 'Wuthering Heights', and we were an item. I even got her to go to Shannon's four-in-a-row victory ball at the end of the season.

I'd be fairly stuck in my ways, but it's fair to say Olive

brought me out of myself a bit. This may have something to do with the fact that she loves music, dancing and amateur dramatics, and is a qualified speech and drama teacher. She used to have great crack getting me to deliver the line 'Father's car's a Jaguar and Pa drives rather fast.' She worked in the bank, as she still does, albeit part-time now. The weird thing was we were going out a good six months before she discovered what I did for a living. Of course, she knew I played a lot of rugby. She just didn't know it was my job (maybe I hadn't figured it out myself, says you). This came out on the eve of the Ireland tour to South Africa, as a few players' wives and girlfriends were sitting chatting in the Glenview Hotel in Wicklow.

'A nice job in the bank, that's what Anthony needs,' Olive announced confidently to Anna Clohessy and Trudy Gatland.

'But I have a job already, Ol,' I said, surprised.

'And what's that?' she asked.

I think Gatty still uses it as one of his after-dinner gags.

At least we knew enough about each other to figure out we wanted to spend the rest of our lives together. Around six months later, on St Stephen's Day 1998, I proposed to Olive in Reddan's Bar, Killaloe – romantic devil that I am – and she accepted. We were relatively young (I was twenty-five, she was twenty-four) but we were lucky because we could afford to get married. After some wise and gentle persuasion from my mother, I bought the house where we currently live, on the edge of Killaloe. Olive didn't move in until after we were married – we were far too respectable to live in sin – but we decided on a short engagement and managed to scramble a church and a hotel for a Saturday in early July, a couple of weeks after Ireland's tour to Australia in 1999. We'd originally planned a date for August, which was very early rugby season, but the Munster Branch politely ordered me to get married on my own time.

As it turned out, we needn't have worried about clashing with the tour, for Gatty didn't pick me in the thirty-man squad. For this to happen in World Cup year was disastrous. Even worse was the way my demotion came about. I'd had what I considered to be a reasonable season. Munster had finally qualified from the pool stages and even if we'd lost our quarter-final 23–9 after an undisciplined performance in Colomiers, at least we appeared to be heading in the right direction. Shannon's AIL run finally came to an end but I reckoned that had to happen at some stage. The Ireland A team won just one of their games in the championship but I started all four, and also played in a comfortable victory over Italy A in early April.

The trouble started with some fitness tests carried out by Craig White a few days before that Italy game. It was bad enough that some of us recorded scores that were down significantly on previous tests. What was really embarrassing was that Craig's report to the IRFU was leaked to the *Sunday Independent* a week or two later, and they had a field day with some of his comments. The juiciest bits were about individual players:

1. Strength and aerobic fitness a million miles away from international competition.
2. Body fat too high at 20 per cent. Also, his bleep test has significantly decreased.
3. Not strong enough and hasn't made significant improvements.

4. His upper body strength has not improved in three years. I would guess that his leg strength is also poor.

5. Body fat has significantly increased from 18 to 21 per cent. Additionally, his bench press has gone down 7 kg since 1996 and his bleep test score has gone down from 13+ to 12.

That last one was me. The public didn't find out immediately as the *Sunday Independent* didn't name any players 'for legal reasons'. Unfortunately, *The Sunday Times* had no such scruples and seven days later, the culprits were all fingered. Embarrassment wasn't confined to five or six individuals, however. Munster players in general came in for some criticism from White, who had written: 'I would like to make comments about differences between provinces but this is difficult because I am missing players, especially Munster players.'

Meanwhile, critical comments from unnamed Connacht player sources appeared in the *Sunday Independent*. 'It's a joke among the provincial players and the Munster guys laugh at how hard we have to work,' said one player. Another added, 'It guts me the way guys who are acting the bollox get recognised ahead of guys who are putting the work in. To be honest, I feel a bit cheated by the whole thing.' Brendan Fanning, who wrote the article, said it didn't help that Munster's fitness advisor Dave Mahedy was working with us part-time but the real root of the problem was that the Cork and Limerick players trained separately. 'The notion of a provincial team splitting into two groups, training simultaneously in two venues, is bizarre,' he wrote. 'There cannot be a competitive training environment where two players chasing the same place are separated by sixty-three miles. And there is no solution in sight.'

No solution, perhaps, but there was plenty of bitterness in Munster. The day the original newspaper article appeared, Cork Con just happened to be playing Buccaneers in an AIL semi and after they had won convincingly, Con coach Packie Derham took the opportunity to proclaim that, 'We breed rugby players in Munster, not athletes.' As for the rugby players themselves, we were busy buying into the 'them and us' routine, figuring out who had leaked the report and swearing to do him grave injury if we ever laid our hands on him – instead of looking at ourselves in the mirror.

In some respects, we weren't helped on the fitness front. No coherent structures existed, and nothing like the resources that players have now for rehabbing injuries. We'd train at 10 a.m. and then 6.30 p.m. so that the part-timers could fit in a working day, and then a couple of evenings a week we were with our clubs – once we'd been knocked out of Europe in December, the AIL became our bread and butter.

That said, the attitude of some players, myself included, was all wrong. Dave Mahedy was monitoring us to some extent but he was also running the university's sports programme, so there were plenty of short-cuts you could take. We were professionals in name, yet we were so far from real professionalism, it wasn't funny. It wasn't the same across the board. Dominic Crotty was so dedicated he probably went too far the other way, but some of us had the same attitude to our bodies that my father's generation had. In Limerick, we even had a Monday night drinking club. No kidding. We didn't meet every single Monday, and definitely not in the week of a game, but it was regular enough to be called a club. You can imagine the quality of the training we'd do the following morning. The routine on

AIL Saturdays was pretty old-fashioned, too, probably finishing off with some fast food in the early hours.

We needed a wake-up call and we got it when Craig White's findings went public. A few of the back-sliders were brought to Santry for extra fitness training but were still left out of the tour party, which would be led by Dion O'Cuinneagain. Meanwhile, in Munster, the *Sunday Independent* article was cut out and pinned to the wall in the weights room at UL, where it remained for many months as a constant reminder, and one of several catalysts that turned us from misguided wasters into genuine contenders.

In the various histories of Munster's march on Europe, a game that is often cited as a turning point was the poorly attended Friday night interpro we lost to Leinster early in the 1998–1999 season at Dooradoyle. Certainly, we took to heart the comments of Trevor Brennan, which filtered back to us after the game. Apparently, during the warm-up, Trev had drawn the Leinster players' attention to the fact that we didn't look like a team on the pitch – we were in small groups, and all wearing different gear. Having that pointed out by someone in Leinster had a big effect on us, and just the simple fact of losing to Leinster at home was a sore point. Some of our lads reckoned they had gone even further than winning. Months later, at the rematch in Donnybrook, when we went into a pre-match huddle, someone began with, 'Look, these bastards think they can come down to Limerick, beat us on the pitch and then ride our women.' We'd use whatever it took to get those hatred levels soaring, I suppose. We won the interpro title that year, as it turned out.

More important, however, was what happened in the off-season. Fergal O'Callaghan had actually been appointed as fitness coach by the time the infamous *Sunday Independent* article appeared but he didn't get his hands on us till June, when we underwent our first proper pre-season as professionals, with training programmes put in place, monitored and followed through. I had never come across anything like the pain of it, yet it was enjoyable in its own strange way. It was rugby-specific, well thought out, with a definite purpose.

We were also inspired – there is no other word – by our new recruits. John Langford, the rangy former Brumbies and Wallabies second row, just blew us away with his fitness levels. While most of us were doing a three-kilometre test run in twelve minutes, he was running it in ten and a half. He was lapping us. I think he may have lapped Hayes twice. He would revolutionise our lineout and bring general Brumbie know-how but it was his attitude that helped us as much as anything else. We had also acquired Irish Kiwis in Mike Mullins and Jason Holland, more understated than John but influential in their own quiet way.

And we had Woody back. This being World Cup year, and as Harlequins were looking to save a few bob, a Munster sabbatical made sense. If any of us had forgotten how painfully direct he can be, we were reminded at an early training session, when he bollocked Killian Keane from a height for dropping a pass. Killian was taken aback but he got over it. Woody's attitude set the tone for the season. At one goal-setting session in UL, Dave Mahedy asked us our main goal for the season and when Woody piped up with 'Winning the Heineken Cup', there were giggles in the room. But the more time you spent with him and the new guys, the less funny the idea seemed.

The other change I had to get used to was on the domestic front. Olive and I were married in Tuamgraney on 4 July – Independence Day, ironically. Olive stood up for herself in the church, literally, correcting Fr Bluett when he referred to her as 'Orla' for the second time. No better woman! We had a large reception in the Abbey Court Hotel, Nenagh, which was well attended by Shannon members, including Gaillimh. As best man, he crucified me in his speech. After a lovely honeymoon in Barbados, it was back to the new house and the adventure of putting up curtains and generally getting the place furnished. I had to get used to the fact that I would never again be waited on hand and foot by my mother – no more vast plates of sandwiches served to me on the sofa. Olive is a brilliant cook but she is petite and doesn't serve Foley-sized portions. Dad still tells a story about me complaining to Mam about the size of the tomatoes Olive was giving me, and how I hadn't seen cherry tomatoes before. It's untrue, of course – but the smaller portions did me no harm, and neither did the discipline of having to do more for myself.

There were worse hardships to endure at work. On a bonding/orienteering weekend in Kilkee, Claw, myself and a few others had to swim 500 metres and then run five miles in wet rugby shorts to get back to base. Claw bitched and moaned the whole way back, and I walked like John Wayne for a week afterwards. But there was a good buzz in the squad, which improved when we beat Ulster, reigning European champions, at Queen's University. We allowed ourselves a few celebratory drinks in the Europa Hotel and were entertained by the singing of our newly appointed team manager Brian O'Brien, who had taken over from Jerry Holland. Briano is quite a character.

There will be just one word on his tombstone – honesty. He was sixty-one that season and his party-piece was to grab both luggage racks on the team bus and do a full 360-degree swing. He's mad, but good mad. Briano sang a lot of songs that night in Belfast but the one that struck a chord with all of us was 'Stand Up and Fight' from *Carmen Jones*. It would become our anthem:

> *Stand up and fight until you hear the bell,*
> *Stand toe to toe, trade blow for blow,*
> *Keep punching till you make your punches tell,*
> *Show that crowd what you know!*
> *Until you hear that bell, that final bell,*
> *Stand up and fight like hell!*

Some of us became proper professionals for the first time that season but we still drew on traditional Munster sources of inspiration at times, such as the time Ireland played a World Cup warm-up game against us at Musgrave Park. Munster v. Ireland might sound a strange concept now but only five of us had been selected for the World Cup squad of thirty – and that included Woody and our second- and third-choice scrum-halves, Tom Tierney and Brian O'Meara. We were pissed off because the squad had been announced ahead of schedule – we'd been led to believe that Ireland's games against us and Ulster would effectively be trial matches. Now we'd been told it didn't matter what we did in this game because we were surplus to requirements.

To be honest, I never expected to be picked for the squad but the Musgrave game was an opportunity to vent some frustration, and not just for me. Put it this way. Deccie didn't need to psych us up for that one, and when we won, we went wild. It was a strange scene with all these Irish people celebrating an Ireland defeat like crazy. Later, after the World Cup, Donal Lenihan conceded that playing the provinces as warm-up games had been a dodgy idea.

The World Cup barely interrupted our preparations for Europe. Quinny and David Wallace were called up when Corks was injured and Trevor Brennan was suspended – despite the fact that they were supposedly struggling with injuries. Quinny had what he said was a torn calf and Wally had a bad ankle, which reduced their participation in the orienteering camp we were on in Delphi, County Mayo. We'd been doing obstacle courses blindfolded and climbing rope ladders among other things. On our way up one hill, the boys' legs were so bad they needed a lift – until word came through that they were needed in Dublin. Mannix – as we called Lenihan, after the 1970s TV character – had been on the phone. The two boys spun on their heels, sprinted down the hill and basically raced each other to Dublin to join the World Cup squad. One minute they were practically in need of operations, and the next, as soon as Mannix was on the blower, they were gone!

It might sound mean-spirited and almost unpatriotic to say it, but my only hope of redemption came from Ireland's failure in the tournament. I can clearly recall where I was on the night we lost to Argentina in a quarter-final play-off in Lens. It's a strange and little-known fact that Munster lost to Garryowen in a 'friendly' that same evening, under lights at Musgrave Park. We then watched the Lens game in the Dolphin clubhouse. These days, people give Argentina the respect they are due but at the time, it seemed like the rugby world had been turned on its head. I knew there would be a fall-out and if I got myself in the right place, I could benefit. Driving from Cork to Killaloe that night, I had the sense of a door being reopened. I told Olive as much when I got home.

11

LONDON CALLING

Saturday, 5 February 2000, Twickenham

England 50 Ireland 18

If Lens was a low-point for Irish rugby, Twickenham the following February was rock bottom. To leak a half-century of points for the first and only time in Five or Six Nations history was embarrassing. I think we also broke the record for recycling the ball for the highest number of phases without making one positive yard. It was so dispiriting, and I know because I was there. My first taste of test rugby since England had walloped us at Lansdowne three seasons earlier wasn't quite the resurrection I'd planned.

I felt sorry for Gatty because he was getting it in the neck from all sides. Some of the newspaper headlines the next day were way over the top: 'In the Name of God, Go!' and 'Gatland: Wanted for Crimes Against Irish Rugby'. It was a tough time for him. I don't think he'd been made to feel particularly secure by the fact that Eddie O'Sullivan had been parachuted in as his assistant coach on a contract that was longer than his own. He subsequently admitted that if we'd lost the next game to Scotland, he would have walked. I was probably feeling extra sympathy for him because he found time at the after-match function to tell me that he thought I'd kept going well despite the problems we were having against a decent England side. Coming at a time when everyone was feeling vulnerable, this was reassuring.

Earlier that week, when Donal Lenihan presented me with my jersey in front of the assembled team at the Chelsea Harbour Hotel, he admitted he hadn't expected me to play international rugby again. In private, he told me any time he'd watched me in the preceding couple of years, it looked as though I was half-limping around the pitch. He had a point. It was some time in November 1999 that Wally and I went to see Dr Dermot O'Farrell in Croom with similar ankle injuries. Dr O'Farrell, who had worked with American footballers, said we had 'footballer's ankle', a spur or bony growth caused by constant friction. He offered us the choice of an operation and a six-month lay-off or a course of injections under general anaesthetic to reduce the pain and increase mobility. I took the needle option and it had the desired effect.

The other major factor in my resurgence, of course, was Munster. If you're looking for a real lift-off point for our European quest, it has to be beating Saracens at Vicarage Road on Sunday, 28 November 1999. You have to remember how glamorous Saracens seemed to us at the time, with their pom-pom girls, the pounding music after every score and their multinational line-up – Francois Pienaar, Richard Hill, Scott Murray, Thierry Lacroix, Danny Grewcock, Roberto Grau, Tony Diprose. They were quality. Us? Well, we had won once on the road in Europe – in Padova, the previous season – but we prepared for this one as though we meant it. We went over on the Friday for a Sunday game, and scouted the ground when Watford played Sunderland on the Saturday.

The next day, we were in serious trouble at 34–23 with ten minutes to go but our fitness showed in a strong finish. I sickened Saracens with a try off a quick tap and then Mikey Mullins, who had a stormer, threw out a beautiful pass to Jeremy Staunton and his try left us a point behind, with Ronan O'Gara's conversion to come. Saracens were moaning afterwards that Rog's kick drifted wide of the very short temporary posts at Vicarage Road but Rog said it didn't and that's good enough for me. It's hard to get video evidence because the match was televised live only by British Eurosport, which shows you where the tournament stood then in terms of profile. That didn't stop us celebrating like madmen. Quinny and I draped ourselves in a Tricolour to pose for the snappers, and our few hundred supporters ignored the man on the PA telling them it was a public-order offence to encroach on the pitch.

One of Deccie's favourite psychological ploys has always been to set us new goals for every match. Next, it was to win our first game on French soil. We'd talked at length about the mental block we had when it came to playing there. Deccie had produced a flip chart, and we listed all our various grievances, from the local food to the hotel beds, the hole-in-the-ground toilets and the grease-proof jacks roll. Then we looked at the ones we could do something about and the ones we just had to live with.

Food is particularly important to rugby players – how much, how often, how tasty – and it's no coincidence that our improving results coincided with the beginning of our ongoing relationship with Vincent Lacrampe-Camus, the catering manager at the Sofitel in Bordeaux, who to this day oversees the preparation of Munster's food for every game in France, making sure the porridge is the right consistency and the green beans are not too soft. Deccie also recognised the value of travelling on our own terms and started chartering flights. The last time we stayed overnight after the game was in Padova the previous season, when one drunken player shoulder-charged his hotel-room door off its hinges when he couldn't find his key. After that, it was decided we'd be better flying back on the night of the game, no matter how late, and hitting our own pillows. As for the toilet roll, I'm sure some players packed sensibly.

We had only revenge on our minds when we flew into Toulouse to play Colomiers two weeks after Saracens – they had beaten us in the previous year's quarter-final, which was a niggly, narky affair. This time, we were probably a bit lucky that Colomiers' own stadium was being rebuilt, so we were practically on neutral territory at Les Sept Deniers, home of Toulouse. We were less fortunate with a spate of injuries. Claw had to be replaced by a young fella called Marcus Horan from Shannon, on a development contract at the time. Jason 'Dutchy' Holland, an accidental Kiwi tourist playing for Midleton, came in for Killian Keane. When John Hayes departed injured at half-time, we had Ian Murray of Cork Con at prop and when he departed, Woody had to fill in at tight-head for the last five minutes. No matter. By then, we were out of sight. Dutchy, the accidental tourist, had scored two tries and Marcus had scored another after the dummy of the century. We won 15–31. So that was three games played, three wins, including two away from home. Qualification, anyone? We won the return game against Colomiers the following week, so it would all come down to Saracens at Thomond Park on the second Saturday of the new millennium, one of the great Thomond days.

It was the last 'over-the-wall' game, those days when stewards turned blind eyes to young fellas being hooshed up and over by their mates. The place was heaving. God knows how many people got inside but the fire officer would set a strict limit of 13,500 from that point on. Nicole Langford set up her camcorder on a tripod in the stand, and to watch it all again a while later – to see it from a supporter's viewpoint, with all the mayhem in the crowd – was an almost eerie experience.

Another ebb-and-flow, one-point game came down to another Rog conversion and the width of another goalpost. The only difference was that this time, Saracens had taken the lead very late through a Mark Mapletoft try and the possibility of a home defeat heaped incredible pressure on us. But we produced the right plays, with Mikey darting up the middle and winning us a penalty. Rog stuck us into the corner, Langford gobbled up another ball at four, we all piled in and Woody got the touchdown. Deccie and Niallo were probably the only people who knew we didn't actually need the conversion as things stood – we were already ahead of Saracens on head-to-head and through as pool winners. But the drama

– with Saracens charging early, Rog having to start all over again, then knocking it over via the post – was unbelievable. Nicole even got the perfect ending to her home movie as her husband stretched a telescopic arm to block Mapletoft's last-gasp drop-goal attempt.

Claw, Mikey and myself were rewarded with selection for the Six Nations game in Twickenham, while Woody got the Ireland captaincy back.

Munster had a big influence in the preparation for the second championship game, at home to Scotland. In particular, there was a famous training session on the back pitch at Greystones, a sort of last-man-standing practice match without a referee when Gatty basically just let us go at each other full pelt. After the England result, there were bound to be changes, and this was the last chance to stake a claim. Gaillimh and Claw were in their element, of course, and so too was Hayes, who was called up for his first cap against Scotland. Strings and Rog also made their debuts, while Gaillimh was recalled for the umpteenth time – you've seen the famous photo with him shepherding our two baby-faced half-backs during the anthems. That made eight Munstermen, a far cry from the World Cup.

Ten minutes in, we were 10–0 down and facing yet another defeat by the Scots (we hadn't beaten them in twelve years). But we dug in – maybe that blood-and-guts session in Greystones helped – and got a few lucky breaks. A Scottish advantage that referee Joel Dumé forgot about, which ended up with Shane Horgan scoring at the other end, is one that gets mentioned, but we won 44–22 and had earned ourselves a little breathing space. When we walloped Italy 60–13, we even began to feel good about ourselves. All we needed was a decent showing in Paris and our first-ever Six Nations campaign would be heading towards respectability.

Brian O'Driscoll, like Woody before him, wasn't interested in respectability. I'd heard a lot about Drico before I saw him. At Irish squad sessions, you'd hear Denis Hickie and Victor Costello raving about this kid from Blackrock and UCD who was causing carnage with Leinster's A team. At first, we were more interested in his centre partner, Dermot O'Sullivan from Tralee, who was also handy, but when I finally did see Drico at close quarters, in a Munster v. Leinster interpro at Temple Hill, I realised the hype was justified. Not only did he have pace that would scare the shite out of you, he had brilliant feet and was willing to do all the dirty stuff, including making the big hits, and robbing balls on the ground. He had only just turned twenty-one when we went to Paris but was already a fixture in the side and wasn't remotely frightened by the idea of playing in front of 80,000 people at the Stade de France. He relished it.

His hat-trick was the main story of that sunny afternoon in Paris, but other bits and pieces have stayed with me. We ate pizza the night before the game – not recommended by the nutritionists but the grub at the team hotel was absolutely shocking and sometimes you need comfort food. Pizza became a regular pre-match feast in Paris after that trip. I also recall blowing hard for the first ten minutes as the French threw everything at us; the restlessness in the crowd when the points avalanche never materialised; Denis Hickie's tackle on Marc Dal Maso, which saved our hides and removed any doubts about Denis' appetite for defence; Paddy Johns coming off the bench; Paddy Johns being sin-binned two minutes later and the distraught look on his face; packing down in the second row and how our seven-man scrum survived; David Humphreys kicking the penalty that saw us home, 27–25 winners; the unconfined joy on the faces of the Irish supporters in one corner of the stadium as they celebrated our first win in Paris for twenty-eight years. Come to think of it, we haven't won there since, have we?

Kitty O'Shea's on rue des Capucines was lively that night. Later, Olive and I got a lift back to the team hotel from the French traffic police – we'd been unable to pick up a cab and when the cops enquired about these two foreigners walking the streets in formal attire, Olive had enough French to explain who we were, where we were coming from and where we were going. A police escort down the Champs Elysées wasn't a bad way to end an amazing day. The euphoria lasted through to the next morning. At Charles de Gaulle airport, I tried to conduct a phone conversation with Marian Finucane for her show on RTÉ Radio with Drico roaring at me in the background. The hat-trick hero might still have been a little tipsy – he'd been stuck to the bed when I went to wake him up that morning.

'Who's that shouting in the background?' asked Marian.

'Girvan Dempsey,' I replied. As if.

After all that, it was annoying to lose to Wales 23–19 at home in the final game. We were probably a bit complacent, what with all the hype, such as the Carphone Warehouse offering millions for the first Irish player to score a hat-trick. A third-placed finish was our best in the championship since 1987 and represented a big step forward after the disappointment of the World Cup, but we already knew that if we were taking ourselves seriously, we should have been beating Wales at home and we should have been finishing second in the championship behind England.

At least the season was still rolling for the Munster contingent. Two weeks later, Stade Français, the Manchester United of rugby as Deccie called them, were coming to Thomond Park for the Heineken Cup quarter-final. The big talking point in the build-up was the selection of Halvey ahead of Quinny, which showed Deccie and Niallo weren't afraid to make the tough calls – and it was a tough call. Halvey was incredibly talented but not exactly cut out for the professional game. I remember talking to Richard Hill, who shared a house with Halvey during his brief spell with Saracens in 1996, and he had been astonished by all the smoking and the junk food. By now, Halvey was back working, and playing part-time, but he hadn't lost that incredible raw talent and Niallo, especially, would have recognised his potential for disrupting the Stade lineout.

That's exactly how it panned out. The selection was hard on Quinny, who had done nothing wrong, but Halvey offered something out of the ordinary. As it happened, we didn't need anything too extraordinary to beat Stade. The supposed Manchester United of rugby failed to show up. We hit them with everything for the first quarter, led 12–3 by the break and extended that to 27–10 by the end. Next, please.

Toulouse. Away. Bollocks. We heard the semi-final draw on radio the next day at home, where we were hosting a christening celebration for Connor Langford – John and Nicole had kindly asked Olive and me to be godparents – and that was our initial response. We could have got Northampton or Llanelli but we got Toulouse, in Bordeaux. Toulouse had put sixty points on us three seasons before and since then had been strengthened by the arrival of Fabien Pelous, Franck Tournaire and Christian Labit. Only as the afternoon wore on did we find a way of dealing with the news. Sure, if we were going to win the tournament, we'd have to play them at some stage, wouldn't we? That's exactly how Deccie put it to us when we went back to work on Monday. In one way, the pressure was off us, because no one expected us to go to the south of France and beat the best side in the competition.

Come the week of the game, my only preoccupation was with being fit to play. On the Monday, I ricked my back running over a humpback bridge in UL and barely trained for the next few days. By Thursday evening, I was in bits, lying on my back on the floor of my room in the Greenhills Hotel while the rest of the lads were in town at *Alone It Stands*, John Breen's brilliant play about the 1978 win over the All Blacks. I ended up having to wear a corset to play in Bordeaux. You can see the extra layer around my midriff in the team photo that was taken just before the game – it looks as though I'd been eating and drinking my face off. It was roasting over there, which didn't make the corset any more comfortable, but adrenalin soon took care of that.

I'd never experienced a pre-match atmosphere like it. Toulouse's supporters are more like soccer supporters in the way they chant, and we'd wound them up further by warming up at their end. We couldn't get over how many Munster supporters had made the trip, although Deccie had told us that a good few had travelled. You don't always know with him whether you're being fed a line, but lots of red was to be seen. Granted, Toulouse wear red but when we saw someone in a Santa outfit, we knew he wasn't French. The number of Munster supporters was eventually put at 3,000 – nothing amazing by today's standards, but an astonishing effort back then.

I just wish more people could have seen that game. It's pretty hard to get a copy of it (Dad has it on video, of course) but it's worth the effort. Already we'd been pigeon-holed by most commentators as a kick, chase and push side but we played some brilliant rugby that day. Watch the approach work for Hayes' try in the first half. The continuity play to set up the try is outstanding. You can see Hayes on the deck taking a long breather just before he receives the scoring pass from Dom Crotty. It became known as 'the seventeen-second wait' – we counted out the seconds at the video review the following week. After the break, Jason Holland's intercept try was a great example of timing and anticipation. Luckily, he didn't have far to travel after getting the ball. When you run at Dutchy's pace, there's only one thing worse than intercepting a pass, and that's intercepting a pass with fifty metres to run. I should know. Rog's try, our last, was sensational. It started with him hitting Mikey with a miss-pass outside our twenty-two and then it seemed everyone got a touch before Rog was dotting it down under the posts and doing a tumble in celebration. He still counts it as his best-ever try.

We had a lot of work still to do. In the back of our minds we were thinking maybe Toulouse would lie down. They looked knackered at half-time, and didn't even make the long walk back to the changing rooms, where we were being draped in iced towels. As Claw put it so eloquently, they 'looked like they'd shot their load'. They hadn't. They kept running at us. The last few minutes were very sweaty, with us just six points ahead at 25–31, and Gaillimh and Woody both watching from the sideline having been replaced. The referee, Jim Fleming, allowed a ridiculous amount of injury time and, once again, we had to tap into all that fitness work we'd done with Fergal throughout the year. On the final whistle, we all felt this enormous emotional release. There are pictures of Niallo and Deccie hugging and crying. They weren't the only ones. Doing a lap of honour was probably a mistake, seeing as we hadn't won a trophy yet, but in the circumstances, with that massive travelling support, it was the only thing to do.

That wasn't our only mistake. I think it was Gaillimh who said maybe we had to lose a final or two to win one, the theory being that if we'd won our first one, maybe we wouldn't have taken the steps necessary to become a real force in Europe, an ongoing force. Perhaps. All I know is that losing to Northampton was horrible at the time. It still rankles even now, and that's because we made things harder for ourselves than they should have been.

For starters, I reckon we bought into the idea that by beating Toulouse, we'd practically one hand on the trophy. The media were saying that Northampton, who'd squeezed into the final with narrow wins over Wasps and Llanelli in the quarters and semis, were knackered and over the hill. It's true they were a motley crew but they were battle-hardened, with a grizzled old pack including Federico Méndez, Budge Pountney, Pat Lam and Tim Rodber. Some other peripheral incidents didn't help. For one thing, the IRFU had called to see if a few of us would be able to parade the trophy at Lansdowne Road the day after the final, when Ireland were due to play the Barbarians. Players don't need to hear those sort of assumptions before a final.

Then our coach spent ages stuck in London traffic because we flew into Gatwick and not Heathrow. Canterbury hadn't provided us with enough socks so we had to go and buy O'Neill's socks – those things would never be allowed to happen now, but we were still finding our way. To top it all off, at the team meeting the night before the game we all got far too emotional. Not everyone wants to talk in these situations but it was felt everyone should say something. Another mistake.

I still haven't watched the game on video – too painful. Northampton were hard and cute, and they got to Rog more than we should have allowed them to. We got a good start, with Dutchy dropping a goal and Wally scoring a great try, the only one of the game. But then we got drawn into a slugging match and Northampton were pretty good at that. A couple of refereeing decisions by Joel Dumé were annoying, particularly the binning of Gaillimh in the second half. Dominic Malone – who would join Munster a couple of years later – tapped a free kick, ran at Gaillimh and fell over. It was well inside their half so it wasn't as though this was some cynical attempt by Gaillimh to prevent a certain try. The most annoying thing was that we just didn't do justice to our ability. We left it behind. We had a chance to win with Rog's penalty from wide on the left but the wind tugged the ball to the left. Later, a safe distance later, we used to take the piss out of him over it. You'd have forwards having a shot at goal from roughly the same distance after training, knocking it between the posts and saying, 'See, Rog? Easy.' But I felt for him at the time. Twickenham was a horrible place to kick when it was open at one end. Then you think back to the kicks he did get for us in that campaign and you realise there's no one else you'd rather have taking a shot at goal for you.

I took a bad knock to my shoulder early on and needed a jab at half-time to numb it, which didn't help. The discomfort was nothing to the frustration I felt during a stop–start second half, or the sense of helplessness at the end, packing down at the scrum and hearing the referee say, 'Last play,' knowing it's their put-in, they can hoof the ball out and it's all over. Northampton 9, Munster 8. We were distraught, wondering if we'd ever get another opportunity like that one. Our supporters, 30,000–40,000 of them, were amazing. We're standing in the middle of the pitch, maybe sixty seconds after the final whistle, and 'The Fields of Athenry' is ringing around Twickenham. They weren't going anywhere. We could have done without Richard Harris and Peter O'Toole turning up in the changing room afterwards, joking and laughing, but our non-celeb supporters were brilliant. I suppose you could look back and say that moment, as we stood in the huddle, was another starting point as well as the end of an incredible campaign.

The following week, Simon Easterby had to room with me in Buenos Aires. I wouldn't be the chirpiest of room-mates at the best of times but on Ireland's short tour to the Americas that summer, I think I walked around with a permanent storm cloud above my head – all because of what had happened at Twickenham. I didn't sleep well, partly because of jet lag, partly because I was replaying scenes from the final in my head, over and over. I don't think any of the Munster contingent were in great mental shape heading to Argentina, and nothing prepares you for the Ferro Carril Oeste, a lively little soccer stadium on the outskirts of the city. Lively is probably understating it. The Pumas hadn't played since the World Cup seven months previously, so this was their glorious homecoming. It was quite a show.

The signs weren't good when we arrived in the dungeon-like changing rooms to find the place flooded. Meanwhile, up on the pitch it was carnival time. The local supporters were hopping and chanting, flares were being lit, confetti was twirling everywhere. On the tower blocks outside the stadium, you could see flags draped from windows and kids squeezed onto balconies to get a look. We had to stand around waiting a good ten minutes while our opponents were being filmed by a gaggle of snappers and TV cameras. Unfortunately, the local media got the story they were looking for, with the Pumas winning 34–23. Obviously, we had gone there seeking revenge for the World Cup but it didn't help that we'd lost Girvan, Denis and Drico when they were injured in that Barbarians game. We actually scored four tries to their three but Humphs had a rare bad day with his place-kicking and some of us were definitely running on empty by the end.

It's one of the privileges of being an international sportsman that you get to travel to cities such as Buenos Aires, Boston and Toronto, as we did on that tour – some of the lads went up to Niagara Falls on one day off. From a rugby-playing point of view, though, this one was a trip too far, and provided an ordinary ending to what had been a good season for Ireland and Munster. We walloped USA 83–3 in Manchester, New Hampshire, but then got out of jail against the Canadians with a 28–28 draw, by which time everyone was just living for their holidays.

Probably the only memorable thing about the week in Toronto was the punishment Gatty meted out to eight tourists who caused a stir by running naked through a college campus – poor old Brian O'Brien, who'd just replaced Donal Lenihan as national team manager, was woken in the middle of the night by an irate security officer. The next morning, Gatty told the pranksters that for the rest of the week, they weren't allowed leave their rooms unless they were wearing their number ones – team code for blazer, slacks, shirt and tie. This doesn't sound too bad until you realise how warm it is in Toronto in June. Photos from Niagara feature the lads in their best bib and tucker, drenched to the skin. By the Friday of that week, the eight of them were all just camped in one room in shorts and T-shirts, watching Canadian television until it was time for grub, and then they had to put the blazers on again. It was hilarious – for the rest of us.

Hayes and I had been rested for the USA game and took things easy. Manchester is one of the dullest towns on the map so there wasn't a hell of a lot to do other than sit in steakhouses and mull over what had been an eventful season. I was happy for Hayes. The farmer from Cappamore, County Limerick, had come to rugby late, and to propping even later, but with five international caps and a European Cup runners-up medal he was doing all right for himself. I was happy enough myself, too. All things considered, I was in a much better place than where I'd been twelve months previously. I wasn't about to start patting myself on the back, though. I'd made that mistake before. Time to kick on.

12

HARD-LUCK STORIES

If 2000 was the year Irish rugby started to feel good about itself again, 2001 was when we learned how to feel hard done by. A few years later, in Munster, we realised that self-pity is a waste of time but back in 2001, we allowed ourselves to wallow in it a little bit. A highly promising Six Nations campaign was shut down because of foot-and-mouth and didn't resume for seven months, by which time we had lost precious momentum. With Munster, the failure of the Heineken Cup organisers to provide television match officials, even for the knock-out stages of the tournament, denied us the try that could have put us into our second successive final. This was a sickening end to an anti-climactic season.

Ireland first. Our confidence was boosted by a decent November during which we put seventy-eight points on Japan and then stood up to the South Africans both on and off the pitch. The pre-match will be remembered for Claw leading the charge onto the back pitch at Lansdowne Road, where the Springboks' team training run had lasted well beyond their allocated time-slot. Their management claimed they had started late because the team bus had got caught in Dublin traffic, but Claw wasn't in the mood for excuses.

'Fuck this, lads, they're on our pitch. C'mon!' he croaked, marching out of the changing rooms and onto the pitch, while the Boks were still going through their routines. They soon left, as they were asked to do, although clearly not happy about it. Relations between the sides weren't great as it was. The hits were hard and heavy the next day.

The Boks won 28–18 but were guaranteed their victory only when Corné Krige scored a try at the death. A couple of things had changed since the last time we'd played them, two years earlier. For one thing, we now posed a threat out wide. Drico and Hendo provided a nice blend of rapier and bludgeon in midfield, while Denis had genuine gas, so we used a lot of lineout ball off the top to get those fellas into the game as quickly as possible. The Boks crowded their midfield defence but still couldn't stop our wingers scoring a try apiece, including a cracker by Tyrone Howe in the second half. The other thing was that we were fitter and therefore able to go the full eighty minutes. They had the control and the composure to score when they needed to at the end but they knew they'd been in a battle – not that they'd ever grant you that respect, of course. We'll only get that when we start to beat them consistently. At least we knew we were improving.

The Six Nations had come up with a reasonably kind

schedule. We had England and France at home, and Italy first up, in Rome – amazingly, Ireland hadn't won its opening game since 1988. Everyone was in favour of having Italy in the tournament, especially Olive, who saw an obvious shopping opportunity. My folks came along, too, and missed Rosie's international debut in Barcelona the same day. She would win a further thirty-eight caps so, I'm pleased to say, there were many more opportunities for the whole family to see her represent her country.

We were all feeling a bit touristy that week. Brian O'Brien arranged an audience with Pope John Paul II, who seemed happy to pose for a photo with us. Even the northern Protestants, including Humphs and Jeremy Davidson, cracked a smile. It's not something that will happen again – an Irish team visiting the Vatican, I mean. Standing around all day waiting to meet Il Papa isn't the best preparation for a test match and Gatty was pretty cranky afterwards. Sure enough, we were a bit slow out of the blocks on match day, but eventually got home 41–22 winners, thanks mainly to a twenty-minute hat-trick by Hendo.

Once we beat France in the next game, 22–15, we were motoring. Consecutive wins over France! That was virtually unheard of. We actually led 22–3 before the French made things difficult for us at the death. The key score came from Drico, who by now had established himself as a world-class player. Afterwards, people questioned the decision of television match official Brian Campsall, who, after looking at replays for an age, decided Drico had, in fact, applied downward pressure before he brushed the corner flag at the Lansdowne Road end. He had so much work to do when he got the ball twenty metres out, it was amazing he even got close.

So there we were, two from two and facing a trip to Cardiff, where we hadn't been beaten since 1983. Despite the strong Munster influence in the squad, with nine players in the side that beat France, there were no cliques. We broke up for a few days and went back to our provinces, but couldn't wait to get back together again. Success can do that to a group, especially when success arrives after a long period without it.

We'd heard some of the scaremongering about foot-and-mouth cases in the UK – as a farmer, Hayes was particularly interested in keeping up to date – but on the Monday of the week we were due to travel, scientific and veterinary experts in the press were claiming the disease posed no threats to racing or rugby, and that sounded good enough for us. The next morning, at a snow-covered Glenview Hotel, Gatty announced an unchanged side. All was going to plan – until we were called to a meeting in the afternoon, to be told the match was postponed, indefinitely.

Our reaction might seem a little surprising. We went wild, with snowball fights and fellas stripped and dragged naked through the snow. Then we went into Dublin and stayed out for the night. We let our hair down. Why? It's hard to understand unless you've been in that situation. You have a big emotional and physical build-up to the intensity of a test match and when someone suddenly says it's off, it's like a switch has been flicked. There has to be a release. This was how we let go.

We didn't think we'd be waiting long before the remaining games were played. We assumed there was too much at stake for too many unions, too many plans in place. Gatty was talking about organising a few games in South Africa against Vodacom Cup teams, to keep us match sharp until the crisis passed. But it didn't pass – not quickly, anyway. As the number of foot-and-mouth cases continued to rise, the seriousness of the situation hit home with us. Eventually, the Six Nations committee rescheduled our three remaining games for the autumn. For the Munster lads, it would be near the end of April, and a Heineken Cup quarter-final in Lille, before we got to play some top-level rugby again.

There had been an urgency in Munster to bounce back from the disappointment of the Twickenham final. As someone put it, it wasn't just about the players and the coaches any more. There were now 30,000–40,000 people involved who'd been let down and were owed. That's a huge motivation. We lost Woody back to Harlequins and Halvey had been lured to London Irish but Frankie Sheahan and Quinny were more than decent replacements. John Langford also knocked back lucrative offers from France because, as he said himself, he had unfinished business with us. As if we'd have allowed him to leave anyway.

We'd been drawn in a nasty enough pool with Castres, Bath and a decent Newport side who pushed us close at Thomond in our first game. Immediately, people were questioning our ability to emerge from the 'Pool of Death'. The following Saturday, when we were trailing 6–20 in Castres with Quinny in the sin-bin, it looked like they had a point. We won 32–29, crowning our comeback with a brilliant try by Rog. Winning again in the south of France was a massive confidence booster for all of us.

It turned out that our only pool defeat was away to Bath, which was an experience. One of the biggest clubs in England stuck us in the smallest imaginable changing room, having first filled the old-style communal baths with piping hot water to steam the place up. It was incredibly claustrophobic – and then you open your kitbag to find one of the messers has crammed a load of hotel cups and cutlery inside for the crack. Ah, for fuck's sake. Bath beat us well, 18–5. They proved a different side from the one we'd walloped in Thomond – same names on the team-sheet, different intensity on their own patch. Home advantage was, and still is, a massive factor in this tournament, which made winning in Newport in early January a special effort. Five wins out of six meant we topped the pool and bagged ourselves a home quarter-final against Biarritz at the end of January.

There's no way of tiptoeing around this story. Biarritz was the game where I earned myself free pizza for life. Brian McGoey, a good friend and former Shannon team-mate who owns the franchise for Domino's Pizzas in Limerick, suggested to the Munster Branch a couple of days before the game that he'd give a free lifetime account to the player who scored the first hat-trick in the tournament – I suppose hat-tricks were still topical after Drico's heroics in Paris the previous year. Funnily enough, Brian told Niallo the offer was there so long as I didn't win it, because he was afraid I'd eat them out of business. He must have been suspicious when he saw me hanging out wide in the first twenty minutes, and slipping in at the corner for number one. Two more opportunities came along in the second half and what could I do but take them? Anyone for the Super Deluxe with all the toppings?

At least I'm not the only one to have benefited. Over the next while, my account number somehow got into the wrong hands and a few people made hefty orders – Paulie (Paul O'Connell) wasn't even in the squad back then but he remembers ordering sixteen large pizzas to be delivered to the Corner Flag in Henry Street, in my name, and all his mates having a good feed. To be honest, I didn't do the dog on it. I was trying to cut down on fast food and, besides, Domino's don't deliver to Killaloe.

We'd beaten Biarritz 38–29 in a hard old game to reach our second consecutive semi-final. Naturally, we were a bit miffed when we were drawn away to Stade Français, in Lille, scheduled for the third Saturday in April. This wasn't the problem, though. Once foot-and-mouth took over, we were struggling just to get some rugby. Basically, we had a couple of months to prepare for a semi-final but some of us had no one to prepare with. I say some of us because most players could at least play for their clubs in the AIL. Shannon, however, weren't interested in Gaillimh or me. I'm sure the coach, Conor McDermott, had his reasons, but I found it hard to take. Two former captains of the club are shooting for international honours while also trying to prepare for a Heineken Cup semi-final and they're being denied game-time by their club. It was petty, bizarre kind of shite to be carrying on with, and incredibly frustrating. Then, when I finally did get a run with the club, off the bench against the Cookies, I hurt my knee in a tackle by Mike Mullins. And I was on as a sub for Quinny, who had broken his thumb. A brilliant afternoon's work all round.

Around 10,000 supporters followed us to a drab old soccer stadium in a drab old city in northern France, where the bars apparently ran out of beer before the game. There was disappointment at the stadium, too. When you look at our preparation, it's a wonder we were so competitive against Stade. Our only game together since the quarter-final was a Good Friday friendly against an Ireland XV in Thomond the week before Lille, while Stade had been playing week in, week out in the French championship. Quinny's injury meant twenty-two-year-old Donncha O'Callaghan played out of position at number six, while Wally played on one knee and I wasn't 100 per cent either. We'd even called Dion O'Cuinneagain away from his medical studies in Cape Town as short-term emergency cover. Our set-pieces were a shambles. Rog didn't kick particularly well. The only things that kept us in it were doggedness, determination and Stade's mediocrity.

That didn't stop us being really pissed off when we found out for definite after the game that John O'Neill had been denied a perfectly legitimate try. He'd been pretty confident at the time that he'd got the ball down before hitting the corner flag and when referee Chris White got a shake of the head from his touch judge, Steve Lander, Gaillimh suggested White 'go upstairs' to the TMO. It was only then that he learned there wasn't one – ERC, the tournament organisers, argued that as not all stadia in the tournament were adequately equipped to use the technology, they'd have none rather than some. Great. It was bad enough getting phone calls after the game from people telling you Johno's try was good. Seeing it for yourself back in Limerick that night was worse. Lander later apologised for his mistake but that didn't make us feel any better. For the second year in a row, we'd travelled a long way in the tournament only to be pipped by a point. Those slow, sorrowful laps of honour were beginning to get to me.

A strange season ended in a strange place – the National

Stadium in Bucharest. It was strange mainly because there were maybe only a thousand people in this vast, 60,000-seater arena, where the spectators were distanced by the running track around the pitch. A good few of those thousand were there for Shane Byrne's stag weekend. Shane, or 'Munch' as we called him because of his resemblance to former England flanker, Mickey 'The Munch' Skinner, was on the bench and the loudest roar of the day came when Gatty finally put him out of his misery in the final quarter and gave him his first cap. He grabbed the match ball on the final whistle and didn't look like someone who was about to let it go.

To be honest, no one else would have been in a rush to challenge him. It had been a bit of a nothing match, which we won 37–3. We were without Woody, Drico, Rog, Malcolm, Hendo and Jeremy, who were in Australia with the Lions. I'd received an availability letter and read that Graham Henry, the Lions coach, was impressed with what he'd seen of me in that Munster v. Ireland XV game. But I saw myself as a long-shot once foot-and-mouth disrupted our Six Nations. I knew I'd be spending a good chunk of my summer in eastern Europe – Bucharest, first of all, and then Spala, a hell-hole in Poland that was to become a regular destination for pre-season fitness camps. We spent three weeks there that summer and they were three of the longest weeks of my life.

From a training point of view, Spala is great. It's a vast Olympic training facility used by athletes from all over Europe, who come for the famous cryotherapy chambers. The basic drill is as follows: after training, you stand for two and a half minutes in an atmosphere cooled to minus 140 degrees by liquid nitrogen, wearing a mask, a headband, boxer shorts, knee-length woolly socks and clogs. The exposure to extreme temperatures speeds up your recovery dramatically and allows you to train with greater intensity for longer periods. Effectively, you can get two weeks' strength and conditioning work done in the space of seven days, and Irish players have definitely felt the benefits in the past few years. The only problem with Spala is that while you get twice as much work done, time moves twice as slowly there as it does anywhere else in the world.

The camp is set in the middle of a forest an hour and a half from Warsaw and near nowhere in particular. When you're not training or deep-freezing, the options are fairly limited. You wouldn't be in a rush to eat the food at the canteen. You can go back to your very basic dormitory-like accommodation for a kip, slap on some more mosquito repellent or watch the Tour de France on Eurosport. The other thing we did on that particular trip was to curse Wally. We were in Copenhagen on the way to Spala when he got another call from Mannix to say he was needed – by the Lions! Just as the Lions saved Paul Wallace from a development tour to New Zealand, they saved the younger Wally from Spala. Where is the justice in that? Then, just to make our day, Quinny and I got wind of the fact that Deccie had signed Jim Williams, the Wallabies back-row, for the following season. How depressing was that?

That first visit to Spala was our longest. We broke it up with a trip to Warsaw – where we popped into Michael Bradley's brother's bar to watch the Lions beat Australia in the first test – and another to Kraków. From there, we travelled the fifty kilometres to Auschwitz, site of the Nazi concentration camp. More than half a century after being closed down, it's still a horrific place. Historians reckon well over a million people died there, in the gas chambers and crematoria, through starvation and in so-called medical experiments. They still have the personal belongings of some of the prisoners – shaving materials and things like that. It was eerie. You feel physically sick walking around the gas chambers. It was a warm day, so someone took off his T-shirt and was told by one of the guides to put it back on out of respect. Our visit made us feel embarrassed for having moaned about the boredom of Spala. That said, we didn't complain when, before returning home, we got to spend one night of luxury in a five-star hotel in Warsaw. We had air conditioning, soft pillows, lovely food, BBC World – how had we survived without BBC World!?

After all that work, we were feeling pretty good about ourselves when it came to completing our Six Nations programme – in October, which felt weird. We tried to ignore the talk of grand slams, knowing we'd only two wins in our back pocket and three games still to play. But we welcomed the idea of travelling to Edinburgh as narrow favourites, even though no Irish team had won there in sixteen years. Then we blew it. Scotland 32 Ireland 10.

It was warm and sunny at Murrayfield, nothing like your normal Six Nations afternoon, and we played nothing like we had played back in February. Gatty had made changes, with Guy Easterby, Rog, Jeremy Davidson and Kieron Dawson all coming in, and Shane Horgan taking over from the injured Hendo at twelve. We tried to play with plenty of width, which was a mistake. We thought we could play rugby but we ran away with ourselves. The Scots read us and pounced every time we turned the ball over. It felt like they knew everything we'd do in advance. Maybe they'd been secretly filming our training sessions. There had been rumours of that happening on previous trips to Edinburgh. I've even asked Andy Nicol, who was on their bench that day, about it and he says it wasn't the case. They just played well, with Gregor Townsend and John Leslie running the show in midfield, and we just played badly. This time there was no feeling hard done by, only the empty feeling of a brilliant opportunity wasted.

13

CHANGING OF THE GUARD

I was paying for petrol in Parteen when I heard that Gatty had been sacked.

'Looks like you've got a new boss,' says the fella behind the counter.

'And who's that then?' I ask.

'Eddie O'Sullivan. It was just on the one o'clock news.'

I knew it was true when I got back to the car and saw five missed calls on the mobile. I rang the folks just in case, and they confirmed it. Gatty had been given the bullet. I was shocked, and so were the players I spoke to over the next few hours. When I rang Gatty to commiserate, he sounded a bit bewildered himself. This was at the end of November 2001, a couple of months after that Scotland defeat, which was a setback, obviously, but results in general had been pretty good. We won seven of our last ten games under Gatty, a pretty high win ratio compared with what had happened before. What's more, our performances promised further improvement down the line.

We had reacted to the Scotland disaster with a 36–6 victory over Wales in Cardiff – a record margin of victory for either side in that fixture. A week after that, we put the kibosh on an England grand slam with an excellent performance at Lansdowne Road. We'd had two warm-up games and they were missing Martin Johnson and Lawrence Dallaglio, so they were vulnerable, while we were in the mood for a bit of mayhem. A few memories stand out: popping the ball to Woody as he peeled around a lineout move we'd only rehearsed in the warm-up that morning, then watching as he ploughed through Neil Back for a famous try; Iain Balshaw, England's full-back, being given the runaround by Humphs; Strings hand-tripping Dan Luger to save us near the death; the sight of the England players being made to wait to receive the Six Nations trophy while we did a lap of honour; and Taoiseach Bertie Ahern dropping in to a noisy changing room afterwards. Not a bad old day.

Next, a few weeks later, came Samoa – a proud occasion for me, as I led Ireland out at Lansdowne Road. Unfortunately, I remember practically nothing about it because of the bang I took in the first half. I vaguely remember being back in the changing room and wondering where everyone else was but by that stage, I didn't know my arse from my elbow.

I do remember the next week, though. We had the All Blacks well rattled when Denis scored early in the second half to leave the scoreline Ireland 21 New Zealand 7. Sadly, that ended up Ireland 29 New Zealand 40 after the Kiwis went up a couple of gears and scored thirty-three points at over a point a minute. It took them just a couple of phases to set up a mismatch, or so it seemed – where one of their strongest runners was charging at one of our smaller or slower defenders – and then exploit it ruthlessly. We conceded five tries, each one a kick in the guts. Sometimes I look back and wonder what might have happened if Norm Maxwell, their lock, hadn't deliberately blocked a Stringer pass as he was running back from an off-side position late in the game – referee Andre Watson let him away with it. The pass was intended for me and I had a free run to the right corner. I've replayed that moment a few times in my mind. But the All Blacks did what they needed to do to win.

That defeat was a real sickener, made worse by the knowledge that no Ireland team had ever beaten them. Gatty tried to lift our spirits in the changing room afterwards, thanking everyone for their efforts, trying to be upbeat. He'd wanted to win that one as much as anyone but he could also see the positives in defeat. Once I'd got over the disappointment, I would have been thinking along the same lines myself. But the powers that be decided change was necessary, and it all seemed to happen so quickly. I know Woody's views were canvassed but I was pretty low down the food chain, so I wasn't consulted on the decision, and we hadn't discussed it. Later, I learned that senior players had been pushing for a more specialised coaching set-up for over a year. England, under Clive Woodward, had been upping the ante by using a range of specialist coaches, guys who'd been brought in to deal with one specific area, such as defence, or lineouts, or kicking. Woodward was probably losing the run of himself when he hired a 'spatial awareness' coach but there you go. The feeling among some of our lads was that we were being left behind in terms of the resources we needed to compete at the top level.

It was true – there was too much work for too few people. Gatty did ask Leinster coach Matt Williams to come in and do a few defence drills with us but it was pretty basic stuff and only for a couple of sessions. Our lack of a proper defence system was ruthlessly exposed by the All Blacks. The market for specialists wasn't really buzzing then – you had to go to the southern hemisphere or to rugby league – but some people clearly felt Gatty had been too slow to search.

He had political problems, too, although as players we weren't really aware of that at the time. We knew he wanted to take us to the 2003 World Cup, to make amends for what had happened in 1999. Having helped us to our best championship finish in ages – second place to England on points difference – he must have felt he'd earned the right. The problem was he didn't seem to have the trust of the IRFU committee men. He didn't seem to trust them, either. When Hayes and I bumped into him a couple of years later, just after his Wasps team had beaten Munster in the Heineken Cup semi-final at Lansdowne, he told us the thing he liked most about his new gig was not having to answer to committees.

There has been plenty of speculation about Eddie's part in Gatty's downfall. All we saw day-to-day was two fellas doing their jobs. You could tell they weren't inseparable friends. In Spala, for example, while Gatty used to take us for runs in the woods, Eddie would be in the gym working on his six-pack. We had a fair idea Eddie was after the number-one job sooner rather than later. He hadn't been there long when we were handed sheets of paper on which was outlined a new 'pod' system for the forwards for attack off scrums, lineouts and so on – basically a road-map for each play – and Eddie had signed his name at the bottom of the sheet. It was like he was pissing on the lamppost, marking territory. Gatty would never have done anything like that.

I felt sorry when Gatty was railroaded out of a job he was doing well. On the one hand, he was being told he was going to lose Craig White, an excellent fitness coach with whom he worked really well; on the other, he was having other people, such as Eddie, forced upon him. Gatty was a decent technical coach, strong on set-pieces, and an excellent man-manager – he knew how to motivate, how to make it personal. He helped get a lot of players back to Ireland. I thought that, with the right structures in place, he had a lot to offer, and I'm not at all surprised that he's done so well with Wasps, Waikato and Wales.

We all had to move on, though. One of the positives about Eddie being in charge from my point of view was that he viewed me as a senior player. I was twenty-eight, had played in the side solidly for two calendar years and he saw me as part of his plans. We had a sit-down chat and he assured me the players wouldn't want for anything in terms of resources, within reason. Our coaching team was certainly ramped up. Deccie had been installed as assistant, although he was staying with Munster till the end of that season – at the time, it seemed like a great opportunity, a stepping stone, for him but things changed later. Eddie went out and hired, among others, ex-rugby league international Mike Ford to take charge of defence, Niallo to look after the forwards (like Deccie, he would be double-jobbing for the remainder of the season) and Mikey McGurn as fitness coach.

Training sessions were a lot different – short, sharp and purposeful. Fordy might have twenty minutes to work on a drill with us and once those twenty minutes were over, the hooter would sound and it was on to the next discipline. This isn't always the most effective format – sometimes things evolve during a session, and you need the flexibility to spend a bit more time on one aspect of your game if things aren't going well, or even if they are going well and you want to bring it on to a new level. But at the time, training was fresh and novel and everyone bought into it.

It was an exciting time generally. A new national coach meant extra competition for places, which in turn meant that the interpros we played in December 2001 at Lansdowne Road were cut-throat affairs. They were, in fact, part of a new competition, the Celtic League, involving Scottish districts and Welsh clubs, which was a welcome development. The league took a while to catch the public imagination but the Irish end of the operation was boosted by having three of the provinces – Leinster, Ulster and Munster – in the semi-finals leading up to Christmas 2001. We took quite a bit of pleasure in beating Ulster in the semi-final. The previous time we'd played at Ravenhill, we'd heard quite a bit beforehand about how they were the only Irish side to have won the European Cup. There was even a banner at one end proclaiming 'Ulster, European Champions 1999, Northampton, 2000' which was a not-very-subtle dig. Deccie used to watch the games from behind the posts in those days and, somehow, he got hold of that banner afterwards. He'd produce it in our changing room at appropriate moments over the next few years.

The final, a week later, was the real beginning of the modern Munster–Leinster rivalry. Instead of the 300 we'd had watching us at Dooradoyle three years earlier, 30,000 people packed into Lansdowne Road, full of Christmas cheer. Eric Miller mustn't have been feeling so Christmassy that day because he gave me a right kick in the bollocks – I never found out what his problem was, even when we roomed together at the next Ireland squad session. Anyway, when he kicked me, the referee was standing right beside him, so he was duly sent off but, as so often happens, this worked to the advantage of the team down a man. Leinster were excellent in the second half and deserved their 24–20 win. It wasn't easy hanging around Heuston Station that night, waiting for the train home with all these disappointed Munster supporters. But we did get a giggle a few days later when we heard Leinster had lost the trophy while they were out celebrating.

That season's European campaign wasn't without its fair share of drama. We had a stronger squad thanks to the arrival of Jimmy Williams and Hendo – although at first Hendo wasn't fit to play – but we failed to guarantee ourselves the all-important home quarter-final thanks to a cock-up at the end of our final pool game in Castres. Even though we were trailing by three points deep into injury time, we knew we'd done enough to top the pool on points difference, which would have given us that home quarter-final. We were in a position to clear our lines but the instinct to try to win the game took over. We moved the ball, didn't execute well, turned it over and they scored – advantage tossed away. The complex points system is one of the things that makes the Heineken Cup such a great competition, the fact that almost every score has a bearing on the outcome. But that result was another pain in the arse.

Claw had more than a pain in his arse after that game.

During the second half, he'd been bitten on the forearm – a serious bite that drew blood. Ismaella Lassissi, the Castres back rower, was banned for a year because of the incident but then had the ban lifted on appeal. According to the Castres doctor, the wound to Claw's arm was 'not consistent with a human bite'. I'll leave you to figure that one out yourself. It was a disgusting thing to happen to anyone – Claw had to have his blood tested, and take an AIDS test. This was another chapter in his hate–hate affair with the French – and it just so happened we'd drawn Stade in the quarters, in Paris two weeks later.

That was one of the most satisfying Munster victories – even though I was responsible for letting my opposite number, Christophe Juillet, slip over for a try early in the second half. The filthy looks I got from my team-mates for that one can be imagined. We'd worked our arses off to build up a 16–3 lead on the strength of a gale blowing straight down the Stade Jean Bouin pitch, and in the second half we were just going to protect that lead. Letting Juillet score wasn't a good start – but we all worked harder as a result. Kicking into the gale wasn't an option, so our recycling had to be spot on, and it was. The key was not allowing Diego Dominguez any shots at goal, and that meant putting up with all sorts of provocation from Stade. Ironically, the only one of us to lose his temper was Hayes. It's pretty hard to get Hayes angry but as one scrum broke up, he clocked Sylvain Marconnet an awful box, which stunned everyone, not just Marconnet, who was taken off a few minutes later. But, in general, we kept our cool, defended hard and held on for an excellent 16–14 win, which had Gaillimh chaired off the pitch by hundreds of very happy Munster supporters. Paris had been taken by storm.

This performance was, as a young Paulie put it afterwards, 'unreal'. He actually said it fifteen times in a TV interview – someone counted them later. He was unreal himself. He'd been invited to train with the squad the previous summer but a few weeks after that Stade game, he'd be making his international debut. I liked the cut of him. He was wiry and aggressive and, most of all, he was incredibly keen to play for Munster – he'd turned down the offer of a full Connacht contract for an academy contract with us because he was so determined to join us. His only problem was he was almost too keen. I remember watching him play a Munster Senior Cup final between Shannon and the Cookies, when he charged off the bench so pumped up that he was in the sin-bin three minutes later. Deccie had to give him a stern talking-to about his discipline – another irony, when you think of how big Paulie is on discipline now.

He remains a proud Cookie, but he is a completely different Cookie from Claw in one sense. As someone who obsessed over individual sports – swimming and golf – in his younger years, Paulie will avoid absolutely anything that might compromise his performance in the slightest. Claw – well, Claw is just different. A few weeks before our semi-final – against Castres, of all teams, in Beziers – he badly burned his arm and his face in what was reported as a gardening accident. We reckoned he'd poured petrol on the fire at home after he'd been out on the beer. He turned up at training a few days later in an awful state. The session actually stopped and we walked over to him. He had his arm in a sling, his face was scalded, his hair singed, and he was looking pretty sorry for himself. Someone giggled and then we all burst out laughing. We couldn't stop. It was hilarious. We showed no mercy, maybe because he'd have shown no mercy himself.

Still, his injuries were serious enough for people to wonder whether he'd ever play again, let alone play in the semi – he was retiring at the end of the year anyway. But those people didn't know Claw. He wasn't going to miss a rematch against Castres. He was told he had to pass a fitness test a few days before the semi but that was no bother to him. He played a game of indoor five-a-side soccer at UL, declared himself fit, and that was that – bitten, burned but not beaten, as it said on the T-shirt.

He was also binned in Beziers but it didn't affect the result. We won our fifth game against Castres in two seasons, 25–17, despite various handicaps. As well as it being an away match, we had no Jimmy because of a calf injury and soon enough, no me either. I hurt the A/C (acromio-clavicular) joint in my right shoulder fifteen minutes into the game. This meant Wally moving to eight and Donners (Donncha O'Callaghan) filling in out of position at six, a job he'd found tough going in the previous year's semi. This time around, he was outstanding – six foot, six inches of raw, non-stop energy and aggression. I was delighted for him, because he'd had a frustrating time of it waiting in line behind Gaillimh. I was happy for Claw, too, because he flew home with Lassissi's blue jersey stuffed in his kitbag. He reckoned it would look good on the wall of his new bar in Limerick.

I wasn't so delighted with my own situation. I flew out of Montpellier that night with my arm in a sling, to find out the next day that the medics rated me 'a major doubt' for the final against Leicester four weeks later. Two of those weeks were supposed to be given over to complete rest but I found various ways to accelerate the healing process. Orla is a qualified physical therapist, specialising in craniosacral therapy, so I had her working overtime, and I found acupuncture particularly good for improving the range of movement. A few prayers may have been said, and a few candles lit, as well. In any event, I made the final. Deccie had a tough selection call to make between Jimmy and me, two players badly short on match fitness but just about available. I think he reckoned on my shoulder lasting longer than Jimmy's calf and so started with me – as it happened, I lasted fifty-two minutes. I just felt lucky to be involved – especially compared with Hoggy (Anthony Horgan), who broke two bones in his hand messing about after a game of tip between backs and forwards at the Vale of Glamorgan Hotel on the Thursday night before the game. What a sickener.

Our preparation was generally far smoother than it had been in 2000 but this was still another of those Munster days overloaded with emotion. We knew Deccie and Niallo were moving on. Claw was definitely retiring, having agreed to play this season only because of the disappointment of the previous year in Lille. Gaillimh knew he was coming to the end, while Dom Crotty was emigrating to the States. So, of course, there was a lot of talk about this being Munster's year, almost as if we deserved to win because we'd been unlucky in the past. Were Leicester going to do us a favour? I don't think so. They beat us because they scored two tries to zero, did a number on our lineout than we did, and were by far the better side. While we were heartbroken walking up to receive a second collection of losers' medals, I think we all probably realised that much.

And Neil Back? He became a hate figure in Munster for paddling the ball out of Strings' hands into Leicester's side of the scrum just as we were lining up to attack the short side, six points down with time almost up, but to make him out as some sort of villain is rubbish. I don't hold any grudge against him. If I'd been in the same situation, I'd have been happy to get away with it.

For professional rugby players – and especially professional back-row forwards – cheating is part of the job. You do what you can to slow the opposition's ball, and if you can get away with stealing it – legally or illegally – then all the better. I'm not saying anything goes on a rugby pitch. You can't kick a fella in the head, gouge his eyes or deliberately injure him. I hate spitting, as well. But other things are acceptable, such as provoking an opponent into losing his rag, so that he either gives up points or sees yellow or red. That's an important part of trying to win a rugby match. You pull and drag at an opponent, you get in his ear, to see how he'll react.

Shannon used to do it all the time to Trevor Brennan – I got him sent off in one AIL match for lashing out. When Trevor asked me to write a letter pleading on his behalf to the IRFU Disciplinary Committee, I had no problem in helping out, but equally I'd no problem in getting him sent off in the first place. You do what you have to do, and this isn't just the attitude of a cynical professional. In my old man's time, Andy Haden won a test for the All Blacks in Cardiff by diving out of a lineout to earn the penalty when no one had gone near him. I'm sure the Welsh were pretty disappointed but they should have been disappointed with the referee. It was his job to spot that sort of play-acting, just as it was the officials' job to spot Back at the

Millennium Stadium. Maybe if the touch judge had seen him, we'd have won the penalty, knocked it in the corner, driven over and Rog would have kicked the winning conversion. Maybe. But that would have been an even bigger steal than what Neil Back did to us.

A week after the final in Cardiff, the Irish squad was due to leave for two tests in New Zealand. If I'd been ultra-cautious, I'd have stayed at home and minded my shoulder, but with just over a year to the 2003 World Cup in Australia, this was no time to be ultra-cautious. Having privately set Australia as the scene of his departure, Woody was even more determined and driven than normal, and the energy in the camp was positive, despite a mixed Six Nations.

In one sense, Eddie was on a hiding to nothing for his first championship, because it was going to take some effort to match the previous season's final standing when we had trips to London and Paris. It was fairly predictable that we'd beat Wales, Italy and Scotland at home, which we did. What surprised people was the margin of defeat by England and France – 45–11 and 44–5 respectively. A good bit of it was down to the fact that we were in the process of getting used to the defensive system being implemented by Mike Ford. Not only did this involve a new language, with its 'turfs' and 'wedges', but also learning to communicate and trust each other. This was tough enough in training; when the French are running at you at 100 mph and the brass bands are playing, it's very easy to slip back into old and bad habits. That uncertainty, together with the fact that Niallo had been given very little time to prepare with the forwards, was our main problem in those games.

One of the good things about going on tour is the opportunity to do a lot of quality work uninterrupted. Useful preparation for our two tests also came in a warm-up game when we hammered a NZ Divisional XV in Timaru on the same night the All Blacks were putting sixty-four points past Italy. The only disappointment that night was that the match officials wouldn't allow John O'Neill, who had replaced Hoggy, to tog out as our twenty-third man. He's a great bloke, and it would have been nice for him to wear the green once, even in an uncapped game.

We were all delighted for Rags (John Kelly), though, who was picked to start at twelve in Dunedin the following week. Centre was our problem position on that tour. Hendo, Shaggy (Shane Horgan), Maggsy (Kevin Maggs) and Jonny Bell were all unavailable. Rags had played just a couple of tests on the wing but he did an outstanding job with Drico in shutting down Aaron Mauger and Tana Umaga. To be honest, we all did well, and we should have won. Jesus, we should have won. Leon MacDonald, their full-back, scored a late and slightly lucky try to ensure a 15–6 victory for the All Blacks, who were roasted by their own media the next day. It wouldn't have crossed their mind to credit the other team, who had defended brilliantly, scrummed well and posed problems at the lineouts, or to mention that Geordan Murphy had come within inches of scoring after gathering Drico's cross-kick early in the second half. It seemed the only Irishman they mentioned was Rog, who'd played well but missed three penalties with a ball later described by Andrew Mehrtens as 'a pig'.

We were all livid that we'd let slip an even better chance than we'd had the previous November, and on New Zealand soil at that. To rub it in, a week later in Auckland, we were refereed off the park by South African official Tappe Henning, and then leaked a load of points in the final quarter. The guy I felt really sorry for was Mel Deane, who was on the touchline near the end, preparing to come on and make his international debut, when Eddie had to change things because Quinny had been binned. And how long had Quinny been on the field? One minute. For a while, the lads nicknamed him Nicolas Cage, because Nicolas Cage stars in a movie called *Gone in 60 Seconds*. We lost 8–40.

If you were cynical, you could compare the first and last of our three tests against New Zealand that season and say we'd gone backwards under our new coaching team, but that would be unfair and inaccurate. Dunedin showed we were coming to grips with Fordy's new defence system, while the set-pieces were in decent order, and there were other positives. Reggie Corrigan had established himself as a decent replacement for Claw, who had said his farewell to international rugby in Paris (where else?). Keith Gleeson got the sort of shoeing in the second test that the Kiwis reserve for opponents they respect, while Paulie was quickly establishing himself as a serious talent. Even allowing for some truly scary rain the week we were in Auckland, it had been a happy touring party. For the time being, all Eddie's ducks were in a row.

Me, Rosie and Dad – over 100 caps between us.

Me and my little man, Tony, May 2005.

Ireland v. England, 21 January 1995, scoring a try on my debut.

Ireland A v. South Africa A, 12 November 1996,
being tackled by Tinus Linee.

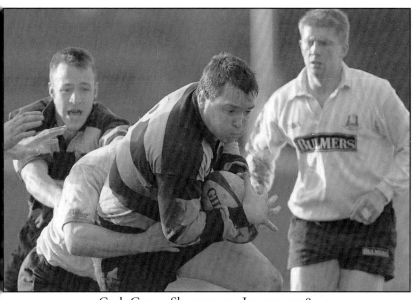

Cork Con v. Shannon, 10 January 1998,
as a skinny Anthony Horgan looks on …

Six Nations 2000, down
but not out …

Scoring one of my three tries against Biarritz,
ERC quarter-final, Thomond Park, 28 January 2001.

Celebrating with Alan Quinlan,
European Cup 28 November 1999, Saracens v. Munster.

© Ted Kirby

Venue	Referee					Kick-off
Thomand Park	Mr Judge					14:45
EAM OBJECTIVES			Munster	Gloucester		
e clock is our friend. ur defence is their enemy. arget 30 minutes concede no score. OME ¼ FINAL DRAW		Targets	No tries	2 tries +	OPPORTUNITY IS SELDOM CHERISHED UNTIL IT IS LOST	

GLOUCESTER						
LINEOUTS	**SCRUMS**	**RE-STARTS**	**DEFENCE**	**STRIKE MOVES**	**ROLLING PLAY**	**KICK CHASE**
EFENCE: First three have be clinical in killing omentum.	Tight bind Think smart about loose head.	Split 3 to start. Sinbad to chase. Onside for 10.	Pro-active defence. Pressure at ruck.	Out-half: Simple, direct, straight - look after the ball.	3 pod will work if we use width. Narrow channels.	Our 22 touch. Middle third - Snape A, B, C (bring them
ery physical.	Options on wheel.	Think quick	8-man chain.	Attacking half: 3	3 pod Kiwi lines -	up - kick to space).
TACK: Front three to ay up, support quick to jumper - patience in ive, throw high - think nart - be bold.	Referee management. Scrummage straight. Good option for PRIORITY THINKING	doesn't mean you have to do quick (Hartpury).	Inside O'Gara at lineout time.	pod attack, use width and keep our depth.	more depth. Clear 9-10 channel. No pick and go in 3 pod.	Attack option - England off a slug or Aberavon. Chase hard.

MUNSTER						
w four man format counter their throw.	Hayes very straight.	Stay high on line - good drill will quell big start they want.	Tight around ruck.	Blindside wing inside 10.	They will try to use their width.	Right-footed 10.
curate hooker will row long in defence: ust have air off all	Looks for gaps between 1-2.		Rush up in mid-field. Front 5 slow to re- organise.	10-12 cut.		Kicks in behind to dissect 11-15.
mpers think smart out using Springbok - s - staying down.	Good contest.	Standard 1 but expect change.	Stringer follows play.	10 dummy cut and go. Double miss for width.	Defend their narrow channels.	Chase hard, pressure 10 right foot.

The infamous Gloucester game plan
that was found in Tom O Donnell's taxi.

Celebrating my fiftieth cap on the final whistle, England v. Ireland, 6 March 2004.

© Billy Stickland/Inpho Photography

A nice, relaxing ice bath in the City West Hotel.

Celebrating our first European Cup victory in the Millennium Stadium,
20 May 2006.

Myself and Deccie showing off the cup
to our supporters in Thomond Park.

The four of us at home in Killaloe.

14

MIRACULOUS

I now had a new boss at my day job – Alan Gaffney. An Aussie coaching Munster. Who would have thought it? We're supposed to be clannish down here – clannish and conservative. Well, our chief executive Garrett Fitzgerald and Munster's management committee used some pretty lateral thinking when they approached Leinster's assistant coach to replace Deccie. It was brave move by Gaffer, too, who said he took the plunge because his mantra in life is 'Don't die wondering'. He could never have dreamt up some of the stuff that he'd experience with us.

By his own admission, he was in a comfort zone at Leinster, trundling along almost unnoticed. The Leinster Branch had their hands full trying to hold on to their director of rugby at the time, Matt Williams, and probably took their eye off Gaffer. That's when Munster made their move, and what a move it was. I know, he may have bought in some dodgy foreign imports in his time (as Claw would say, not naming names, but Clinton Huppert?) but he also employed some good helpers, such as Brian Hickey as assistant coach and Paul McCarthy as scrum specialist. After a while, Graham Steadman arrived to work on our defence. Gaffer was an outstanding technician himself, and encouraged us to think about the game in terms of a process, or a series of processes. He probably figured out soon enough that the emotional side of things would look after itself.

Even though he eventually ended up going back to Leinster, we always reckoned he was more one of us. We got a bit of mileage out of press interviews where he said that he came originally from a working-class part of Sydney – we slagged him for licking up to the Limerick Munster supporters – but he does have the common touch. He loves a pint and a chat. My family got to know him pretty well because he and his missus, Lorraine, are roughly of an age with my folks, and he loved coming out to Two Mile Gate, a leisure spot in Killaloe, for water sports.

I would have liked to have been his first captain but when it was put to the squad, Jimmy pipped me by one vote. Gaffer spun the result by saying I was better off not getting it because of my international commitments, but I'd have been keen enough. I liked the idea of being in charge, making the calls out on the pitch. No matter. Jimmy had made a huge impression on the lads in the space of a year – he was abrasive on the field, intelligent and helpful to the younger lads. He was a good choice. My time would come. For Gaffer, the problem was trying to emulate the coaches he had succeeded. For all the disappointments, two European finals and a Celtic League final all in the space of three years was a fair effort by Deccie and Niallo. They invited him along to Cardiff for the Leicester final so he could see what he was letting himself in for. Six months later, as we were pulling out of the Stade Aimé Giral in Perpignan, he must have seen himself as the first coach in six years not to get Munster out of their Heineken Cup pool.

In one sense, Gaffer was lucky that we had drawn an Italian club in our pool, because this enabled him to experiment a little – Viadana at home was the first Heineken game that Paulie and Donners started together in the second row. The flip side was that we also had Gloucester and Perpignan, two of the toughest teams in Europe to beat on their home patch. Sure enough, we lost at Kingsholm first up and then at the Aimé Giral in round five, and that seemed to close the door on qualification. The changing room was like a morgue afterwards. The supporters we met in the airport on the way home were thanking us for the memories of the previous few seasons. All they asked from the following Saturday was that we beat Gloucester and preserve our unbeaten record at Thomond. We met just one couple who said they were certain we'd be back in France again later in the season. I haven't forgotten them.

The question I'm asked most often is whether I actually knew before the Gloucester game what we required to qualify, and the answer is no. Even as I was waiting to be interviewed by Fred Cogley after the game, I still wasn't sure. I should have known, of course. I hadn't trained till the Thursday because of back spasm, so I'd had time to figure it out. Afterwards, when the fuss had died down, I was reminded by Brian Hickey that we'd been told before the Perpignan game that we'd need to beat Gloucester by twenty-seven points if we lost in France. Telling us that had been part of the motivation for beating Perpignan. In the lead-up to the Gloucester game, though, we'd been brainwashed into concentrating on the process rather than the outcome – getting the nuts and bolts right, rather than watching the scoreboard. I saw myself saying as much in a television interview, during the build-up. I thought, 'I don't even speak like that.' Gaffer had got us thinking that way and while it may sound crazy that professional sportsmen wouldn't be clued up to the exact requirements of the situation, his way worked.

We were sorted on the emotional side, naturally. Gaillimh, who'd stepped aside for Donners, got us going in the changing room with some well-chosen words. Claw even stuck his head around the door, after receiving some award on the pitch designed to get the crowd going – Marcus, who'd waited long enough to get his chance, had some choice words for him, as I remember. The fact that two of our tries would come directly off the scrum was a source of pride for Marcus, who'd been criticised for not having a big enough arse, among other things.

But I don't need to go into detail about how each try came. What I'd love to be able to describe is the surge of energy that coursed through my entire being when Rog launched the first bomb for Gloucester's full-back Henry Paul, and the crowd went ballistic. I'd love for you to see up close the look of bewilderment in the eyes of Ludovic Mercier as the impossible became increasingly possible, and I wish I could recreate the sheer hysteria when Rags touched down for the fourth try. The photo of his celebrations gives some clue. Look at his eyes. The soft-spoken engineering graduate goes nuts.

Did Gloucester fail to show us enough respect? I'm not so sure. We got some value out of Andy Gomarsall's comment, mentioned to us by Gaillimh, that the Premiership leaders were looking forward to coming to Thomond Park. It was hardly the biggest insult I've ever heard but you take these things out of context and skew them to suit your purposes. The real mistake Gloucester made was coming with the attitude that all they had to do was protect their points advantage, rather than coming to win. They weren't properly prepared mentally, so when the heat was on, they unravelled. As a result, they were on the wrong end of one of the most amazing results in sport – and certainly the most amazing game I was ever involved in.

In my memory, it seems like we took the momentum from that 'Miracle Match' straight to Welford Road, where we were playing Leicester in the quarter-final – strange how this tournament finds a way of throwing old friends together. In reality, we had the usual three-month gap for the Six Nations, and also the minor matter of a Celtic League final against Neath in Cardiff. The league was still finding its feet – we played a total of ten games to win it – but it was a big deal for us. As I mentioned earlier, we had lost three finals in as many years and we craved silverware. So did the 15,000 supporters who travelled to watch us. Remarkably, we had more fans in the Millennium Stadium than Neath had. We won 37–17 and enjoyed every minute of it.

Unfortunately, only 2,000–3,000 of those supporters were able to get into Welford Road – Leicester knew that going to a bigger stadium would play into our hands – but those few thousand made their presence felt. As our bus reversed into the stadium that Sunday afternoon, I noticed Barry Gleeson senior, a neighbour from Killaloe, directing the driver. Welford did have a fortress feel to it. Leicester had lost there just twice in nearly six years and they were on course for their third Heineken Cup win, but we stuffed them – no other way to describe it. They scored a try early in the second half to lead 7–3 but the way Donners chased Rog's restart – flinging himself through the air like a madman and actually landing on his head – said everything about our attitude. He later admitted he went out there to make an impression on his hero, Martin Johnson. I think it's fair to say he succeeded. He and Paulie were phenomenally good and, together with Quinny, they managed to pinch twelve Leicester throws. Other memories include Hendo missing Geordan in the lead-up to that try but then making the hit on Austin Healy that led to Rog getting one back. It was also really satisfying to maul the Tigers back forty metres in injury time, 20–7 up and the result in the bag.

Having beaten the champions on their own patch, there was the usual talk of this being our year – the final was scheduled for Lansdowne Road, after all. But the same storyline had been laid down for us, and it never had a happy ending. Incredibly, for the fourth year in a row, the semi-final draw sent us to France. It had gone beyond a joke. The least funny bit was the 'neutral venue' where we'd be playing Toulouse – the soccer stadium, in Toulouse! We gave it our best shot, as usual, and we were beaten by a painfully tight margin, as usual. Toulouse 13 Munster 12.

They probably just about deserved it, because they scored the only try of a seriously physical game. The scorer was Freddy Michalak, who started at nine but moved to ten when Jean-Baptiste Elissalde came off the bench. Gaffer had warned us he was capable of swinging a game. Rog had the chance to win it with a drop-goal at the death and, afterwards, we couldn't help thinking that surely we were due a break. We couldn't allow ourselves to think that way, though. The most important lesson to take from the game was that Toulouse had been able to use their bench. They had fellas waiting who were capable of changing the game, including Elissalde, Finau Maka and Cedric Heymans. We used our bench in case of emergency. We needed more depth in our squad. At least we had that thought to take home with us, if nothing else.

For Ireland, it was the busiest season in history, with an incredible fourteen fixtures, ranging from Limerick in September to Samoa in June. Three of those games were in the schedule because we needed to qualify for the 2003 World Cup. As I kept reminding the lads who'd played in the previous tournament, we wouldn't have had to play against Russia and Georgia if they hadn't made a balls of things against Argentina in Lens three years previously. Losing in Lens effectively meant we were sent to Siberia.

It was tough trip but a fascinating one. For starters, we were playing a European qualifier in Asia – the Russians hosted us in Krasnoyarsk, a rugby hotbed by all accounts, which just happened to be seven time zones away. To give you an idea of how far that is, when the charter Boeing 737 we shared with committee members, supporters and media stopped in Moscow to refuel, we weren't even halfway there. Moscow turned out to be a four-hour stop-over. As we hung around in a transfer lounge, we were told there was an issue with baggage handlers –

even though our bags weren't leaving the plane. Eventually Briano twigged that there were people on the other side of a glass partition who were waiting to be bribed. He managed to organise a quick whip-round without our friends in the press noticing anything untoward, and then made eye contact with a friendly face in a position of authority. No better man. Once he'd handed over a fistful of US dollars, euro and roubles, together with a few bars of chocolate, we were ushered through security. The things we had to do to get to a World Cup.

We realised Krasnoyarsk was indeed a rugby hotbed when we disembarked at Yemelyanovo airport at 3 a.m. local time to find a TV team waiting to speak to 'Keith Woods'. The entire trip was a disorienting experience in general. Siberia was warm, for starters – or at least that part of Siberia at that time of year. We arrived the day before the game because Martin Murphy, who'd scouted the place for us, said there weren't the training facilities to justify going early and acclimatising. Our hotel was a lot better than Martin had warned us it would be, but I couldn't stomach the tasteless food and survived on a box of Kit-Kats my old man had carried out on the plane. We were in a city of a million people and there wasn't one McDonald's sign, not one Irish bar. Hardly anyone spoke English, yet on the day of the game, the local rugby fans seemed almost grateful we were there, as if we had gone out of our way. We won 35–3 at the crumbling Centralny Stadium, despite the jet lag, the tiny, rock-hard pitch, the midges, the dodgy ball, the dodgy changing rooms, the big Russians and their illegal South African. Then, we were told to stay up as late as possible to prepare for getting back on Irish time – we had Georgia at Lansdowne Road the following Saturday. What else could we do but go to the local nightclub, an amazing spot where they sold only vodka after 11 o'clock. Some trip.

I captained Ireland twice that September but, again, not in the circumstances I would have liked. Our warm-up for Russia was against Romania in Limerick and I stood in for Woody because, tragically, his brother Gordon, a good friend, had died of a heart attack, aged forty-one. Then I led the team against Georgia because Woody had aggravated a neck injury on our cramped plane journey home from Russia. Almost exactly a year out from the World Cup, this was a worrying development for someone with a history of neck and shoulder injuries. For our November tests against Australia, Fiji and Argentina, Eddie gave the captaincy to Drico. I wasn't too put out – I had a good chat about it with Drico over dinner and as it turned out, his record over the next few seasons was exceptional. I suppose the rationale was that if there was a doubt over Woody returning, the skipper had to be somebody who was a cast-iron selection all the way to the World Cup, and even though I'd been a regular starter, the back row was a competitive area.

Hayes and I were the only starting Munster forwards in the pack that November but our mix of Leinster, Shannon and Gary Longwell worked pretty well. Woody's injury opened the door for Shane Byrne. Like his hairstyle, the Munch takes a bit of getting used to but I was happy for him – he is one of the Rotorua Five after all, and had to wait a while to get his chance. When it came along, he took it – his 100 per cent return at the lineouts in the lashing rain against Australia was exceptional. Woody's absence also meant a recall for Victor Costello, because we needed another ball-carrier in the pack. Victor was another fella I could identify with because he'd had a stop–start international career. He repaid Eddie's faith with big performances against both Australia and Argentina.

We've beaten Australia again since then, also at Lansdowne Road and also in the wet, so it's easy to forget how big a deal it was for us back then. They were the reigning world champions and we hadn't beaten them since 1979, when my old man was in the squad. The key to our 18–9 victory was that we more than matched them physically, which was where they normally had it over us. In a constant downpour, collisions were going to be plentiful and, for once, we were operating on the same level as they were. The other thing was the control we were given by Strings, Rog and Girvan. Rog also kicked six out of six, which was a nice way to bounce back after his experiences with the pig in New Zealand. He managed four from four against the Pumas two weeks later in another deluge, a game we won 16–7. We'd beaten two of our pool opponents in the World Cup – maybe not in the same conditions we'd experience in Australia, but a nice psychological boost all the same.

Throw in a cake-walk against Fiji and we had six wins in a row, which was a record for Ireland. We didn't read too much into this but when we beat Scotland 36–6 at Murrayfield – at last, a win in Edinburgh – a sense of momentum started to build. Humphs scored a mountain of points to take advantage of an injury to Rog, so the out-half debate was up and running again, which was all part of a healthy mix. Next, we beat Italy 37–13 in Rome, then France 15–12 in a real dogfight on yet another ugly day at Lansdowne Road. Afterwards, Drico even dared to mention the words 'grand' and 'slam' in a television interview – he was still young, still getting used to the media game. It was obvious where he was getting the confidence from, though. While the French had obliterated us in Paris twelve months previously, here we had overcome them in the scrums, where Marcus did really well in his first start, and in the lineouts, where Malcolm O'Kelly and Munch were immense. Our defence was good, too – we'd conceded just one try in three games. Suddenly, the survivors of the 1948 team, our only slam winners, were being wheeled out for interviews.

The whole thing was set up for us – Wales in Cardiff, where we just didn't lose, and then England, also unbeaten, at Lansdowne Road the following Sunday. Hard though we tried to play down expectations, they were clearly getting to us and we did our best to bottle things against Wales. We were awful. I remember Eddie losing it at half-time, kicking the lid of an ice bucket and nearly decapitating me. This was around the time when Alex Ferguson kicked a boot at David Beckham, and I actually got a fit of the giggles there in the changing room, even though I already had an ice-pack on my cheek thanks to Leo Cullen head-butting me towards the end of the first half. Despite Eddie throwing a strop, we were still poor after the break and, in the end, we needed Rog to come off the bench and kick a forty-metre drop-goal – and then Denis to block Stephen Jones' own drop-goal attempt, heroically – to squeeze home 25–24.

We really needed Lansdowne to be a cauldron when England came there the following week but it wasn't. We used to get a much better atmosphere for the November tests against southern-hemisphere teams, when the crowd would be almost completely Irish. Six Nations games attracted a fifty-fifty crowd, and the place wasn't intimidating at all. Then we had Martin Johnson's refusal to move, which was a bit of a farce but a psychological boost for them, I'm sure. I was more annoyed that their first score, by Lawrence Dallaglio, came directly off a scrum under our posts when I failed to control the ball at my feet. It was also irritating that they got so many soft points at the death when we chased the game and got sloppy. I didn't think 42–6 remotely reflected the game. That said, they were an awesome side, at their peak, probably playing better than when they won the World Cup. They had a great pack, a brilliant back row and Jonny Wilkinson was untouchable. He dropped goals off his left and right that day, and he has such a brain for the game. You could tell he was thinking two or three plays ahead.

Once over the disappointment, I started looking ahead to the World Cup. I was ruled out for the June tests in Australia, Tonga and Samoa because my shoulder had been giving me some grief and I needed to rehab it properly. I wasn't complaining about staying put. I'd had a full season of thirty games, most of them high-intensity. My thirtieth birthday was approaching and I had yet to participate in rugby's biggest showpiece. I wanted to be ready for this one.

15

CRASHING DOWN UNDER,
CLIMBING BACK UP

I was sitting next to Frankie Sheahan when he won AU$93,000 for a dollar bet on one hand of Caribbean Stud. It was in the Melbourne Crown Casino on Wednesday, 5 November 2003, and this moment is probably my happiest memory of the World Cup – which tells you all you need to know about the sort of trip I had. A tournament I'd been quietly building towards for three years turned out to be a massive anticlimax, so it holds a fairly prominent place in my bitterness bank.

I'd been so optimistic heading out to Australia. We had a tough draw but we felt we could do some damage. Everyone was feeling sharp. We'd won our three warm-up games against Wales, Italy and Scotland, and we'd never been in better physical condition. Admittedly, I'd strained my hamstring against Wales and had to sit out the other two warm-ups but my travelling was never in doubt. We had a warm-weather training trip to Bilbao, where it rained, as it tends to do on these occasions, but our camp in Athlone was sunny and so was everyone's mood. Eddie did his best to keep things fresh and different. He brought in a biokineticist to assess our physical make-ups and individual training requirements – we never heard of her again after that but it was certainly novel. Later, back in Dublin, we had a fascinating talk from Sir Ranulph Fiennes, the Arctic and Antarctic traveller and holder of several endurance records. We also listened to Marvin Hagler, the champion middleweight boxer and another inspiring individual. Sometimes, you'd go down to breakfast in the team hotel wondering which visiting celeb you'd bump into at the cereal counter. I'm not sure how relevant or beneficial any of this was – we were all pretty psyched up anyway – but it was interesting nonetheless.

Some of the lads had said they found Eddie a bit unapproachable. I found him okay to deal with, although I'd had the advantage of playing a round of golf with him and Woody in Portumna when he was good company. So my advice for anyone who thought he was a bit distant or uncommunicative was, 'Play a few holes of golf with him. He's a grand fella.' It became a bit of a running gag for the lads.

In general, we were a happy bunch, especially while we were in Terrigal, a beautiful seaside resort an hour and a half north of Sydney and our base for the first two pool games, against Romania and Namibia. I was rooming with Paulie, who's easy enough. He read books while I played Tiger Woods PGA Tour on the PlayStation. He liked going to sleep with the telly on, I liked watching telly late. Our training sessions up at the local school were going well and instead of ice-baths afterwards, we'd all go for a dip in the Pacific Ocean. Everything was good as gold, mate – until we played Romania and I did my knee.

The frustrating thing was I didn't even know how I'd done it – Gary O'Driscoll, the team doctor, looked back through the video to try to spot some collision that might have caused the damage but he found nothing. I just remember going to lead the defensive line-up and feeling my knee lock. It transpired I had a badly bruised meniscus, and the stiffening got worse. I went from cursing the fact that I'd miss the Namibia game – which I needed to play in because I was short on game-time – to being relieved that I wasn't being sent home, which looked a distinct possibility before a specialist prescribed a series of jabs.

Still, I hated Adelaide, mainly because I had to sit through the Argentina game, one we'd all been brooding over for ages. There was so much history between the sides, so much bad blood. I love playing in those games. Instead, I found myself acting as a minder for Hayes when he got split early in the game and had to get treatment in the changing room. The drama was only starting. While I was down there, I heard an almighty roar, definitely an Irish roar. It was Quinny scoring, but by the time I got to the end of the tunnel, he was being stretchered past me with a busted shoulder. He was in bits and I'm there in my blazer, feeling generally useless.

At least we won, by a point, which was an enormous relief. From a personal point of view, the other bit of good news was that I'd come through a game of tip that morning unscathed. By the following Tuesday, I was declared fit to face Australia at

Melbourne's Telstra Dome, and then, even better, I was selected to start. To top it off, the snappers got a shot of me being stripped stark naked at the end of training, to mark my thirtieth birthday, and the picture made all the local papers. Was I bothered? No. I was getting a crack at the Wallabies, in a city where the World Cup had barely registered with the locals, while the number of incoming Irish supporters was growing daily. We reckoned it was a bit naive of the Aussies to bring us down to Melbourne, an Aussie Rules town where they had very little public support, only a year after we'd beaten them in Dublin. We saw it as a brilliant opportunity to beat the hosts and holders and set ourselves up for a quarter-final against Scotland in Brisbane.

We lost by a point, 16–17. On the one hand, it was our best performance in a long time; on the other, it was a glorious opportunity blown. Unlike the Argentina game, when we'd been shackled by fear of losing, we actually played some rugby. A slow start meant we had to chase the game but we did it with purpose. Paulie announced himself on the world stage by terrorising the Wallabies' lineout, so we had plenty of ball and we were happy to use it, especially in the second half when we pulled a 6–14 deficit back to 13–14 thanks to Drico pulling a rabbit out of a hat in the left corner. When they stretched the lead to four points, Drico brought it back to one with a drop-goal. We kept hammering away but probably took a few dodgy decisions, and then had to watch as Humph's forty-five-metre drop-goal attempt stayed right – later, he said he'd allowed for a metre of right-to-left movement but connected too well. That's not a game I've been able to watch again.

So we'd have France in the quarters. It wasn't the worst

option. We'd beaten them in three of our previous four meetings and were back at the Telstra Dome, on neutral territory. You wondered whether some of the lads who'd featured in four straight games were beginning to feel the pace. Fatigue certainly wasn't a problem for me. I was confident enough I'd be picked. I'd spilled a few balls in contact against Australia but that could be put down to lack of match practice. I was always someone who needed games under my belt to be at my best, to be in the thick of it. I hadn't been dropped since my comeback game in Twickenham, nearly four years previously, so that gave me a certain feeling of security. It seemed that people had faith in me.

I started getting worried the following Tuesday, the day before the team was due to be announced. It was Melbourne Cup day, the biggest day in the racing calendar in Australia and a public holiday, so the locals were all in good form. We were chirpy enough ourselves. We had a day off, too, and travelled up to a winery in the Hunter Valley. I'd a feeling all day, though. You're out for lunch with thirty-odd fellas, all very pleasant, but certain people won't make eye contact with you. Deccie isn't talking to me. Niallo isn't talking to me. Eddie isn't talking to me – although Eddie was barely talking to anyone. Looking back, I suppose I could have asked Woody for clues but I never liked compromising him in that way. Besides, I was blocking all negative thoughts. We were playing Ireland's biggest game in four years the following Sunday – no time for negative thoughts.

Back in Melbourne, Woody, Paulie, Hayes, Marcus and I were going out for a bite to eat, and as I was walking into the team hotel to go and get ready, I bumped into Eddie. He asked if he could have a quick word.

'You're not in.'

'Jesus.'

'You're not in the twenty-two.'

'Ah, Jesus—'

I think he said something about needing Victor's extra power as a ball-carrier against the French but I'm not sure. I wasn't hearing him any more. I took it on the chin because I knew there was no point in arguing the toss with him and also because all you want to do in those situations is walk away. First, you've a sickening feeling in the pit of your stomach, then you feel like hitting something or someone.

I'd reached the anger stage by the time I got back to my room, where Paulie was lying on the bed, reading as usual. I told him the news, with a fair few expletives about Eddie thrown in. Paulie commiserated – but then he couldn't help himself.

'Sure, play a few holes of golf with him. He's a grand fella,' he says, bursting out laughing. The pup. Is nothing sacred?

My mobile rang before I could throw something at him. With uncanny timing, it was Gaillimh. If there was one fella I needed to talk to then, it was the man who's had the biggest number of let-downs in the history of Irish rugby. Even chatting to him on the phone gave me a lift. I hopped into the shower, threw on some fresh clothes and went out to meet himself, Langford, Wally, Frankie, Ronan Barry and Packie Derham for a beer. It became known as 'The Extraordinary Night'.

It actually wasn't that extraordinary until we were walking back to the team's downtown hotel at around 2.30 a.m. Across the way, the Crown Casino could only be described as a gambling mall, a series of vast rooms that never seemed to close – perfect for rugby players, especially on match nights when it's usually well into the early hours before you can put your head down. We had lineouts in the morning but I was in no mood for lying down and having to contemplate my situation. Frankie and I wandered in and just as we were strolling past a busy Caribbean Stud table, two fellas got up out of their seats – not their best move of the night.

All you need to know about Caribbean Stud is 1) it's five-card stud poker played against the house and 2) you can place a $1 jackpot bet before the cards are dealt. The rules also state that you're not supposed to consult with any other players but I couldn't help myself when I took a peek at my cards and saw I had a straight.

'Frankie,' I said out of the corner of my mouth. 'You won't believe what he's after dealing me.'

'And you definitely won't believe what he's after dealing me,' he replied.

He'd a royal flush in his hands. Holy shit. A royal flush! The probability of being dealt that straight up is 0.000001 per cent. The standard jackpot for the Crown Casino was AU$93,000 – just over €50,000. He would have won considerably more had the dealer been able to open the betting – he needed an ace and a king or better to open – because that would have allowed us to plough more money on. That didn't seem to matter at the time. Frankie was standing up on his chair, roaring and shouting, buying drinks for the table. We went baloobas – all except the poor fella who'd been sitting in Frankie's chair a couple of minutes before him. We rang a few of the lads to tell them and to ask them to come down and collect us – we didn't feel comfortable, just the two of us walking out of there with a cheque for AU$93,000. Naturally, when they arrived, we stayed to celebrate a little bit longer. Frankie deserved it. Earlier that year, he'd failed to tick a form stating he was an asthmatic and when a subsequent drug test showed illegal levels of salbutamol, he'd been handed a two-year ban. The fight to reduce the ban and clear his name was a difficult, draining business, which also cost him a six-figure sum in legal fees. At least this win would put a fair-sized hole in that.

You're wondering what I won on my straight? A few hundred bucks. 'The Extraordinary Night' gave us something to talk about for a while but it didn't take away my acute disappointment at being dropped. Woody didn't need to say anything to me. We'd known each other so long that words weren't necessary. I'm pretty sure he would have argued for my inclusion but he wasn't going to undermine his coach by letting that out. He had enough on his hands anyway. He was preparing for a World Cup quarter-final that was potentially his last game of rugby ever. I'd have loved to play in that game but it wasn't to be. I just had to get on with things and hope that if we made the semis, I'd be involved.

Any hope of that happening was blown away in a disastrous first half, by the end of which we'd conceded twenty-seven points to the French. We were flat, looking a bit like a side that had peaked in getting past Argentina and nearly beating Australia. Fordy had talked beforehand about making sure we picked up Imanol Harinordoquy, the French number eight who liked to hang wide for cross-kicks – I knew all about it because I'd had to fill the Phil Neville left-back role against him in the past. But within three minutes, he was tapping a ball down unchallenged for Olivier Magne to score.

Offensively, too, our game-plan was way off the mark. The idea was to play them down the blind-side, then come back into the middle of the field with a pod before reloading on the other side. But the French didn't go where we wanted them to go, which was a bit inconvenient, and we made mistakes. When Malcolm pulled out of catching a pass, it bounced up for Christophe Dominici and he ran the length of the pitch. We made the score a respectable-ish 43–21 with three tries in the last half-hour, but it was really a tonking.

Eddie tried to talk things up by saying we'd had a 'very, very good World Cup', but we all knew it had been a failure. Limping out at the quarter-final stage didn't add up to success for a squad that had aimed for a first-ever semi. It left us feeling unfulfilled. I certainly won't ever be releasing my *Greatest Ever World Cup Moments* DVD.

Normally, when you come to the end of a tour to the southern hemisphere, it's the middle of June and you're off on your jollies. This time we were pretty much straight back into the daily grind with our provinces, and thank God for that. One of the great things about playing sport for a living is that moods and results can change very quickly, and there is no better mood-enhancer than a few days back in the Munster set-up. If you're feeling a bit hurt or a bit precious, they'll knock it out of you sharpish. And there's nothing better for the soul than a win in France – which is what we got when we travelled to Bourgoin in early December. It's been suggested that some fellas prefer playing for Munster than for Ireland, which is rubbish, of course. Playing for your country is always the pinnacle, but the buzz you get winning with your province can feed into the national side, and that's what happened post-World Cup. For all the disappointments in Australia, 2004 turned out to be a bloody good year for Ireland and for me.

On the face of it, the Six Nations schedule didn't look promising. First up were France, who by now really fancied themselves against us anywhere apart from Lansdowne Road. Then we had a Wales side that had put the frighteners on both England and New Zealand during the World Cup, followed by a trip to London to act as extras in a homecoming parade – England would be playing their first game at Twickenham since becoming world champs. All this and Drico, now officially skipper, was out injured with a hamstring tear. I'm pretty sure I read some people predicting zero from three.

We were zero from one, it's true. France beat us 35–17 at the Stade de France but there were encouraging aspects. This hadn't been a repeat of Melbourne where the French had hammered us for the first fifty minutes. If anything, the damage was done in the space of five minutes after the break when they took advantage of defensive lapses to change an 11–10 scoreline to 25–10 with a couple of tries. We'd lost but we'd regained a bit of respect. Gordon D'Arcy had been a revelation as a replacement for Drico at outside centre; Rog looked very composed and in control; and Ireland's number eight snaffled a try on his 'comeback'.

After Wales had walloped Scotland, there was all sorts of talk about a Welsh revival but they offered nothing at Lansdowne Road – we should really have beaten them by more than 35–16. Their media had been talking up Iestyn Harris, a rugby league convert and their inside centre, but Drico and Darce owned the midfield. Wales' fringe defence was awful, allowing me to score one of the softest possible international tries, while Munch scored a couple of softies from short range. Out of respect, Woody was forced to don a mullet wig on *Rugby Special* that night.

The real story of that championship was Twickenham. It might not seem such a big deal now because we went on to beat England four times in a row, but, back then, I associated Twickenham with forty- or fifty-point beatings. They had put forty-two points on us at Lansdowne Road the previous year, and this was their homecoming match. The Webb Ellis Trophy had been paraded from one end of the country to the other and now it was coming home. But they were vulnerable. Martin Johnson had retired, Jonny Wilkinson was injured along with Danny Grewcock and Simon Shaw, Neil Back had been dropped and Jason Robinson was picked at outside centre. Clive Woodward was way out, hiring aromatherapists. I'm all for alternative medicine but lavender in the changing room?

Puma were kind enough to give me a pair of boots to mark the occasion of my fiftieth game for Ireland – I have them at home, and wore them only on that day. Drico asked to me run onto the pitch ahead of everyone else, which was decent of him. It was probably the only time you saw me that day, because it was a game played mainly in the trenches. We won the aerial battle, too – their hooker Steve Thompson looked a broken man by the time Clive hauled him ashore – but mainly it was about grinding out the inches and Rog keeping us moving forward. There were moments of individual brilliance. Darce made three or four line-breaks and a corner-flagging tackle on Ben Cohen – the TMO may have done us a favour there. Strings produced his trademark ankle-tap, this time on Robinson, and Malcolm produced some heroics to stop Mark Regan from scoring. But for all the individual contributions, it was fitting that our one try was a team effort, started by Darce and carried on by a dozen pairs of hands before Girvan slid in at the left corner. A thing of beauty was that try, but probably my abiding memory is of the endgame – making one tackle and then dragging my ass off the floor to make another, with England all the while trailing 13–19 and still capable of stealing it. They didn't. We won. And it felt bloody good.

We'd beaten the world champions and it was my fiftieth cap – I was aware that I was being lined up as part of the evening's entertainment. Guy Easterby, our resident comic, got me to sing a few songs on the bus back to the Chelsea Harbour and then, after the post-match banquet, which was not quite the celebratory affair England had planned, I had to hide in a cupboard to have a chat with Woody on the mobile while outside people were keen to pour drink into me. By now, I was a lot cuter than I'd been on the occasion of my first cap and knew how to duck and dive and dilute while at the same time getting proper value out of a great night.

I'm not sure who first mentioned the words 'Triple Crown'. I do know we were glad that we had something to play for when Scotland came to Dublin for the last game of the championship – glad also that Scotland made us fight for it, when Allister Hogg scored in the third quarter, there was a danger we'd waste our backs' excellent work before the break. But Wally and Strings scored tries, which enabled us to enjoy the last ten minutes or so. We enjoyed the lap of honour, too. A couple of people had a go about us doing a lap without a trophy and, to some extent, they had a point. France would win the championship and the grand slam in Paris later that evening, but I was proud of what we'd achieved, and I certainly enjoyed my pints afterwards with Willie Duggan and Brian Spillane, two other Irish Triple Crown-winning number eights.

It would have been nice to end the season with a win on South African soil, as if to confirm progress made. Even the locals had us down as favourites before the first test of two, in Bloemfontein. Back in 1998, the local media barely acknowledged our presence before the tests. This time, they were all over us, looking for snaps of Drico in particular. There didn't seem to be the same reverence for the Boks. They hadn't played since a disastrous World Cup and their new coach, Jake White, had picked a new team, including a few of the Baby Boks he'd coached to an Under-21s World Cup win two years earlier. For all the good work of our superb video analyst, Mervyn Murphy, we'd never heard of Schalk Burger or Fourie du Preez, but we knew plenty about them after the Boks had beaten us 31–17. South Africa gave us a tough time in the set-pieces and took their opportunities, simple as that. Suddenly, the locals were back to their normal, arrogant selves.

We got closer to winning in Cape Town a week later but narrowish defeats don't cut any mustard out there. In a newspaper interview after the series, White went on at length about how his boys had a genetic advantage over us, as if they were some sort of rugby super-race. He said Drico was the only guy who'd get into their squad, 'and maybe one of the locks'. It passed most of us by at the time – we were lying on a beach somewhere – but, thankfully, it was dredged up the week before the rematch in Lansdowne Road that November. I say 'thankfully' because it gave us extra motivation – not just Eddie, who took White to task in the media, but all of us. I'm sure White believed that what he was saying was correct – that inexperienced Boks team had gone on to win the Tri Nations that summer, after all – but it didn't show much respect to repeat it on the eve of a test match in Dublin, so we rammed it down his throat.

We had the advantage of being in peak physical condition, whereas they were coming to the end of their season. It was also a blustery old day at Lansdowne Road, which we were used to, plus Paul Honiss was reffing. We couldn't get enough of Paul Honiss around that time. Things seemed to go our way with him, and it happened again that day. After a stoppage in play, he allowed Rog to take a quick tap near the Boks' line without calling the game clock back on again. Rog got in for the try and it ended up a five-point win, 17–12. The Boks grumbled about it afterwards but that sort of thing happens in rugby. Get on with it. I thought we deserved to win, anyway. We stood up to them physically and we managed to reduce the threat of Burger – sometimes, when you're up against a flanker of his or Richie McCaw's calibre, you have almost to devise a plan to take him out of the game. The fact that he spent ten minutes in the bin was a measure of how difficult we made it for him. We also took our chances and then defended like demons at the death.

Rog was a bit good that day, and he got us out of jail against Argentina two weeks later with a forty-five-metre drop-goal in injury time, helping us to pinch it 21–19. That was a nasty game. A few of our guys complained of being gouged, which wouldn't have been a first for the Argentinians, while Agustín Pichot, their captain, threw a hissy fit, saying we'd been trying to get some of his players sent off. Look at the scoreboard, pal. We'd drawn them in our World Cup pool once more, so it was a good one to win – and seeing as we'd had a clean sweep in our November tests, the force was with us. We had England and France at home in the Six Nations, so we could quietly consider the possibility of a grand slam. And the best news of all? Olive was pregnant.

16

SURPLUS TO REQUIREMENTS

There's another reason why I was especially 'up' for 2005 – it was Lions year. No player ever promotes his case in the run-up to the Six Nations in Lions year for fear of falling flat on his face but, quietly, everyone is lining up the competition and trying to calculate his own chances. As someone who has watched all the old Lions videos with my old man, I was as keen as anyone. I received my Lions rubber bracelet and my 'Power of 4' Christmas card from Sir Clive Woodward and tried to ignore the fact that seemingly every rugby player in England, Scotland, Wales and Ireland had received them too. Being in the Irish team was no harm. We'd finished highest of the four 'home' nations in the previous championship and Drico was runaway favourite to lead the tour. Another decent Six Nations could only help our representation.

I knew I wasn't going to walk into any pundit's projected test team. I remember Nigel Melville, the former Gloucester coach, once picked me in his 'Team of the Six Nations' but that was the only time that sort of thing had happened in the UK press. I was, apparently, an 'unfashionable' number eight. Certainly, I didn't fit the identikit of the explosive power player. If selection was based on gym scores, I hadn't a hope in hell. One of the tests they run to determine leg power is the counter-movement jump, where you do a standing jump on a mat with power-sensors. Wally has scores that are almost off the chart. My score is barely off the ground. Paulie used to say it would be a good test of your reaction speed to see if you could slip a Rizla paper under my feet in the millisecond they were in the air.

Against that, I had a good engine. The only physical test I actually liked doing was the lactic-acid test. We did it in Spala a couple of times. They'd take a pinprick of your blood before and after an intense, five-minute workout, to check the levels of an acid that, in layman's terms, can slow you down. My reading was exactly the same before and after – almost zero. Must be something to do with all the cross-country running I did as a kid. I may not have had five gears, but the ones I had were reliable. One year, the afternoon before a Munster Christmas party, Paulie and myself did a short, two-man training session that involved two sets of eight 150-metre sprints. While he was beating me by five or ten metres for the first few, it was the other way around for the last three or four. Stamina was never a problem for me.

By 2005, there seemed to be a perception that I was getting on in years, which probably had something to do with the fact that I was capped at twenty-one. Now is as good a time as any to point out that I played Under-20s rugby with Quinny, whose boyish looks have fooled people for years, and also with Hayes, who's actually only three days younger than I am. I passed my thirty-first birthday early in that 2004–2005 season and I'm a year younger than Lawrence Dallaglio. Obviously it's for others to say whether they think I was good enough to go on a Lions tour. I just felt I could still do a job for a team.

I soon had more than enough to keep my mind off the Lions. I was Munster captain. As Jimmy had found out before me, it's a time-consuming job and a lot of that has to do with our split personality – half of us live in Limerick, the other half in Cork. Jimmy had publicly highlighted the problems caused by bilocation after we had lost yet another European semi-final, against Wasps at Lansdowne Road in April 2004. He ruffled a few feathers when he said we were hamstrung by the time we were spending on the road between Limerick and Cork, time that could be spent profitably in the gym or on the training pitch. I had mixed feelings on the issue. The old-fashioned side of me felt having two camps actually gave us something because we were fresher for seeing less of each other; the realist in me knew it didn't make sense for guys playing in the same unit – say back row – to have maybe only two field sessions together in the week before a game.

Our bilocation wasn't the only reason we'd lost that epic semi against Wasps. First, the excuses – we lost Rog early in the game with a hamstring injury; Donncha was binned very harshly by referee Nigel Whitehouse; touch judge Nigel Owens put his flag out for Josh Lewsey's blatant knee into Paulie's back but then inexplicably changed his mind because Whitehouse was binning Hendo for hitting the ruck at the side;

Whitehouse failed to go upstairs to the TMO for Trevor Leota's crucial late try, although Strings appeared to dislodge the ball – either we're suffering because there's no TMO or we're losing out because he's there but they won't use him. But that's enough excuses. The bottom line is we were ten points up with ten minutes to go, in front of something like 45,000 Munster supporters, and we couldn't close the deal. We didn't hold our discipline, and our defence just wasn't good enough – we leaked five tries that day, and four in the quarter-final against Stade Français. I'm not a subscriber to the Kevin Keegan philosophy of 'You score four, we'll score five.' Basically, Wasps were ruthless and efficient, and we weren't. After three losing semi-finals and two losing finals, the sense of debt to our supporters was truly overwhelming.

We kept trying to evolve, trying to find the extra couple per cent. We took Jimmy's advice, cut down on the travelling and did more of our training in UL the following season. Gaffer brought in Steady (Graham Steadman) to shore up our defence. The problem was the big English and French clubs were also evolving, at an alarming rate, and they had bigger budgets for foreign investment. We had less money to invest, so we had to make it count. Our biggest investment was in Christian Cullen. For all the admiration we had for Cully, you couldn't say we got a good return on the outlay.

Outsiders wonder why the Munster players all spoke so highly of Cully when clearly he didn't have the impact everyone hoped for. It's because we know that he gave absolutely everything he had to the Munster cause and that was all we could ask of him. He just happened to be followed around by a series of cruel injuries. If somebody who joins our squad, especially a high-profile player, is not pulling his weight, we will eat him alive – we won't say anything publicly, but, behind the scenes, no one will be left in any doubt about what we think. There was never a hint of that with Cully because of the standards he set in terms of training and rehab. When he did play, you could see he didn't have the old pace any more but he was still a second or two ahead of everyone in terms of anticipation, so he was a joy to play with.

There was a certain irony in Cully being signed in the same season as a supposed journeyman, Shaun Payne, who ended up being one of our two best imports ever. For what Payne brought to the cause, and will continue to bring as manager, he has to rank up there with Jimmy, even ahead of John Langford. I think of him as a modern-day Pat Murray – and although he won't know who the hell Pat Murray is, he can take it as a massive compliment. He may be slow to open his wallet, he may take about fifteen practice swings before finally hitting a golf ball, but for consistency and reliability on the rugby pitch, he has been unbelievably good value.

Considering Gaffer came originally from Randwick, a club with a tradition for running rugby, he must have been disappointed that he never transformed us into a team that could hurt opponents in every part of the field. If you look at our pool statistics for the 2004–2005 Heineken Cup campaign, you'll see most of our twelve tries were scored by forwards, including a couple for a kid from Tipperary with a lot of talent and unnaturally large paws, who had struggled with injuries for the first couple of years of his career – Denis Leamy.

We ended up travelling to play Harlequins in Twickenham, without Rog, who was injured, needing to win and score four tries to have a chance of getting the all-important home quarter-final. We won but managed only two tries. All we could offer our supporters was a new quarter-final destination – San Sebastian, the Basque stronghold where we played Biarritz – and a gutsy second-half fight-back during which we overcame Rog's continued absence to play some great rugby. Our only try in a 19–10 defeat came from David Wallace directly off the back of a scrum but we showed we could play the offloading game. We just couldn't finish things off.

I didn't have too long to ponder the reasons for defeat because after I'd finished doing a post-match interview, team manager Jerry Holland ushered me outside to Rosie, who gave me the tragic news that my Uncle Gerard, Dad's older brother, had died of a heart attack the previous day – Mam and Dad had flown back from Biarritz within hours of hearing the news. He was a good man, full of fun, heavily involved in rugby with the Presentation club in Limerick, and a frequent spectator at Munster's and Ireland's away games. He was also a keen rower with the Athlunkard and Limerick boat clubs. To lose him at the age of fifty-seven was a tragedy for my Auntie Marie and their three children, Brian, Elaine and Shane, and came as a shock to all of us.

There were other family matters to consider. This was April, and Olive, seven months pregnant, was wondering whether her husband would be at home for the first few weeks in the life of our first child. The situation was complicated by the fact that there were two tours that summer – the Lions in New Zealand and Ireland in Japan. However, when the forty-four-man Lions squad was announced after the Six Nations, I hadn't made it, which may have had something to do with our grand slam never materialising, despite a promising start. Having scraped a win in Rome, we mauled Scotland off the park at Murrayfield two weeks before hosting England at Lansdowne Road on the last Sunday in February.

We had won our first two games, they had lost both theirs – which made them very dangerous. Sure enough, they shocked us with an early try by Martin Corry. But we were an experienced side by now, and not about to be bullied as we had been in the corresponding game two years previously. We also had the ability to produce something a bit special and we did just that midway through the second half. On a day when space was virtually non-existent, Geordan Murphy created a yard or two with a brilliant dummy, before passing to his right. Drico somehow held on to a pass that was a yard behind him while running along a tightrope, and scored in the Wanderers' corner. A special try, that.

There were a few contentious moments in our 19–13 win – I remember England coach Andy Robinson losing it with referee Jonathan Kaplan in the tunnel at half-time because he had disallowed what video replays suggested was a perfectly legal Mark Cueto try. But we held on, and were beginning to look decidedly like a team that had learned the winning habit. That's why losing to France two weeks later was such a kick in the guts, although it has to be said they were comfortably the better side.

Unusually for them, they came with a game-plan designed specifically to play against Ireland, rather than just to play as France. They attacked one of our strengths, the lineout, and attacked it effectively. They knew the wind blows at Lansdowne, so they mauled, and they mauled superbly. They also produced a fella with savage pace by the name of Benoît Baby. He's barely been heard of since but, that day, he made one try, scored another and head-butted Drico into the bargain. The wonder was we were still in it when Drico scored near the end – for some reason, France had started making silly substitutions in the final quarter. They were very good and should have beaten us by more than 19–21. No slam then, but we had no complaints, either.

Instead, the slam went to Wales. They hadn't been rated at the start of the tournament but by the time we arrived in Cardiff, on a warm, sunny afternoon in mid-March, the force was with them and we were swept aside. They broke one of the supposed rules of rugby in winning a grand slam without having a decent set-piece, but when the game opened up, they played some superb, instinctive rugby. They should have had more than ten Lions but then the squad was picked by Sir Clive, who selected twenty Englishmen.

I wasn't too sore at being left out – I almost expected it once we'd lost to France and Wales. What I was sore about was being omitted from the Ireland squad for Japan. It wasn't so much that I relished the prospect of playing in Osaka or Tokyo, more their relative proximity to New Zealand. I was on the Lions reserve list and being in Japan would have improved my chances of getting the call from Clive if anyone got injured. But Niallo, who was Eddie's deputy while Eddie was with the Lions, told me they wanted to have a look at a few younger players with a view to the 2007 World Cup – which would have been fine, except they took Reggie Corrigan, David Humphreys, Girvan Dempsey and Kevin Maggs! Not being in Japan effectively took me out of contention as a Lions reserve. I couldn't help but notice that Simon Easterby and Ryan Jones got the call to join the Lions and ended up being two of their better players, both starting the final test. I'm not sure where I was on the reserve list in relation to Ryan, and I don't want to know.

The Lions hadn't seemed very important on 24 May when Tony Edward Foley came into the world. It wasn't a straightforward delivery. Olive was unhappy when the obstetrician announced he'd have to conduct an emergency caesarean section, but both of us were massively relieved with the decision when Tony emerged with the umbilical cord wrapped around his neck. This wasn't the last scare he has given us. The following January, local GP Maureen Ryan mercifully spotted the symptoms of meningitis – Tony seems intent on following in his father's footsteps in everything. I realised there was trouble when I came in from training and saw five missed calls on my mobile, all from Olive, along with the unforgettable text message: *In ambulance with Tony. Don't panic*. Grand, so! A couple of worrying days later, we got the all clear and we will always be enormously grateful to everyone at the Children's Ark Ward in Limerick Regional Hospital for all their help.

It had felt strange to be at home for almost the entirety of June – after a while, you get used to the idea of spending a large chunk of that month every year on long-haul flights or in hotels in the southern hemisphere. I was glad to be with Olive and Tony, of course. Professional rugby players are away from home a lot and the house must seem very big at times. A few years ago, I had a panic button installed beside the bed, with a line connected to the Killaloe garda station. When I was growing up, everyone in Killaloe left their front doors open. Now, sadly, it's all electronic gates and intercoms.

Anyway, my only rugby for that June was the Martin Johnson/Jonah Lomu testimonial at Twickenham, which amounted to just a few days away. It was a pretty relaxed affair, involving quite a few people who were coming to the end of their careers. I was asked whether I'd retired from the international game myself, which was a fair question, I suppose. It was ten years since I'd made my test debut. I'd missed the cut for the Lions and was stretching it to think I'd be in the frame for the 2007 World Cup, by which time I'd be approaching my thirty-fourth birthday. But I hadn't retired, and for two very good reasons. One, I wasn't in a position to retire, because I was on an IRFU national contract up until June 2007 and was required to be available if selected. Two, I was still only thirty-one and, as far as I was concerned, had plenty of rugby in me.

That attitude was vindicated when Eddie included me in his squad for the November tests against New Zealand, Australia and Romania. He was a bit short on experience, with Drico, Paulie and Denis Hickie all out injured, and he was short on back rows, with Quinny and Eric Miller injured, and Wally strangely omitted. That left Simon Easterby, Johnny O'Connor, Leams – who had made his debut against the USA – the uncapped Neil Best and me. When Simon smashed his nose playing for Llanelli a fortnight before the New Zealand game, it complicated matters somewhat – but the situation would become even more complicated for me. About ten days before the test, I was in my room with Hayes at the Citywest Hotel when Eddie called and asked if he could come up for a quick chat.

'That's it,' said Hayes, getting ready to vacate the room. 'You're captain against the All Blacks. That doesn't mean you can start bossing everybody about, now.'

But that wasn't it, not exactly. Eddie explained he wanted me to lead the side if Simon didn't make it. And if he did make it? Then I wouldn't be in the twenty-two, and Leams would be starting at number eight. How do you get your head around that one? With difficulty, that's how. My head was wrecked for the weekend. I knew it was highly unlikely a broken nose would keep Simon Easterby from playing against the All Blacks, whether he was captain or not, and I didn't want to wish him any ill, but I was also mad keen to have a cut off them myself. At the same time, I could see where I figured in Eddie's plans – basically, as an emergency babysitter.

Simon made it, of course. The only good thing was that after his fitness was confirmed, Eddie cut me loose, and didn't expect me to hang around and hold tackle bags for the next few days. I congratulated Leams, of course. I was delighted for the kid. And then I pointed the car in the direction of Killaloe. I was reminded of another journey home, roughly six years previously, after watching Ireland crash out of the 1999 World Cup from the Dolphin clubhouse, when I realised the door to international rugby had been reopened. Now, as I headed down the N7, I could hear the sound of that door slamming behind me. If I was going to achieve something else substantial before my career ended, I knew then it would have to be with Munster.

17

GETTING THERE

'I'm no Nostradamus, but we're going to win the European Cup at some stage in the future and when we do, a lot of it will be down to what Alan has done with us during his tenure as coach.'

I was speaking on the occasion of Gaffer's going away bash, in May 2005. No doubt I was still slightly euphoric after our 27–16 triumph over Llanelli in the final of the Celtic Cup at Lansdowne Road – Gaffer's second trophy in three years with us. Now he was off to start a new job as assistant coach with Australia.

No doubt Munster's critics would have laughed at the idea of us ever winning the Heineken Cup, especially around Christmas of that year, when we were losing Celtic League games to Leinster and Ulster and were long odds even to get out of our pool. That Christmas was a time for straight questions and honest answers.

I didn't lose faith, because I simply couldn't afford to lose faith. Munster was now the sole focus of my professional life, so winning the Heineken Cup was my only real objective. I knew I was running out of time so that added a certain urgency. I'd been glad to renew a working relationship with Deccie, who had returned from Leinster in controversial circumstances. He got quite a bit of stick for leaving them just one year into a three-year contract but I can't say I was too surprised that he went for the Munster job when it was advertised, or that he was appointed. It's a very specialised role and insider knowledge is hugely beneficial. I also knew he would be highly motivated because the three years since he'd left us had often been difficult ones for him.

Things had changed considerably in the time he was away. Instead of just him and Niallo preparing the team, a coaching staff of five now did the job. Altogether, fifty people made a living from the business. Typically, he wasted no time getting up to speed with the mechanics of the entire operation. He had inherited a decent squad from Alan. When Jerry Flannery was capped later that season, I was the only non-current inter-national between numbers one and ten. He also inherited some Gaffer signings, two of whom worked out very well. Not only was Trevor Halstead a powerful presence at twelve, he had test experience with the Springboks and was bitter at the way he had been treated at Natal Sharks – made for Munster. Freddie Pucciariello brought with him plenty of political ideas, a fascination for biofuel and a good sense of humour but, most importantly, he too had international experience and could play in all three front-row positions.

I distinctly remember Freddie trying to take responsibility

for the fact that we came away empty-handed from our first pool game, away to Sale in October – he had dropped a ball in midfield, which enabled Jason Robinson to scoot away and deny us a losing bonus point. No one was having any of that. We all took responsibility for the defeat. I was annoyed that they'd scored directly off our put-in when we were down a man with Frankie in the bin – the ball squirted out past my feet and their scrum-half pounced. A massive pain in the arse, that. We tried hard to put a positive spin on things – Sale were a good side, top of the Premiership, a few things hadn't gone our way, we'd lost our first pool game before and still qualified, and so forth – but the mood was very down afterwards. Poor Quinny had ruptured his cruciate and looked like he was out for the season – and this was only a matter of months after he'd recovered from a serious shoulder injury. Frankie had hurt his neck more seriously than anyone realised at the time. We couldn't afford to lose another pool game. Not good.

Hammering Castres in Thomond the following week only partially lifted the gloom. Ireland had a poor November, getting hammered by the All Blacks and allowing Australia to end a long losing streak, and that affects players, obviously. We allowed Ulster to nick a Celtic League win at the death in Musgrave Park, which wasn't the best preparation for our December back-to-back with Newport Gwent Dragons. Fortunately, one of their props had a go at us, calling us 'Dad's Army'. I saw it in the local paper the night before the game in Newport, along with a comment from their out-half Ceri Sweeney about Rog and Strings being easily intimidated. That wasn't very clever, when you think we still had to play four games against them that season. Sure enough, we won in

Rodney Parade, but still got criticised for not picking up a bonus point – some people failed to remember that any Heineken Cup win on the road is a good win. The Dragons then gave us a scare at home the following week – once more, we had to be happy with a straight win, no bonus point. I almost lost it at the press conference afterwards, when Charlie Mulqueen of the *Examiner* asked me if we were now playing for second place in the pool. Maybe I was beginning to feel the pressure.

The pressure was certainly there when we lost 35–23 to Leinster at the RDS on New Year's Eve – Paulie's first game back after a long lay-off. Leinster were cock-a-hoop afterwards, especially Felipe Contepomi, who was gloating after their last try, running up to our supporters with his hand cupped behind his ear as if to say, 'What have you got to say about that?' That wasn't the only time he got up our noses that season. He's making a good living in Ireland. He should have minded his manners.

From our point of view, the one positive to come from the game – apart from Paulie coming through unscathed – was Barry Murphy. He'd made a few mistakes but he was playing opposite Darce and Drico, so that was allowed. He'd also shown some special touches in attack and we needed something different. In a fortnight's time we were travelling to Castres, where we'd lost on our previous two visits, but couldn't afford to lose again.

For that game in France, not only did Deccie chuck Baz in for his first Heineken Cup start, he did the same with Ian Dowling, who came in for Hoggy. We seemed to pick up on Deccie's sense of adventure that Friday night in the Stade Pierre

Antoine, scoring seven tries in a 46–9 victory – a record home defeat for any French side in the Heineken Cup, and surely the only time French supporters have been out-shouted in their own ground. Suddenly, we had the right balance in midfield between Trevor and Baz, and rediscovered the sense that anything was possible.

Someone branded the Sale game in Thomond as Miracle Match 11, and you could see fairly obvious similarities with the Gloucester game three years earlier – the top side in the English Premiership comes to Limerick needing to stop us from winning and from scoring four tries while we are at it. I just remember the fear I felt beforehand. People talk about the familiarity of playing at Thomond and the lift you get from the crowd, but the place can be intimidating for us. You don't want to be part of the first Munster team that loses a Heineken Cup game there, and their team was crammed with internationals – Jason Robinson, Jason White, Andrew Sheridan, Ignacio Fernández Lobbe and especially my opposite number, Sebastien Chabal. I was shitting it beforehand.

Chabal took some punishment that day but I couldn't help having a sneaking admiration for him. The hit by Paulie, followed up by the cavalry, was a real YouTube moment, and a match-turner, but there was something heroic about the way he refused to go to ground even as he was being driven back twenty metres. He kept scrapping till the end that day, despite the constant attention we were giving him. His problem was he kept getting isolated, and that was really the difference between the two packs. We hunted as one. We got our slices of luck, too. Fla (Jerry Flannery) could easily have been binned along with Fernández Lobbe for throwing punches early in the game, and it was while Fernández Lobbe was off that I was driven over for our first try. Baz's try – our second – was a brilliant piece of individualism but a fortunate ricochet was involved. We'd scored three tries by the break, and people tend to forget that we only secured the bonus point in the second minute of injury time when Wally ploughed over.

Still, what a day! I was persuaded to go up into the stand to say a few words of thanks to our supporters afterwards. I was reluctant only because we'd won nothing yet, but the occasion demanded some gesture of gratitude. The next day, I considered sending my thanks to Drico, because his brilliance in Bath ensured we would have a home quarter-final against Perpignan at Lansdowne Road, after the Six Nations. Our luck dried up a bit after that, however. In early March, Baz broke and dislocated his ankle playing a Celtic League match in Ravenhill. His timing couldn't have been worse – just after he'd been called into the Ireland squad, and four weeks before the quarter-final. To make matters worse, there was some nasty jeering from the terrace as he was being stretchered off. We also learned that we'd drawn yet another away semi-final, most likely in Toulouse, if we beat Perpignan. That would be our fifth away semi out of six.

The international players rejoined the fold in good spirits after winning a Triple Crown but the squad was shocked ten days before the Perpignan game by the news of Conrad O'Sullivan's death. Conrad had played a few Celtic League games for us the previous season and was a real character, a guy who could light up the room by his presence. Even now, thinking back to the day of the funeral gives me a shiver. I feel for everyone close to him. His passing was deeply affecting for the players who knew him best, including Leams, Stephen Keogh, Rog and Donners. Deccie had a difficult job leading up to the quarter-final, trying to get the balance right between giving guys room to grieve and preparing them for a game of rugby.

We hadn't played together as a team for nearly two months. The forwards had to prepare for a brutal confrontation with Perpignan's unique mixture of Catalans, Romanians and Argentinians, plus an Englishman and a Kiwi. If anyone typified their spirit, it was their skipper, Bernard Goutta. He was an unbelievable player who'd crawl everywhere to kill ball and was just incredibly aggressive at the breakdown. He didn't play as it turned out, but we had to prepare to deal with that sort of approach, so we had a brutal confrontation among ourselves the Tuesday before the game. It's standard to have fifteen against fifteen in the build-up, where the guys not in the starting team run all the opposition plays against you. This time, they were told to be as niggly and aggressive as they could be. So there were punches, kicks, rakings, quite a few flare-ups and a lot of verbals. Some of the lads thought it was dangerous to go so hard that close to the match, but Mick O'Driscoll assured us we were only preparing for what we would experience five days later – Micko played a couple of seasons in Perpignan, so he'd know. And that in-house pitched battle paid off, like he said it would.

Our conundrum had been the outside centre slot. Baz's injury left us with a big hole to fill. Gary Connolly, our rugby-league recruit, who'd played the earlier rounds alongside Trevor, was injured, and Hendo and Cully were both on their way back from injury but not quite there yet. So Deccie took another punt on a youngster and picked Tomás O'Leary in a position completely unknown to him, opposite David Marty, a seasoned French international. Tomás is some talent but his inexperience showed in the build-up to Perpignan's try at the end of the first half, giving them a 10–7 lead at the break. We got away with it in the end, though. It was a dogfight, as expected, but we gradually took control in the second half. Our discipline held, while theirs didn't. They had two fellas sent to the bin and Rog kicked the points that got us home safely.

As if we needed any extra motivation, we'd been given it before the game when we watched Leinster giving Toulouse the runaround, in Toulouse. We knew we'd meet them in the semi, and so our away match would be played in Dublin, in three weeks' time. What a result! Maybe we were due some luck. But no one was celebrating. From the harrowing minute's silence for Conrad before kick-off, through the eighty minutes of trench warfare, it had been a draining day.

Living out in Killaloe was a blessing for those three weeks because it provided a few hours' break from the hype and the frenzy. Someone compared it to the build-up to an All Ireland final but that doesn't come close to describing the madness of it. An entire region bought into the them-and-us affair. There wasn't a car on the road that didn't have a red flag poking out of the window, and the fascination was not confined to Munster. A journalist from *L'Équipe*, the French sports newspaper, travelled over to interview me and various other people about the cultural differences between Leinster and ourselves. I was careful what I said, of course. Such was the interest in this one game of rugby that you could be sure any disrespectful comment would get back to the other side, no matter what language it appeared in.

It would have been easy to get caught up in the emotion of it all. I had been brought up to view Dublin as the source of all injustice in the world. Dublin was home to the selectors who hadn't picked my dad for Ireland as often as they should have done. Dublin was home to the newspapers that had an anti-Munster bias. I'd picked it all up in the changing room at Thomond Park, but I had to put it to one side. The lads didn't need their captain getting over-emotional. They needed psyching down rather than up. They had to understand that losing was not an option and neither was settling scores. Getting involved in one-on-ones, going after Contepomi and trying to kick his head in was not going to help. We needed to be more focused than that. The game-plan would be simple. We would crowd the midfield, where they were most dangerous – as it turned out, Wally would play a massive role – and we would attack them where we thought they were most vulnerable, in the forwards. Of course, there were a million technical nuances on top of this but that was the essence of our plan.

We had plenty of distractions in the weeks leading up to the game – 'counter-worries' as we called them. Marcus damaged his calf in a scrummaging session three days after Perpignan and never looked a runner for the semi – this was where Freddie was invaluable. Rog was a different matter because he wasn't replaceable. He'd played against Perpignan with a hamstring strain, and picked up a nasty gash on his knee, which became infected and required that he spend five days in hospital. He missed both Celtic League games between the quarter and semi – away to Dragons, home to Edinburgh. Never before has one limb been the subject of more medical attention or public scrutiny; never before has there been such relief when Rog was declared fit. Meanwhile, Deccie decided to move Rags from the wing to the troubled outside centre slot – he had test experience in the position and would need it against Darce and Drico. That meant a recall for Hoggy, who was short on confidence but high on experience. I knew he wouldn't let us down. We had a brief scare over Strings the day before the game when he took a bang during the captain's run. People wondered why Deccie chose to mention this at the pre-match press conference. I suppose he was preparing people for the worst, while also knowing that it would be a psychological boost for everyone if Strings was declared fit on the day of the game.

Deccie was clearly determined to win the psychological battle. For example, while Leinster had drawn a home semi-final, according to tournament rules the game had to be played at a neutral venue and, therefore, we had to toss for who got the home changing room. We won, and Leinster had to remove their sign from the door. I know that annoyed a few people in their camp, but tough. We were determined to scrap for every inch, on and off the field. Leinster's Australian coach, Michael Cheika, had said in the build-up that he was in a way fortunate to be an outsider, without any psychological baggage – I suppose this was a reference to Deccie. By the same token, Cheika can't have been prepared for the sight that greeted him the following day.

We got a bit of a surprise ourselves as our coach came down the Merrion Road into Ballsbridge around an hour and a half before kick-off. We could have had a contest – spot the person who isn't wearing a red jersey. We knew we'd have more supporters than our official allocation of 21,400 tickets but we were amazed by the way Munster fans took over Dublin 4 that beautifully sunny Sunday. It made me think of the Irish people living in London we'd met after beating England at Twickenham – how grateful they were, how much they were looking forward to going into work on the Monday morning. I'm sure a lot of the red jerseys at Lansdowne that day were worn by Munster people working in Dublin. A lot of them come from GAA backgrounds, so they had the parish mentality. They came to participate, rather than to be entertained, and they did participate, literally. They were making so much noise come Rog's kick-off that Malcolm O'Kelly and Jamie Heaslip couldn't hear each other call and Mal knocked on, which led pretty quickly to Rog's first penalty. We couldn't have planned a better opening. The pace was ferocious but when Leams was mauled over the Leinster try-line in the eighth minute, we had the perfect foundation.

A final score of Leinster 6 Munster 30 gives no idea whatsoever of how tough a game this was. To put it in perspective, we were just ten points ahead in the seventy-fifth minute, when we were also a man down with Freddie in the bin – I remember because I was replaced by Frankie Roche when we needed a front row to take Freddie's place in the scrum. Leinster defended with real guts, especially in the third quarter, but their number ten didn't have a great day. He missed three kicks at goal and cost his side another kickable penalty because he got caught up in a row with Leams – come to think of it, he gave away a penalty in the process, so that was a six-point swing. No, it was a ferocious contest, with just one line-break all day. That just happened to come from Rog, who used his, er, tremendous upper-body strength to brush Mal aside near the end and score. He then did some steeple-chasing into the crowd to celebrate. What an all-round athlete! Seriously, though, I was delighted for him. He'd had to hear and read a lot about Contepomi in the build-up and he couldn't have responded better. Fittingly, he had the last kick of the game, converting Trevor's long-range interception. I think the run nearly killed the poor fella. He's more effective over ten to twenty metres.

We tried to be as humble as possible afterwards, because we knew what Leinster were going through. But we enjoyed the moment, no denying it. We found a nice bar near Heuston Station for a few drinks and a bite to eat with the wives and girlfriends, and then went across the road to the station for a rousing welcome – I loved that, especially as I could remember the depressed atmosphere in the same location after we'd lost the Celtic League final to Leinster five years earlier. Back in Limerick, we went to Fla's pub, which was hopping – by mentioning the pub in a post-match television interview, Paulie had effectively invited all of Limerick to join us. We commandeered the wood-panelled snug, some twenty of us in an area about six-feet square, singing our songs and drinking beers. You could say we felt like a tight bunch.

18

BEING THERE

3 p.m., Friday, 19 May 2006

Millennium Stadium Media Centre

Final press conference. Straightforward questions, straight-forward answers, no controversy. The only inconvenience is caused by the Munster captain, who refuses to lift the trophy together with Biarritz captain, Thomas Lièvremont, for the assembled snappers.

Sorry, no can do. I'm generally not superstitious but I don't believe you should lift a trophy until you've earned the right to do so. Besides, we've enough superstitious people in the side who'll lose it if they hear I've been putting my paws on the European Cup the day before the final. There's a fair bit of hoping and praying going on. John Kelly hasn't played since hurting his A/C joint early in the semi-final but is going to risk starting – Deccie says we should ask if it's okay if he wears 12A on his back instead of thirteen, seeing as that jersey has caused us so many problems. As for Marcus, he hasn't played since the quarter-final, while Paulie was in doubt midweek with his ankle. To top it off, Rog has picked up a tummy bug. At least the captain's run went off without any further hitches. We meet Dominic Crotty, who's home from the States and doing some media work at the stadium. It's good to see him. It's also a reminder of how many people are depending on us.

5 p.m. Room 101, Vale of Glamorgan Hotel

It's nice to have a familiar setting. We stayed here for the 2002 final, and had a quick refresher visit recently for our Celtic League game against the Ospreys. I like having my own room. At first, you miss having someone to chat to, because that helps to take up the long hours you have to spend waiting around. But your chances of an uninterrupted night's sleep are greatly increased by being on your own. It also gives me space to think about what I'll say in the team meeting later this evening.

8 p.m. Team room

The lads say they know I'm getting emotional when they see my lower lip start to quiver. Paulie says that's good because it gets him going as well, but I'm reluctant to go down the emotional route on this occasion. I prefer not to mention the commentators who don't rate us, or say we don't play with enough variety, and I don't want to talk too much about where we're from and who we're representing. Getting too emotional the night before a game drains you. So I basically tweak an old idea of Gaffer's. I tell them to make sure they don't wake up on

Sunday morning thinking about what they could have done but didn't. A lot of us had been in that situation before – waking up the day after and having a load of things we'd change, given the chance. The message is if you think something is on, go for it, and we'll all back you to the hilt. Rog, Paulie and Rags have their say, but we try to keep it short. You can over-talk a situation. Afterwards, I read a few of the fax messages and emails that have been posted on the wall. The Claw had sent this: 'Best of luck and sow it into those French bastards.'

1.45 p.m., Saturday, 20 May 2006
North Dressing Room, Millennium Stadium

'O'Loughlin Gaels. 2001 Kilkenny County Hurling Final' – that's what is written on the side of Ian Dowling's kitbag, the one he's using for a Heineken Cup final, in front of around 75,000 people in Cardiff. The muppet. At least it gives us some light relief, which is in short supply. I was glad to get a good night's sleep and had no problem getting some breakfast into me. But Paulie hurt his neck doing lineouts this morning, which is another worry we don't need. He's been given an anti-inflammatory jab and is good to start. Then we had a helicopter overhead all the way into the centre of Cardiff – it felt like watching the BBC's build-up to the FA Cup final when I was a kid, only now, the camera was on us.

The amazing scenes outside the stadium gave us an idea of the size of our support, but we were still struck by the volume of noise when we jogged out to warm up, and that was a good forty minutes before the start. I lost the toss, which meant we'd be receiving the kick-off. The lads generally prefer to chase and tear into the opposition, but it's not a big deal.

Ten minutes before kick-off, all bar the starting fifteen have left the room. I can't recall what is said after this point. I just know this is the most intense huddle I've ever been a part of. If I held back on the emotion last night, my lips are quivering now.

3.00 p.m. Kick-Off

Julien Peyrelongue kicks off, Payney and Wally fail to hear each other call in the noise, and we turn the ball over. ERC have shut the roof for dramatic effect and the din is deafening. But just over a minute later, it's as though someone had turned the volume right down. Philippe Bidabe, the Biarritz centre, fends Rags's tackle and sends Sireli Bobo tiptoeing down the left touchline, trying to stay in play before diving in at the corner. I see the touch-judge having a good look but as I get there, he's saying, 'No, that's a good try, no question there.'

We're gathering behind the sticks and Rags comes in to apologise and promise that it won't happen again, but he's almost drowned out by the sound of the crowd booing at the replay on the big screen. I look up and see confirmation that touch-judge Dave Pearson got it wrong. I'm thinking, 'Why the hell can't the ref go upstairs for touchline calls?' But this is no time to start feeling sorry for ourselves. Anyway, I reckon the referee, Chris White, has seen the replay. Who knows? Maybe we'll get a fifty-fifty decision later in the game. Dimitri Yachvili lands a superb conversion on his 'wrong' side but we are determined to remain positive.

7 minutes: O'Gara penalty

Munster 3 Biarritz 7

White penalises Biarritz for pulling down our maul, about twenty-five metres out, and we take the opportunity to put points on the board. But the next time we get a penalty in their third, we go after them. We'd decided beforehand we had to get ahead of Biarritz, make *them* chase the game. We'd watched enough of them to know that they are front-runners, who like to build an early lead and use Yachvili's kicking to keep them out of reach. If they're in danger of conceding a seven-pointer, they're happy to give away a penalty, concede three instead of seven, and then go back into your half. That way, they think they can control the scoreboard. So we reckoned we'd knock them out of their comfort zone. We kick the penalty into the corner. Twice. They hold us up, and when Damien Traille gobbles up Rog's chip behind his try-line to give them a twenty-two drop-out, it looks like we've thrown points away. But we've made a statement of intent. It was as though we'd said, 'You can give away penalties but we're still going to come at you. We're not leaving anything behind here today.'

17 minutes: Halstead try, O'Gara conversion

Munster 10 Biarritz 7

Now we're sucking diesel. Rog runs back Peyrelongue's clearance, Fla offloads to Paulie and we're back on the front foot. Once the ball is swept left, what makes the difference is Leams' tight line off Trevor's shoulder. Biarritz are diving in, doing anything to slow us up, but the next time the ball comes, Trevor has enough momentum off Rog's pass to plough through two tacklers and score. Gwan ya good thing, ya! The decision to go after the seven-pointer is vindicated. Rog kicks the conversion.

23 minutes: Yachvili penalty

Munster 10 Biarritz 10

Before the game, much was made of Biarritz's scrum, and their front row is decent – Petru Balan, the highly rated

Romanian, at loose-head, the experienced Benoît August at hooker and at tight-head, the massive Samoan, Census Johnston. Meanwhile, we have three guys in our front five – Marcus, Paulie and Fla – who've played an aggregate of five minutes rugby in the previous month. Here, Marcus is penalised on our put-in, five metres from our line. Yachvili converts from his wrong side. Again. Given the importance Biarritz place on a big start, we'd probably have taken 10–10 by the end of the first quarter.

32 minutes: Stringer try, O'Gara conversion
Munster 17 Biarritz 10

I can remember a time when I feared for Peter Stringer's safety. He was on the bench for a Combined Provinces team that played South Africa in Cork in 1998. He can't have been any more than twenty – in his tracksuit he looked around twelve – and we were playing these massive Springboks. I needn't have worried for him.

Here, in what turns out to be a game of tiny margins, his quick thinking earns us seven massive points. As he puts the ball into a scrum on the right-hand side just inside their twenty-two, I have no idea what he has in mind. But he has spotted Bobo tracking Hoggy infield, leaving a massive blind-side. Later, we learn that Peyrelongue had shouted a warning to Bobo but his words were drowned out by the noise of the crowd – the Munster supporters participating again. Just when we need it to be, the scrum is rock solid. Hayes even gets a slight angle, which is perfect for what Strings is planning.

When I sense him running right, I take off after him in the expectation that he'll be tackled and my next job will be to clear the ball. But no, he's diving over. You wait for the ref to call him back for some technical detail but the whistle never comes. Nice one! Rog kicks the conversion and as we go in for half-time, we are in control. Now it's Biarritz who have to chase the game, and Strings, the man who was pickpocketed by Neil Back the last time we were here, is the man mainly responsible for that.

42 minutes: O'Gara penalty

Munster 20 Biarritz 10

Payney later admitted he was raging that he'd made a couple of errors in the opening minutes. He more than repaid his debt. Having chased his own precision bomb, which lands just outside their twenty-two, he gobbles up Jérôme Thion in the tackle. Thion fails to release, Rog kicks the points and that's the perfect start to the second half.

48 minutes: Yachvili penalty

Munster 20 Biarritz 13

We've been going full throttle since the Bobo try so I suppose it's inevitable we'll ease off at some stage, just as it's inevitable that Biarritz will fight back. They are French champions, after all. They have been using Imanol Harinordoquy to double-team Paulie at the lineout all day, so we've used Donners as our main ball winner and Fla's darts have been spot on every time. Here, though, we go to Paulie and he's forced to slap it back to Strings. Under pressure, Strings runs into trouble, we're penalised at the breakdown and Yachvili kicks the points.

51 minutes: Yachvili penalty

Munster 20 Biarritz 16

Harinordoquy is having an outstanding game for them and when Leams gets the opportunity to take him man and ball, he hits too high, so Yachvili gets another shot at goal. Just as in golf, when you should always expect your opponent to make ten-foot putts, you expect Yachvili to be on target. He and Rog missed nothing between them all day.

It's real trench warfare, the second half, and midway through, when there's a stoppage in play, the Sky producer decides he'll lighten things up by showing shots of the massive crowd in O'Connell Street back in Limerick. A connection was made between the folks at home and the 60,000–70,000 supporters inside the Millennium Stadium and it felt like a jolt of energy through us. I was preoccupied, making sure we were focused on the next play, but fellas said afterwards that they sensed what was going on and were lifted by it. Then again, it's Biarritz who score next.

69 minutes: Yachvili penalty
Munster 20 Biarritz 19

This is an annoying penalty. It's their lineout, thirty-five metres out to the right, and I drag Thion to ground before it becomes a maul, but when Biarritz regroup, we pull it down again and the ref loses patience. Yachvili scores. Even more frustrating, I'm hauled ashore a couple of minutes later, to be replaced by Micko. It makes sense, though. They have five subs on the pitch at this stage and we've replaced just Marcus, who did remarkably well to last sixty-two minutes given his lack of match practice. Micko is an international player and he's fresh, so it's a good call. I'll have to watch the last ten minutes from the side.

73 minutes: O'Gara penalty
Munster 23 Biarritz 19

Once again, Trevor comes up with a big play when we need one. Off a scrum, he takes Rog's pass and piles over the gain-line. Johnston hits the ruck from the side, right under the ref's nose, so White has no option. The penalty is around thirty-five metres out, just to the right of the sticks. Just to increase the degree of difficulty, as Rog is setting up, Sky again show the pictures from O'Connell Street on the big screen. He doesn't need that. But his strike is perfect and for the time being, Biarritz need more than a penalty or a drop-goal to win.

I'm a hopeless spectator. Paulie soon joins me after cramping up, allowing Quinny on for the last five. Looking back, it's great that he was on the pitch for the final whistle, but nothing seems great at the time. Paulie and I are sitting side by side, not saying a word. It's incredibly frustrating. Your mind is still playing the game but your body is forced to be still. I'm an awful clock-watcher, too. It's reading 78:50 when Biarritz have a scrum in front of us near halfway – their final chance. We get away with murder as Wally stands off the scrum at Rog's request, but they don't attack his channel. Peyrelongue passes wide to Bidabe. Rags hauls him down but he gets the pass away to Nicolas Brusque, who's tackled by Trev, just on our twenty-two. Mercifully, Payney prevents a quick release and our defence can reset.

I'm on my feet now – everything is happening on the far side. Two phases later, Bobo takes a pass down the short side but runs into Thion. Munster's scrum. There's madness in the air as thousands and thousands of Irish people everywhere – and surely anyone with a sense of poetic justice – is willing this to be over. Biarritz are penalised for wheeling the scrum, Strings grabs the ball from Leams and kicks it into the stands, and that's it. We're running across the pitch, going ballistic, jumping and hugging and screaming. The joy. The relief. The pride. The tears. The mayhem.

5.15 p.m. Trophy presentation

Claw is having a bit of bother with a Millennium Stadium steward, who won't let him through the barrier and onto the pitch. Luckily for the steward, Sky's man pitch-side is Dewi Morris, the former England scrum-half, who slips Claw his accreditation. So off he goes, along with a swarm of backroom staff and squad members, including Frankie, Cully and Baz, hopping along on his crutches. At one stage, Donners hands me Tony, who's wearing a Munster jersey, with 'Dad' on the back, above a number eight. It's a nice moment, and a nice picture, but within seconds, a security man is telling me Tones will have to be handed back to his Mam. I give Olive a big sweaty hug while I'm at it.

You'd think after ten seasons of playing in this tournament, and seven seasons after our first final, I'd be willing to wait a few more minutes to get my hands on this bloody trophy, but the delay, as everyone else collects their medals from ERC chairman Jean-Pierre Lux, is killing me. I'm also a bit put out that they won't let me bring Deccie up onto the platform to accept the cup. Typically, he's happy to hold back. The trophy is heavier than I thought it would be but it feels like the noise would lift it anyway – none of our supporters appear to have left the building. It's a moment we've watched on DVD on countless occasions and it still brings a lump to the throat.

Even the standard post-match procedure is emotional. When Deccie and I walk in for the press conference, I hear a familiar bark from the back of the room. 'GO ON, FOLEY!' It's Gaillimh, who's been doing radio commentary. The press conference can wait. We go to each other and there's a big hug, maybe even a few tears. This trophy belongs to more than the eighteen fellas who were on the pitch.

12.30 a.m. Shannon airport

After the official function at the stadium, we stop on the way to Cardiff airport at St Andrew's Golf Club in Barry for refreshments with family and friends – we'd requested this because, as we knew from experience, it's often hard after big matches to get a few moments with loved ones. As it turns out, a seating schedule mix-up means we're scattered all over our return flight. No matter. It gives some of us the chance to steal half an hour's kip, in the knowledge that there won't be much sleeping done over the coming days.

Maybe 5,000 people are there to greet us at Shannon, despite the late hour, and they are treated to the rare sight of Deccie leading a rendition of 'Stand Up and Fight', his voice breaking. Then it's a garda escort straight to the Clarion Hotel for a semi-private function. The place is hopping. Some fellas had been talking about saving themselves for the next couple of days but going to bed just isn't an option. And me? I'm sitting in the corner with Paulie, watching the game all over again, pressure off, reliving every precious moment of it. A perfect end to a perfect day.

19

A PROPER ENDING

The party was only starting, of course. I'd hardly any sleep by the time I was taking a call from Marian Finucane on RTÉ Radio early the following morning and, like everyone else, I floated through the rest of the day. The weather was so awful that there were doubts whether the open-topped bus ride through Limerick would take place but I'm so pleased it did. Even though we were soaked, it was great crack, and nice to acknowledge all the folks who'd made the effort.

After a bite to eat back at the Clarion, it was off to the Sin-Bin that evening, where Claw gave us the run of the place before letting his customers in later on. We had a karaoke session with wives, girlfriends and close friends. If you must know, I think I sang Bony M's 'Brown Girl in the Ring' and U2's version of 'Helter Skelter'. On Monday, we took the cup to any number of pubs around town – Angela's, Charlie St George's and so on. By ten o'clock, I know I was in Fla's bar because the nation heard me being interviewed by Vincent Browne on his radio show. I don't recall anything of the conversation but I intend getting a tape of it sometime. Apparently, it's very entertaining.

On it went. We had a civic reception in Cork, going-away bashes for Hendo and Mike Mullins and Stephen Keogh and Trevor Hogan. On the Friday, a few of us were on *The Late, Late Show* – Paulie, Rog, our press officer, Pat Geraghty, and me. I think Pat Kenny was a bit surprised to see Gerty arrive out on stage but there were no rules that week. We even managed to get a Munster shirt over Pat's head, with the Toyota logo there for all to see. Who says we don't look after our sponsors?

The next day was our last Celtic League game of the season, against Cardiff at Thomond Park – a handy piece of scheduling by somebody, for it allowed us to say thanks to our supporters and parade the trophy one final time. In fact, Quinny, Deccie, UL President Roger Downer and I got to show it off to our North American supporters' club in San Francisco later that year, but that's another story. Up in the stand after the game, we presented medals to the squad members who hadn't received one on the day of the final. The lads who were leaving us sang songs – all quite moving, and a nice way to end the week.

It had to end there, especially for those of us who were going into camp with Ireland. Yes, after the disappointment of the previous November, I'd got the call from Eddie for the three-test tour to New Zealand and Australia. As Simon Easterby was injured this time, and Quinny wasn't quite fit enough yet for test rugby, I travelled believing I had a good chance of getting back into the team. After winning the best club competition in the world, I felt ready for anything, and I was wondering whether Eddie might pick Munster's one to ten en bloc to face the All Blacks. But it quickly became obvious that unless Leams, Wally or Neil Best were involved in some boating accident, I wouldn't be playing any part. I even read it in a newspaper article when I came home – I was in the 'Break glass in case of emergency' category, apparently. Those three weeks down under were soul-destroying. I know people might find it hard to believe that I could be so miserable while on tour representing my country, but after a fortnight of holding tackling bags or watching the Auckland rain lash down, I would rather have been anywhere else in the world. That was my last involvement in the international set-up, and I found it a sad way to finish.

I know one of the things I'd said to Vincent Browne was that winning the cup was only the beginning for Munster – I know because I said it a lot around that time. I also knew it was going to be bloody difficult to back it up the following season. We'd put so much of ourselves into winning the thing that it would be tough to reproduce the same intensity consistently, especially seeing as we now had target signs stitched into our jerseys.

Initial signs were good, though. We won our first pool game, at Welford Road, thanks to an excellent all-round performance and a superb long-range penalty by Rog at the death. The only drawback was that I dislocated my shoulder early in the second half attempting to tackle Andy Goode, which put me out for a couple of months. The next game, against Bourgoin at home, was the first Heineken game I had missed since Greg Tuohy took my place for that trip to Harlequins ten years previously.

The 2006–2007 season didn't turn out to be the best crack, to be honest. I worked hard to rehab my shoulder and was back in business just after Christmas but couldn't budge Micko from the starting back row. I had to sit and watch as Leicester took our Thomond record away from us in January – seeing them bullying us off our patch was hard to take. I did get a run in the second half but ripped my calf just before the end, which entailed more rehabbing while the lads were away for the Six Nations. I was ready for the quarter-final in Stradey Park and was told I'd be coming off the bench for the final thirty minutes. We lost, and I never got to take off my tracksuit.

At the end of a season ruined by injury, it sounded like my body was telling me to call it quits. I had been replaced by Paulie as captain, my national contract was up and I was heading towards my thirty-fourth birthday. But I didn't want to end this way, to limp away from the game. I wanted a proper ending. So I negotiated a one-year deal with Munster. By October 2007, I knew for definite that it would be my last season. While Gaillimh was away working at the World Cup in France, I took his place at Shannon and helped out with a bit of coaching with the senior side. I enjoyed it. I reckoned I had a bit of a feel for it, so I stuck with it for the season – we won an All Ireland Cup, the Munster Senior Cup and finished second in the AIB League. I also got involved with coaching the Munster Under-20s and will continue to do so. It's good to have found a way to stay involved in rugby.

This doesn't mean my final contract was what's known in

the trade as 'a Harvey Norman' – one year, no interest, as the fella says on the radio ad. By getting involved in coaching, I was planning for life after playing, but my main focus was still getting picked to play in the Heineken Cup, trying to get out of our ridiculously tough pool and trying to win the thing. I was on the bench for the first two pool games. I actually came on as tight-head prop in the second half of the first pool game, against Wasps in Coventry – uncontested scrums, of course. My real chance came when Quinny was injured and I was picked to start in Llanelli. I wouldn't like to say that the conditions suited me, because they suited no one – at one stage, the referee seriously considered calling a halt – but I suppose you could say it was a roll-your-sleeves-up sort of day, and I can do that. We all could, and we did it bloody well. Our 29–16 victory was the original team effort, and from a personal point of view, it helped banish the memory of sitting helplessly in the stand at the same venue for the duration of the previous year's quarter-final.

We won the rematch in Limerick the following week but the key moment in the pool was nicking a losing bonus point in Clermont Auvergne in mid-January – this meant a straight win at home to Wasps would see us topping the pool. On the journey home from France, someone mentioned the fact that Lawrence Dallaglio had just announced he'd be retiring at the end of the season. The game in Limerick was potentially his last Heineken Cup game, so it was like he was using Thomond Park as motivation for his own troops. I'd already told Deccie and the senior players I'd be finishing at the end of the season and now Deccie suggested I might put it in the public domain in the build-up to the game. But Pat Geraghty and I convinced him that it could be distracting and counter-productive, and it was best to let the players focus on the game rather than the occasion. I'd announce it the following Monday when things had calmed down.

Dallaglio did get a bit of a send-off in Thomond, as it happened, but not the sort he wanted. When he was binned during the second half, the crowd gave it to him with both barrels. He was a pain in the arse that day, constantly mouthing off, but then he was always a pain in the arse to play against. He was the best number eight I came across, and I played against him all the way up. He reminded me of Halvey with his ball skills and the way he could throw in a devastating break, plus he'd give you absolutely nothing on the pitch. I reckon the crowd's reaction to him being sin-binned was as much a mark of respect as anything else.

I got a nice send-off myself, midway through the second half – but this wasn't some orchestrated farewell stage-managed by Deccie in honour of my final game at my home ground. I'd hurt my ribs and needed to come off. If I'd had a choice in the matter, I would have played to the end of what was a great win. The longer I stayed in the game, the longer I was in contention to be picked for the quarter-finals. That's why I played against Connacht on 28 March, the day Dan, our second son, was born. And while I sensed I'd be on the bench for the Gloucester game, and while I accepted it, I wasn't happy about it. Being left out altogether for the semi was hard, too. Donnacha Ryan, who was picked on the bench instead of me for the Saracens game, is a great talent. I was just a bit surprised that when he was used in the semi, he was used as a second row. Maybe I'm just a bad spectator.

But I'm not bitter. When you tot everything up, how could I possibly be bitter? I've spent over a decade making a living from something that I love doing. I have a beautiful, intelligent, loving wife and two lovely boys. My mam and dad and two adorable sisters are all happy and healthy. I have my third family, Munster, plus a whole heap of friends – one of the privileges of a life in sport – and a million happy memories. Dad says I won't have outdone him till I have a son and a daughter who have both won more international caps than I have, which is one way of looking at it. But all told, I'm ridiculously lucky.

And I did get my proper ending, after all. Before the 2008 final, the last thing I said to Paulie in the changing room was that you have to earn the right to lift the Heineken Cup – it sounds an obvious comment now, but he tells me he quoted me in the pre-match huddle, which was nice to hear. There is no doubt that Munster earned their second title, just as they earned their first. They came through the toughest pool ever, won both quarter- and semi-finals away from home, and then beat Toulouse, the greatest team in the history of the tournament, in the final. And I was proud to play my part. I may not have togged out in Cardiff, but I'd done absolutely everything in my power to help us get there.

So, while I'd prepared all week to keep my distance, when the final whistle went in the Millennium Stadium, I obeyed the urge to go out on to the pitch and celebrate, just as Claw had done two years previously. I hugged and I sang and I jumped and I smiled. And when we were delayed at Cardiff airport on the way home, us and a few hundred Munster supporters, I led the singsong. This was no time to be holding back.

STATISTICAL RECORD

Compiled by Des Daly

Legend

R	Replacement
T	Scored try
A	Away game
C	Captain
QF	Quarter-final
SF	Semi-final
F	Final

AIL	All Ireland League
CC	Celtic Cup
CL	Celtic League
ERC	European Rugby Cup/Heineken Cup
IPC	Interprovincial Championship
ML	Magners League
MSC	Munster Senior Cup
RWC	Rugby World Cup

LR	Lansdowne Road, Dublin
MP	Musgrave Park, Cork
TP	Thomond Park, Limerick

ARG	Argentina	JAP	Japan
AUS	Australia	NZ	New Zealand
CAN	Canada	ROM	Romania
ENG	England	RUS	Russia
FRA	France	SA	South Africa
GEO	Georgia	SAM	Samoa
ITA	Italy	SCO	Scotland
IRE	Ireland	WAL	Wales

1   **International Career**

Note: In seasons where Ireland played an opponent more than once, numbers have been used to indicate each game, i.e. NZ(2) refers to the second test Ireland played against New Zealand that season.

1990–1992   8 caps for Ireland Schools.

1993–1994   IRE U-21 v. NZ; v. ENG; v. WAL; v. SCO.
                 Ireland Students v. ENG.

1994–1995   **IRE** v. ENG (T); v. SCO; v. FRA; v. WAL; v. ITA.
                 RWC (1995) **IRE** v. JAP (R).
                 IRE U-21 v. ENG.
                 Ireland Development XV v. USA.

1995–1996   IRE A v. SCO; v. WAL (T); v. ENG.
                 Ireland Students v. FRA.
                 Students World Cup v. Wales; v. Argentina; v. England; v. Uruguay.

1996–1997   **IRE** v. AUS; v. ITA; v. ENG (R).
                 IRE A v. SA; v. FRA; v. WAL; v. SCO.
                 Ireland Development xv v. Northland; v. Bay of Plenty, v. Thames Valley.

1997–1998   IRE A v. ENG(R).
                 IRE v. South West Districts; v. Griqualand West (uncapped games on senior summer tour to SA).

1998–1999   IRE A v. SA; v. FRA; v. WAL; v. ENG; v. SCO; v. ITA (T).

1999–2000   **IRE** v. ENG; v. SCO; v. ITA; v. FRA; v. WAL; v. ARG; v. CAN.

2000–2001   **IRE** v. JAP; v. SA; v. ITA; v. FRA; v. ROM (T).

2001–2002   **IRE** v. SCO(1); v. WAL(1); v. ENG(1); v. SAM (C); v. NZ(1); v. WAL(2); v. ENG(2); v. SCO(2); v. ITA; v. FRA; V NZ Divisional XV (uncapped game); v. NZ(2); v. NZ(3)

2002–2003 IRE v. ROM (C); v. RUS; v. GEO (C); v. AUS(1); v. FIJI (T);
           v. ARG; v. SCO; v. ITA; v. FRA; v. WAL; v. ENG.

2003–2004 **IRE** v. WAL(1); IRE v. FRA(t); v. WAL(2) (t); v. ENG; v. ITA;
           v. SCO; v. SA(1); v. SA(2).
           RWC (2003) **IRE** v. ROM; v. AUS.

2004–2005 IRE v. SA; v. USA (R); v. ARG; v. ITA; v. SCO; v. ENG; v.
           FRA; v. WAL.

For the record ...

- 62 caps (59 starts) against 17 nations, three times as captain (all wins) and score FIVE test tries.

- 55 test at number 8 (an Irish record) and four as blindside flanker.

- Scored a try on international debut, aged 21, against England at Lansdowne Road, 21 January 1995 (L 8–20).

- One half of the twelfth father-and-son combination to play rugby for Ireland. Brendan Foley won 11 international caps in the second row (1976–1981).

- 60 per cent success at test level: played 62, won 37, drawn 1 , lost 24.

- Made 29 consecutive test appearances – from Canada (June 2000) to England (March 2003) – and participatd in 10 consecutive Ireland victories during the 2002–2003 season.

- Participated in five Ireland summer tours – South Africa (June 1998), to the Americas (June 2000), to New Zealand (June 2002), to South Africa (June 2004) and to Australia and New Zealand (no game) (June 2006).

- Participated in two world cups – South Africa (1995) and Australia (2003).

- Started all three games when Ireland won its seventh Triple Crown (2004).

- Joint holder, with three other players, of the record for the most Ireland Schools caps (8).

2 Munster Career

1990–1992   Munster Schools; Schools Interprovincial title
(1990–1991).

1992–1994   Munster U-20; back to back IPC grand slams.

1994–1995   Senior Munster debut v. Edinburgh Districts (TP)   5/6
(22 October 1994).
IPC grand slam.

1995–1996   ERC v. Swansea (W17–13) (TP); v, Castres (W12–19)   4/9
(A).

1996–1997   ERC v. Milan (W23–5) (MP); v. Cardiff (L18–48) (T)   10/12
(A); v. Wasps (W49–22) (T) (TP); v. Toulouse
(L19–60) (A).
IPC grand slam.
Munster v. Australia (L19–55) (TP).

1997–1998   ERC v. Cardiff (L23–43) (A); v. Bourgoin (W17–15)   9/11
(TP); v. Cardiff (L32–37) (T) (MP); v. Bourgoin
(L6–21) (A); v. Harelquins (W23–16) (TP).

1998–1999   ERC v. Padova (L20–13) (MP); v. Neath (W34–10)   14/15
(MP); v. Perpignan (L24–41) (A); v. Neath (D18–18)
(A); v. Perpignan (W13–5) (MP); v. Padova (L35–21)
(A); v. Colomiers (QF, L9–23) (A).
IPC winner's medal.

1999–2000   ERC v. Pontypridd (W32–10) (TP); v. Saracens   17/17
(W35–34) (T) (A); v. Colomiers (W31–15) (A); v.
Colomiers (W23–5) (MP); v. Saracens (W31–30) (TP);
v. Pontypridd (L36–38) (T) (A); v. Stade Francais
(QF, W27–10) (TP); v. Toulouse (SF, W31–25)
(Bordeaux); Northampton (F, L8–9) (Twickenham).
IPC grand slam.

2000–2001   ERC v. Newport (W26–18) (TP); v. Castres (W32–29)   16/16
(A); v. Bath (W31–9) (TP); v. Bath (L5–18) (A); v.
Newport (W39–24) (A); v. Castres (W21–11) (T)
(MP); v. Biarritz (QF, W38–29) (3T) (TP); v. Stade
Francais (SF, L15–16) (Lille).
IPC winner's medal.

2001–2002   ERC v. Castres (W28–23) (TP); v. Harlequins (W24–8)   19/22
(A); v. Bridgend (W16–12) (A); v. Bridgend (W40–6)
(MP); v. Harlequins (W51–17) (T) (TP); v. Castres
(L13–21) (A); v. Stade Francais (QF, W16–14) (A); v.
Castres (SF, W25–17) (Beziers); v. Leicester (F, L9–15)
(Cardiff).
CL runners-up v. Leinster (F, L20–24) (LR).

2002–2003   ERC v. Gloucester (L16–35) (A); v. Perpignan (W30–21)   15/18
(TP); v. Viadana (W64–0) (2T) (MP); v. Viadana
(W25–22) (T) (A); v. Perpignan (L8–23) (T) (A); v.
Gloucester (W33–6) (TP); v. Leicester (QF, W20–7) (A);
v. Toulouse (SF, L12–13) (Le Stadium, Toulouse).
CL winners v. Neath (F, W37–17) (Cardiff).

2003–2004   ERC v. Bourgoin (W18–17) (A); v. Benetton Treviso   14/31
(W51–0) (2T) (TP); v. Gloucester (L11–22) (A); v.
Gloucester (W35–14) (TP); v. Benetton Treviso
(W31–20) (T) (A); v. Bourgoin (W26–3) (TP); v. Stade
Francais (QF, W37–31) (TP); v. London Wasps (SF,
L32–37) (T) (LR).

2004–2005   ERC v. Harlequins (W15–9) (TP); v. Ospreys (W20–18)   18/30
(A); v. Castres (L12–19) (A); v. Castres (W36–8) (T)
(TP); v. Ospreys (W20–10) (T) (TP); v. Harlequins
(W18–10) (A); v. Biarritz (QF, L10–19) (San Sebastian).
CC winners v. Llanelli Scarlets (F, W27–16) (LR).

2005–2006   ERC v. Sale (L13–27) (A); v. Castres (W42–16) (TP); v.   25/29
Dragons (W24–8) (A); v. Dragons (W30–18) (T) (TP);
v. Castres (W46–9) (A); v. Sale (W31–9) (T) (TP); v.
Perpignan (QF, W19–10) (LR); v. Leinster (SF, W30–6)
(LR); v. Biarritz (F, W23–19) (Cardiff).

2006–2007   ERC v. Leicester (L21–19) (A); v. Bourgoin (W30–27)   12/27
(R) (A); v. Leicester (L6–13) (R) (TP).

2007–2008   ERC v. London Wasps (L23–24) (A); v. Clermont   23/28
Auvergne (W36–13) (TP); v. Llanelli (W29–16) (A); v.
Llanelli (W22–13) (TP); v. Clermont Auvergne
(L19–26) (A); v. London Wasps (W19–3) (TP); v.
Gloucester (QF, W16–3) (R) (A).

                                        Total   201/271

For the record …

- The most appearances by any player for an Irish province (201 caps) over 14 seasons – 86 ERC ties, 69 CL/ML games, 31 IPC games and 12 capped challenge games. Played 182 games at number 8, 10 at flanker and was a replacement nine times.

- 72 per cent success rate – played 201, won 142, drawn 4, lost 55.

- Most ERC apperances in the history of the tournament with a success rate of 70 per cent – played 86, won 60, drawn 1, lost 25.

- Scored 22 tries and appeared in three ERC finals (2000, 2002 and 2006), winning in 2006. Gained a second winner's medal in 2008, though omitted from 22-man squad for semi-final and final.

- Played in 24 of Munster's 26 straight ERC victories at Thomond Park before defeat by Leicester in January 2007.

- Scored Munster's only ERC hat-trick of tries (v. Biarittz (TP) 28 January 2001).

- Has five IPC titles, including three grand slams.

- First captained Munster on 28 August 1998 (v. Edinburgh (MP)) and led them on 63 occasions, including 16 ERC games. Captained Munster to two trophies – Celtic Cup (2005) and Heineken Cup (2006).

- Holds career try-scoring record for Munster (46) – 22 ERC, 10 CL/ML and 14 in challenge games.

- Received only one yellow card during his representative career – from referee David Keane (Leinster) v. Connacht (A), October 2005.

- Won 200th cap against Ulster at Ravenhill (ML, L9–19, 30 April 2008) and played last game 10 days later v. Glasgow (L18–21, (MP)).

3   **Shannon Career**

1992–1993   AIL debut as a replacement v. Young Munster (L6–15, 21
            November 1992) (TP), aged 19.

1993–1994   Shannon's top AIL try scorer this season.
            Munster U-20s cup winner's medal.

1994–1995   First AIL title, with a 100 per cent success rate.

1995–1996   Second AIL title, with a 100 per cent success rate.
            First MSC winner's medal, beating Cork Con 15–13 in
            the final.

1996–1997   Third AIL title.

1997–1998   Captains Shannon to its fourth AIL title, beating
            Garryowen 15–9 in the competition's first play-off final.
            Second MSC winner's medal, beating Young Munster
            19–18 in the final.

1999–2000   Third MSC winner's medal, beating Young Munster
            23–13 in the final.

2001–2002   Fifth AIL winner's medal, beating Cork Con 21–17 in
            the final.

For the record …

*   88 appearances in AIL Division One over a period of 16
    seasons, scoring 19 tries.

*   Played in all 48 games during the club's four-in-a-row
    (1995–1998).

*   After an absence of five seasons from the AIL, played final
    game v. Blackrock College at Coonagh, 1 December 2007
    (W26–7).

Index

Aboud, Steve, 55, 73
Ackford, Paul, 72
Ahern, Bertie, 161
All Ireland League (also AIB League), 46, 47, 49, 50–1, 53, 57, 61, 66, 82, 84–5, 90, 96, 101, 109, 116, 123, 125, 126, 239
    1998 final, 114
Anderson, Willie, 55, 57, 73
Andrew, Rob, 74, 75
Argentina, 130–1, 145–6, 181, 183, 184, 189, 190, 194, 200
Ashton, Brian, 91, 92, 100–1, 102, 104, 111, 116–17
August, Benoît, 230
Auschwitz, 157–8
Australia, 21, 44, 47, 79, 82, 98, 157, 183, 184, 190, 191, 194, 211, 215

Baby, Benoît, 208–9
Back, Neil, 161, 171–2, 197, 231
Balan, Petru, 229
Ballymena RFC, 46, 52, 66
Balshaw, Iain, 161
Barbarians, 83, 143, 146
Barry, Ronan, 192
Bath RFC, 152–3
Bayfield, Martin, 72
Beckham, David, 185

Beggy, David, 66
Begley, Brian, 41
Bell, Jonny, 41, 58, 67, 80, 96, 173
Benazzi, Abdel, 82
Benetton, Philippe, 82
Berkeley Court Hotel, 56, 59, 67, 68, 69, 72, 76, 77
Best, Dick, 97
Best, Neil, 211, 238
Bevan, John, 106, 111
Biarritz Olympique, 153–4, 207, 225–35
Bidabe, Philippe, 228, 233
Bishop, Justin, 92
Black, Gordon, 24
Blackrock RFC, 54, 66–7, 74, 81, 102, 138
Blaney, James, 41
Bluett, Fr Garry, 29, 30, 44, 128
Bobo, Sereli, 228, 230, 231, 233
Bourgoin, 113
Bowen, Scotty, 38
Boyd, Clem, 41
Bracken, Kyran, 65, 71
Bradley, Michael, 40, 67, 157
Breen, John
    Alone It Stands, 141
Brennan, Trevor, 126, 130, 171
Brewer, Mike, 102
Bristol RFC, 97
Browne, Philip, 87

Browne, Vincent, 237, 238
Brusque, Nicolas, 233
Bruton, John, 84
Buccaneers RFC, 125
Burger, Schalk, 199, 200
Burke, Matt, 38
Burke, Paul, 39, 65, 67, 72, 73, 74, 75, 82, 97
Butler, Eddie, 71
Byrne, Shane 'Munch', 66, 92, 156, 183, 185, 197

Cabannes, Laurent, 114
Califano, Christian, 110
Campbell, Ollie, 23
Campsall, Brian, 150
Cardiff Blues, XV, 113, 237
Carling, Will, 64, 71, 74, 114
Carroll, Bernard 'Bomber', 9
Castres Olympique, 110, 152, 166–7, 168–9, 215, 216–17
Catt, Mike, 67, 75, 76
Cecillon, Marc, 82
Celtic League (aka Magners League) XV, 165–6, 179, 213, 215, 218, 221, 224, 226, 237
Chabal, Sebastien, 217
Cheika, Michael, 222
Clarke, Andy, 98
Clarke, Ben, 72, 75
Clermont Auvergne, 240
Clohessy, Anna, 122
Clohessy, Ger, 50
Clohessy, Peter 'The Claw', 47, 50, 57, 65, 72, 103, 107–8, 111–13, 117, 128, 135, 137, 142, 149, 166–7, 170, 174, 176, 178, 227, 234, 236, 242
   burn injury, 168–9
Cogley, Fred, 177
Cohen, Ben, 198
Connacht, 124, 241

Connolly, Gary, 219
Contepomi, Felipe, 216, 221, 224
Cooke, Geoff, 71
Cork Constitution RFC, 14, 47, 84, 121, 125, 136
Corkery, David, 38, 58, 60, 63, 65, 68, 69, 71, 73, 80, 88, 95, 97, 130
Corrigan, Reggie, 174, 209
Corry, Martin, 208
Costello, Victor, 95, 97, 117, 138, 183–4
Coventry RFC, 97, 98
Cowhey, Angela, 19, 53, 65, 85
Crawford, Andy, 96
Creamer, Tommy, 117
Cronin, Ben, 61, 82, 102
Crotty, Dominic, 125, 142, 170, 226
Cueto, Mark, 208
Cullen, Christian, 205–6, 219, 234
Cullen, Leo, 185
Cunningham, Paul, 54

Dallaglio, Lawrence, 161, 186, 204, 240, 241
Dal Maso, Marc, 138
Danaher, Philip, 47, 57, 65, 76
D'Arcy, Gordon 'Darce', 27, 117, 196, 197, 198, 216
Davidson, Jeremy, 41, 58, 95, 96, 97, 150, 156, 158
Davidson, Jimmy, 60
Davis, Conor, 41, 42
Dawson, Kieron, 158
Dawson, Matt, 39
Deacy, Bobby, 106
Deane, Mel, 174
Deegan, John, 25
Dempsey, Girvan, 146, 184, 198, 209
Derham, Packie, 125, 192
Dinneen, Len, 61
Diprose, Tony, 39, 134
Dolphin RFC, 111

Dominguez, Diego, 86, 167
Dominici, Christophe, 195
Dowling, Ian, 216, 227
Downer, Roger, 237
Doyle, Mick, 80–1, 83
Dublin University RFC (Trinity), 70
Duggan, Willie, 21–2, 69, 199
Dumé, Joel, 137, 144
Dungannon RFC, 51, 52, 84
Du Preez, Fourie, 199

Earls, Ger, 50
Easterby, Guy, 158, 198
Easterby, Simon, 27, 30, 145, 209, 211, 212, 237
Eaves, Derek, 97
Edinburgh Districts, 61, 222
Elissalde, Jean-Baptiste, 180, 181
Ellison, Rhys, 114, 115, 116
Elwood, Eric, 65, 82, 117
England, 38, 41, 63, 64–5, 67, 69–75, 77, 79, 80, 101, 117, 132, 133, 137, 140, 150, 161, 162, 163, 172, 185, 196, 197–8, 201, 208, 223
English, Alan, 16
Erskine, Dave, 92

Fanagan, Denise, 105
Fanning, Brendan, 79, 124
Ferguson, Alex, 185
Fiennes, Sir Ranulph, 188
Fiji, 95, 183
Finucane, Marian, 139, 236
Fitzgerald, Garrett, 175
Fitzgerald, John 'Paco', 50, 57, 65
Fitzgerald, Terry, 25
Fitzgibbon, Mick, 47, 49
Fitzpatrick, Mick, 17
Five Nations Championships, 47, 64, 90, 95, 101–2, 116, 132

Flannery, Jerry, 214, 217, 224, 229, 230, 231, 237
Fleming, Jim, 143
Flynn, Frankie, 15, 85
Fogarty, Denis, XVI
Foley, Brendan, 1–3, 4, 6, 7, 11, 12–26, 37, 39, 43, 45, 49, 62, 64, 69, 70, 85, 90, 94, 95, 97, 125, 142, 184, 207, 242
    coach at St Munchin's, 32–4
Foley, Dan, 241
Foley, Gerard, 207
Foley, Marie, 207
Foley, Olive (née Hogan), 30, 120–2, 128, 131, 139, 140, 150, 201, 207, 210, 234
Foley, Orla, 2, 3, 4, 27, 31, 115, 121, 170
Foley, Rosie, 2, 3, 4, 10–11, 27, 37, 87, 88, 150, 207
Foley, Sheila (née Collins), 1–3, 6, 7, 10, 16, 19, 22, 23, 28, 31, 32, 62, 65, 121, 122, 207
Foley, Tony Edward, 12, 26, 210, 234
Ford, Mike, 164, 165, 172, 174, 194
France, 17, 23, 82, 83, 90, 150, 151, 172, 184, 191, 196, 199, 201, 208–9, 216
Francis, Neil 'Franno', 58, 73, 74, 75, 80–1
Fulcher, Gabriel, 75, 97, 102, 105
Furlong, Neville, 40

Gaffney, Alan 'Gaffer', 175–7, 178, 180, 205, 206, 213, 214, 226
Gaffney, Lorraine, 176
Galvin, Jim, 52, 62, 115
Galwey, Mick 'Gaillimh', 7, 10, 20, 47, 49, 54, 57, 58, 62, 64, 65, 66, 70, 71, 73, 76, 80, 84, 104, 111, 112–13, 116, 117, 119, 137, 142, 143, 144, 154, 155, 167, 169, 170, 178, 179, 192, 234, 239

best man at Foley's wedding, 128
Pod Four incident, 107–8
Garryowen RFC, 14, 45–7, 49, 51, 52, 53, 54, 62, 84, 94, 96, 114, 116, 130
Gatland, Trudy, 122
Gatland, Warren 'Gatty', 116–18, 119, 123, 132–3, 137, 146–7, 150, 151, 156, 158
sacking, 160, 162–4
Geoghegan, Simon, 68–9
Georgia, 181, 182, 183
Geraghty, Pat, 237, 240
Gleeson, Barry, snr, 179–80
Gleeson, Keith, 174
Glennon, Jim, 20
Gloucester RFC, 177, 178–9, 203, 217, 241
Gomarsall, Andy, 179
Goode, Andy, 238
Goutta, Bernard, 219
Governey, Richie, 92
Grau, Roberto, 134
Gregan, George, 98
Grewcock, Danny, 134, 197
Griqualand West, 119

Haden, Andy, 171
Hagler, Marvin, 188
Hakin, Ronnie, 20
Halpin, Gary, 102, 112
Halstead, Trevor, 214, 217, 219, 224, 229, 232, 233
Halvey, Eddie, 48–9, 57, 60, 62, 65, 82, 89, 95, 102, 103, 104, 115, 116, 140, 152, 241
Harinordoquy, Imanol, 194, 231
Harlequins RFC, 97, 109, 113, 114–15, 127, 152, 206, 238
Harris, Iestyn, 197
Harris, Richard, 145
Hayes, John, XIV, 10, 51, 58, 118, 127, 135, 137, 142, 147, 151, 163, 167, 183, 189, 191, 204, 211–12, 230
Hayes, Liam, 71, 78
Healy, Austin, 180
Healy, Noel 'Buddha', 85, 107–8, 110, 111
Heaslip, Jamie, 223
Heineken Cup games, 95, 96, 97–8, 114, 163, 177, 238, 242
1995, 109–10
1997–8, 111
1999, 130, 132–7, 165
2000, 139–45
2001, 152–6
2002, 166–7
2003, 180 1
2004, 206
2005, 213–17
2006, 225–35
2007, 239–40
organisers fail to provide television match officials, 148
Henderson, Rob, 92, 102, 117, 149, 156, 158, 166, 173, 180, 204, 219, 237
Henning, Tappe, 174
Henry, Graham, 156
Heymans, Cedric, 181
Hickey, Brian, 176, 177
Hickey, Susie, 19
Hickie, Denis, 101, 138, 146, 149, 185, 211
Hill, Richard, 39, 134, 140
Hogan, Eddie, 121
Hogan, Mary, 121
Hogan, Niall, 67, 80
Hogan, Paul, 47
Hogan, Trevor, 237
Hogg, Allister, 198
Holland, Jason 'Dutchy', 127, 135, 136, 142, 144
Holland, Jerry, 98, 128, 207
Honiss, Paul, 200
Horan, Marcus, 10, 32, 135, 136, 178, 185, 191, 221, 226, 230, 232

Horgan, Anthony 'Hoggy', XV, 170, 173, 216, 222, 230

Horgan, Shane 'Shaggy', 137, 158, 173

Howe, Tyrone, 149

Howlett, Dougie, XV–XVI

Humphreys, David, 97, 103, 139, 150, 161, 184, 209

Huppert, Clinton, 176

Instonians RFC, 84

Ireland, 79, 112, 138, 181, 215
  Americas tour (2000), 145–7
  audience with Pope John Paul II, 150
  Australia tour (1994), 57–8
  Australia tour (1999), 122–3
  becomes professional, 95
  Foley's debut with, 63–5, 67, 68–78
  Japan tour (2005), 207, 209
  New Zealand tour (1992), 37, 40–4, 45
  New Zealand tour (2002), 172–4
  selection system, 80
  South Africa tour (1998), 117, 118 19, 122
  'The Under-14s', 56–67
  World Cup warm-up game against Munster, 129–30
  see also Five Nations Chamionships; Heineken Cup; Rugby World Cup; Six Nations Championships

Ireland Development XV
  New Zealand/Samoa tour, 102–6, 108, 111
  Rotorua (1997), 91–3, 104, 107

Irish Rugby Football Union (IRFU), 44, 46, 55, 64, 77, 89, 96, 97, 109, 143, 163, 171, 211
  professionalises the provinces, 111–16
  promotes weights training for players, 98–9
  Rugby Foundation (Academy), 44, 73, 83

Italy, 85, 86, 100, 123, 137, 150, 172, 173, 184, 187

Japan, 87

Jeffrey, John, 59

Johns, Paddy, 63, 67, 82, 88, 95, 97, 117, 138

Johnson, Martin, 72, 76, 161, 180, 186, 197, 211

Johnston, Census, 230, 233

Jones, Ryan, 209–10

Jones, Stephen, 185

Jorgensen, Peter, 38

Juillet, Christophe, 167

Kaplan, Jonathan, 208

Keane, Anne, 6

Keane, Enda, 9

Keane, Killian, 127, 135

Keane, Moss, 6–7, 16, 20, 39, 69

Keane, Sarah, 7

Keegan, Kevin, 11, 205

Kelly, John 'Rags', 173, 178, 222, 225, 227, 228, 233

Kelly, Liam, 9

Kennedy, Terry, 21

Kenny, Paddy, 62

Kenny, Pat, 237

Keogh, Stephen, 219

Kidd, Murray, 46, 94, 97, 100

Kidney, Declan, 'Deccie', XIV, 35–6, 41, 42, 109, 111, 112, 113, 120, 130, 134–5, 136, 140, 141, 143, 157, 164, 165, 168, 170, 175, 177, 191, 214, 216, 219–20, 222, 226, 234, 235, 237, 240, 241

Kiely, Jack, 50

Kiely, Sonny, 18, 40

Kiernan, Tommy, 23

Kierse, Sean, 8

Kingston, Terry, 57
Kirwan, John, 40
Knox, David, 98
Krasnoyarsk, 181–2
Krige, Corne, 149

Labit, Christian, 141
Lacey, Johnny, 115
Lacey, Peter, 3
Lacrampe-Camus, Vincent, 135
Lacroix, Thierry, 114, 115, 134
Lam, Pat, 143
Lander, Steve, 155
Langford, Connor, 140
Langford, John, 127, 137, 140, 152, 192, 206
Langford, Nicole, 136, 137, 140
Lassissi, Ismaella, 167, 169
Late Late Show, 237
Leahy, Shane, 114
Leamy, Denis, XIV, 10, 206, 211, 212, 219, 223, 229, 231, 233, 238
Leicester Tigers, 179–80
Leinster, 126, 138, 165–6, 175–6, 213, 214, 216, 220, 222–4, 239
Lenihan, Brian, 9
Lenihan, Donal 'Mannix', 21, 118, 130, 133, 147, 157
Leonard, Jason, 114
Leota, Trevor, 43, 204
Leslie, Andy, 106, 111
Leslie, John, 159
Lewsey, Josh, 204
Lièvremont, Thomas, 225
Limerick Regional Hospital, 210
Lions games, 111, 112, 114, 118, 156, 157, 202, 204, 207, 209–10, 211
Llanelli Scarlets RFC, 143, 213, 240
Lobbe, Ignacio Fernandez, 217–18
Lomu, Jonah, 43, 89, 211
London Irish RFC, 97, 152

Longwell, Gary, 183
Luger, Dan, 161
Luxe, Jean-Pierre, 234
Lynch, Mike, 104

McBride, Denis, 60, 88, 95
McBride, Willie John, 20
McCall, Mark, 97
McCarthy, John 'Tar', 9
McCarthy, Paul, 176
McCaw, Richie, 200
McConnell, Barry, 105
McDermott, Conor, 54, 154
McDermott, Mark, 115
MacDonald, Leon, 173
McGoey, Brian, 153
McGrath, Alan, 104
McGuinness, Conor, 41
McGurn, Mike, 164
McIvor, Stephen, 53–4, 92, 102, 110
McLoughlin, Gerry 'Locky', 13, 17–18
McLoughlin, Mick 'Bungalow', 17
McMahon, Ger, 13
McMahon, Paul, 115
McNamara, Freddie, 14
McNamara, Madgie, 14
Maggs, Kevin, 173, 209
Magne, Olivier, 195
Magners League (see Celtic League)
Mahedy, Dave, 54, 124, 125, 127
Maher, Kieran, 49
Maka, Finau, 181
Malone, Dominic, 144
Malone, Niall, 56
Malone RFC, 46
Mapletoft, Mark, 136, 137
Marconnet, Sylvain, 167
Martin, John, 88
Marty, David, 220
Matchett, Andy, 92, 105
Mauger, Aaron, 173

Maxwell, Norm, 162
Mehrtens, Andrew, 173
Melville, Nigel, 203
Mendez, Federico, 143
Mercier, Ludovic, 178
Michalak, Freddy, 180
Miller, Eric, 100–1, 102, 166, 211
Minogue, Pat, 10–11, 87, 88
Mitchell, John, 97
Molloy, Dr Mick, 60, 69
Mooney, Dan, 48, 71
Moore, Brian, 64, 71
Moran's of the Weir, Kilcolgan, Co.
    Galway, 18
Moriarty, Jerry, 19
Morris, Dewi, 234
Moylett, Mick, 14
Moynihan, Seanie, 18
Mullin, Brennie, 66, 67, 70, 75, 80
Mullins, Mike, 127, 134, 136, 137, 142,
    154, 237
Mulqueen, Charlie, 216
Munster, 15, 17, 38, 47–8, 59, 61, 63–4,
    90, 93, 94, 106, 107, 108, 109, 111,
    127, 129, 130, 133, 137, 139–45, 148,
    152–6, 163, 164, 165, 167–71, 175,
    195–6, 204–7, 212, 213–24, 238, 239,
    242
  Biarritz game (May 2006), 225–35
  fitness test results, 123, 124–5, 126
  playing in France, 134–5
  professionalisation of, 111–16
  win against All Blacks, Thomond
    Park (1978), 12, 16, 23, 40, 41–2
  win against Ulster (1999), 128
  World Cup warm-up game against
    Ireland, 129 30
Murphy, Barry, XVI, 216–17, 218, 219,
    234
Murphy, Geordan, 173, 180, 208
Murphy, Gerry, 58, 64, 65, 70, 74, 80,
    82, 83, 94

Murphy, Martin, 109, 182
Murphy, Mervyn, 199
Murphy, Noel 'Noisy', 6, 20, 64, 82,
    86, 87, 88–9, 94
Murray, Ian, 136
Murray, Jerry, 36
Murray, Pat, 62, 110, 111, 115, 116, 206
Murray, Scott, 134

Namibia, 188, 189
Neath RFC, 179
Neville, Phil, 195
Newport Gwent Dragons, 152, 153,
    215–16, 222
New Zealand (All Blacks), xv, 11, 12,
    16, 23, 36, 39, 40, 41, 42, 87, 89,
    161 2, 163, 171, 173, 196, 211, 215, 238
Nicol, Andy, 159
Nolan, Tony, 8
Northampton Saints, 143–5

O'Brien, Brian, 17, 19, 128–9, 147, 150,
    182
O'Brien, Padraig, 19
O'Callaghan, Donncha 'Donners', XIV,
    155, 169, 177, 178, 204, 219, 231, 234
O'Callaghan, Fergal, 127, 143
O'Callaghan, Ultan, 114
O'Connell, Ken, 40, 63
O'Connell, Paul 'Paulie', XIV, 59, 154,
    168, 174, 177, 180, 188, 189, 190, 191,
    192, 203, 204, 211, 216, 217, 224,
    226, 227, 229, 230, 231, 233, 235,
    237, 239, 242
O'Connor, Charlie, 9
O'Connor, Johnny, 211
O'Cuinneagain, Dion, 119, 126, 155
O'Donovan, Niall, 18, 52–3, 54, 85,
    109, 111, 115, 136, 140, 143, 153, 164,
    170, 172, 177, 191, 209, 214

O'Driscoll, Brian 'Drico', 117, 138, 139, 146, 149, 150, 153, 156, 173, 183, 184–5, 190, 196, 197, 199, 202, 208, 209, 211, 216, 218

O'Driscoll, Gary, 189

O'Driscoll, Mick, 219, 232, 239

O'Farrell, Dr Dermot, 133

O'Gara, Ronan 'Rog', 134, 136–7, 142, 144, 152, 155–6, 158, 172–3, 178, 180–81, 184–5, 196, 198, 200, 204, 206–7, 215, 219–24, 237–8, 226–33

O'Grady, Paddy, 49

O'Hara, Pat, 63

Ojomoh, Steve, 77

O'Kelly, Malcolm, 97, 156, 185, 195, 198, 223, 224

Old Wesley RFC, 62

O'Leary, Daren, 39

O'Leary, Tomás, 220

Oliver, Anton, 41

Oliver, Frank, 41

O'Mahony, Darragh, 97

O'Mara, Frank, 8

O'Meara, Brian, 36, 129

O'Neill, John, 155, 173

O'Shea, Billy, 52, 61, 62, 66–7

O'Shea, Conor, 80, 88, 97

O'Shea, Paul, 18

Ospreys Neath-Swansea, 226

O'Sullivan, Conrad, 218–19, 220

O'Sullivan, Denis, 50

O'Sullivan, Dermot, 138

O'Sullivan, Eddie, 66, 133, 160, 163–4, 172, 174, 183, 184, 185, 188, 191, 192, 195, 200, 209, 211–12, 237, 238

O'Sullivan, Sean, 9, 28

Oswald, Dean, 66

O'Toole, Peter, 145

Owens, Nigel, 204

Paul, Henry, 178

Payne, Shaun, XIII, XIV, XV, XVII, 206, 228, 231, 233

Pearse, John, 25

Pearson, Dave, 228

Pelous, Fabien, 141

Perpignan, 177–8, 218, 219 20, 221

Peyrelongue, Julien, 228, 229, 230, 233

Pichot, Agustin, 201

Pienaar, Francois, 134

Pinkerton, Stu, 38

Pod Four incident, 107–8, 109

Polla-Mounter, Craig, 38

Popplewell, Nick, 72

Pountney, Budge, 143

Price, Eddie, 18

ProActive agency, 95

professionalisation of rugby, 82–3, 87
early years of Irish professionalism, 93–100
provinces professionalised, 111–16

Pucciariello, Freddie, 214–15, 221, 223

Queensland RFC, 111

Quinlan, Alan 'Quinny', XIV, XVI, 6, 51, 58, 115, 130, 134, 140, 152, 154, 155, 157, 174, 180, 189, 203–4, 211, 215, 233, 237, 240

Randwick RFC, 206

Rauluni, Jacob, 38

Reason, John, 39

Rees, Gareth, 110

Regan, Mark, 198

Reid, Ken, 44, 77

Richards, Dean, 39, 59, 64, 70, 72, 74, 76, 77

Rigney, Brian, 54, 62

Robinson, Andy, 208

Robinson, Brian, 63

Robinson, Jason, 197, 198, 215, 217
Robson, Bryan, 11
Roche, Frankie, 223, 234
Rodber, Tim, 72, 73, 76, 143
Romania, 183, 188, 189, 211
Rugby After Dark, 80
Rugby World Cup
   1991 (England), 47, 72
   1995 (South Africa), 63, 81, 83, 84,
    85, 86, 87–90, 94, 95, 106
   1999 (Wales), 119, 123, 127, 129–31,
    139, 145, 163, 212
   2003 (Australia), 163, 172, 181, 182,
    183, 184, 186, 187–95, 199
   2007 (France), 209, 211, 239
Russell, Gavin, 62
Russia, 181–2, 183
Ryan, Donnacha, 241
Ryan, Dr Maureen, 210
Ryan, Michael Noel, 15, 17–18

St Lua's Athletics Club, 8
St Mary's RFC, 14, 24–5, 32, 52, 54, 62,
   84, 116
St Munchin's College, Corbally, Co.
   Limerick, 5, 8, 27–44
   Foley plays for Irish Schools side,
    37–44
Sale RFC, 97, 215, 217
Samoa, 103, 105, 161, 181, 186
Saracens RFC, 97, 133–4, 135–7, 140, 241
Scotland, 41, 80, 81, 102, 133x 137, 158,
   160, 161, 172, 184, 187, 190, 196, 198,
   202, 208
Shannon RFC, 13 14, 15, 16–18, 20,
   23–4, 25, 46, 47, 48, 49–50, 53, 61–2,
   63, 66–7, 79, 94, 101, 102, 104, 114,
   115–17, 121, 123, 154, 168, 239
   AGM of 1993, 52–3
   AIL winners, 84, 90, 96
   Canada tour, 90, 93

   captained by Foley, 106, 115
   European Cup 1995, 109–10
   refusal to pay players, 51
   Under-14s, 32
Shaw, Simon, 38, 39, 197
Sheahan, Frankie, 152, 187, 192–4
Shelford, Buck, 39–40, 69
Sheridan, Andrew, 217
Sheriff, Rory, 92, 104
Six Nations Championships, 137–40,
   149–52, 158–9, 161, 172, 179, 185,
   196, 201, 202–3, 207, 218, 239
   disrupted by foot-and-mouth
    disease, 148, 151, 152, 156
Skinner, Mickey 'The Munch', 156
Smart, Colin, 59
Smith O'Briens GAA Club, 5, 8, 25, 35
South Africa (Springboks), 63, 118, 149,
   199–200, 214, 230
Spala, Poland, 156–7, 158, 203
Spillane, Brian, 199
Spotswood, George, 89
Spreadbury, Tony, 86
Spring, Donal, 20, 22
Stade Français, 140, 154, 155, 167–8, 205
Staples, Jim, 100
Stapleton, Frank, 11
Starmer-Smith, Nigel, 26
Star Rovers, 8
Staunton, Jeremy, 134
Steadman, Graham, 176, 205
Steele, Harry, 20
Stimpson, Tim, 39
Stoica, Cristian, 100
Stringer, Peter 'Strings', 21, 137, 161,
   171, 184, 198, 199, 205, 215, 230–1,
   233
Students' World Cup in South Africa,
   96
Sunday's Well RFC, 62, 63
Supple, Alan, 49
Sweeney, Ceri, 215

tactical substitutions introduced, 92
Thames Valley, 104–5, 106
Thion, Jérôme, 231, 232, 233
Thompson, Andrew, 61, 62, 84, 116
Thompson, Steve, 39, 197
Tierney, Tom, 129
Toland, Brian, 61
Toulouse, 110, 140–3, 180–1, 220, 242
Tournaire, Franck, 141
Townsend, Gregor, 159
Traille, Damien, 229
Treviso 'friendly' match, 85–7, 88
Troncon, Alessandro, 86
Tucker, Colm, 14, 17, 69
Tuigamala, Inga, 110
Tuohy, Greg, 109, 238
Tweed, Davy, 82

Ubogu, Victor, 76
UCD RFC, 138
Ulster, 128, 165, 213, 215
Umaga, Tana, 173
Underwood, Tony, 75, 76

Waikito, 164
Wales, 22, 39, 41, 84, 87, 89, 111, 139,
    161, 164, 172, 185, 187, 188, 196–7,
    202, 209
Wallace, David 'Wally', XIV, 92, 109,
    118, 130, 133, 144, 155, 157, 169, 192,
    199, 203, 207, 211, 218, 221, 228, 233,
    238
Wallace, Paul, 66, 89, 97, 103, 157
Wallace, Richie, 47, 97
Walsh, David, 81

Wanderers RFC, 46, 70
Ward, Finbarr, 9
Ward, Tony, 11
Warrington Rugby League Club, 111
Warrington, Giles, 88
Warwick, Paul, XV
Wasps, London, 110, 143, 163, 164,
    204–5, 240
Watson, Andre, 162
Western Samoa, 98
Whelan, Pat 'Pa', 92, 94, 101, 108, 118
White, Chris, 155, 228, 233
White, Craig, 123–4, 126, 164
White, Jake, 199–200
White, Jason, 217
Whitehouse, Nigel, 204
Wilkinson, Jonny, 186, 197
Williams, Jim, 157, 166, 169, 170, 176,
    204, 205, 206
Williams, Matt, 163, 175
Wilson, Jeff, 43
Wood, Gordon, 4, 183
Wood, Keith 'Woody', 1, 4–6, 9, 28, 31,
    46, 47, 53, 57, 65, 72, 73, 74, 81–2,
    97, 113, 114, 115, 118, 127, 129, 136,
    138, 142, 156, 161, 162, 172, 182, 183,
    188, 191, 194, 197, 198
    regains captaincy of Ireland, 137
    returns to Harlequins, 152
Woods, Niall, 66, 67, 75, 80, 97, 102
Woodward, Clive, 162, 197, 202, 209

Yachvili, Dimitri, 228, 229, 230, 231–2
Young Munster RFC, 'Cookies', 48, 52,
    66, 96, 116, 154, 168
    1993 AIL win, 47, 50–1